Go Ahead John

The Music Of John McLaughlin

Also by Paul Stump

The Music's All That Matters
A History of Progressive Rock
(Quartet Books, 1997)

Digital Gothic
A Critical Discography of Tangerine Dream
(SAF, 1997)

Unknown Pleasures
A Cultural Biography of Roxy Music
(Quartet Books, 1999)

Go Ahead John

The Music Of John McLaughlin

Paul Stump

SAF Publishing Ltd

SAF Publishing Ltd

First published in 2000 SAF Publishing Ltd

SAF Publishing Ltd.
Unit 7, Shaftesbury Centre,
85 Barlby Road,
London.W10 6BN
ENGLAND

www.saf.mcmail.com

ISBN 0 946719 24 1

A CIP catalogue record for this book is available from the British Library.

Printed in England by Redwood Books, Trowbridge, Wiltshire.

Contents

For Alquimia

"I'm a musician for people who are not musicians."

JOHN McLAUGHLIN, 1974

Preface

It had to happen, really. Me, McLaughlin, and his music. It was meant to be.

Back in the early eighties I was – I admit – a Prog-rock fan. I spent time catching up on all the high-aiming hokum that had gone over my kiddie head ten years previously, and it was only to be expected that I'd eventually come across the Mahavishnu Orchestra, whose rock encyclopaedia entries had always interested but never enticed me. Sure, album titles like *Visions Of The Emerald Beyond* always hinted at the Symbolist decadence which underlay so much of Progressive's inspirational discourse, but there was that pesky omnipresence of the word "jazz" and the Eastern imagery, garlanded like beads around every title. Therefore, what I originally inferred from the existence of the Mahavishnu Orchestra was the almost certain promise of a character which I'd grown used to seeing hung inaccurately on Progressive rock – kitsch piety, self-obsession and featureless introspection; not to mention plenty of cornball blues stylings thrown in for good measure. Which, as all you musicians out there will no doubt concur, proves what morons we hacks can be. I only hope that this admission of such a gratuitous error of good taste, albeit one made nearly twenty years ago, does not colour any reader's evaluation of what comes later in this book.

In any event, I decided to take a chance on a cheap Mahavishnu compilation. Apart from a discovery of Wagner (coincidentally, in the same month, July 1982), few single discoveries have so enriched my musical life. Without McLaughlin, I would have almost certainly come much later to Miles Davis, Bill Evans, Stan Getz, John Coltrane, Pat Metheny – indeed to jazz as a whole.

I finally met McLaughlin in my capacity as a contributor to *The Wire* magazine in January 1996; it was the first time in my life that I had met a real live hero. It had taken me just 31 years to meet one. It was also the first and only time in my career as a journalist to date that an interviewee has enjoyed the interview so much he actually asked for more time to be allotted. When heroes behave the way you want them to behave, hell, it reminds journalists just how frankly piss-easy and wonderful their lives can be.

McLaughlin is, in this author's experience, a genuinely pleasant man. He is a joy to be around; calm and calculating, but with a seam of good humour and childish glee like quicksilver. Now in his fifties, he is an infuriatingly good-looking guy with money to burn on sharp threads which he obviously buys with a couturier's eye. He laughs a lot, and from within. Alternatively, if I was a musician, I might not care to work with this guitarist; the desire for complete immersion in the music in hand is intimidating.

For the above reasons, it has been difficult not to make this book into a hagiography. I admit to adoring McLaughlin's music and own up to the missionary intention of making up for the absurd gap in the bibliography of rock, pop and jazz where a proper biography should have stood for many years.

My previous two biographies have been exercises in ambivalence; here, for the first time, I am dealing with my own dreams, and I have to tread carefully. But avoiding treading on dreams doesn't mean one shouldn't stomp on illusions, and while I have attempted to be as musico-logically impartial as possible, many of my judgements are personal, as they must be – another drawback of taking a pen to a hero.

In writing this book, which took place sporadically between summer 1998 and spring 1999, I also intended to investigate the phenomenon of jazz-rock fusion which, rather like Progressive rock, stands as a genre once hailed as a soundtrack to the future but has subsequently been hideously misunderstood. In particular, the British popular music critical community have, as with Progressive, discounted the possibility that the genre can actually be critically evaluated in terms of good and bad, and not just dismissed with a blanket term – 'self-indulgence' is usually one of the kinder epithets. I was very glad, however, when a work reached the shops from an author with a much securer musicological grounding than mine. I refer to Stuart Nicholson's exceptional and underrated study, *Jazz Rock: A History* (Canongate Books, 1998), from which much information about John McLaughlin has been gleaned, not to mention no little motivation.

Far from diminishing my own work by its appearance, I feel Nicholson's book has immeasurably enriched it by broadening my understanding of the genre as a whole. After reading this book, I can heartily recommend people to Nicholson's. Jazz is after all almost dead on its feet, and needs all the help it can get. During the writing of this particular book, maybe one of the greatest contemporary jazz pianists, Michel Petrucciani, passed away, to a criminally unanimous chorus of indifference in the media throughout the western world (save maybe in France). When obituaries for artistic giants, even little giants, are pygmy-sized, then their art needs its followers to stand tall.

Therefore I make no apologies for the tone and style of this book, which will appeal first and foremost to fans and musicians. If I am branded musically academic, then I will be more than pleased. This, as I'm sure the discerning reader will understand, is less out of a desire to appear didactic, and more about the increasing reliance of music criticism in the UK upon opinions which have been reheated once too often from the intellectual freezer – as well as upon tediously prevalent flip postmodern irony. My limited musicological knowledge can only give the barest essentials of what makes McLaughlin's style so distinctive. But in the context of a biography, I feel this to be preferable. This book is about the man *and* his music. Those wishing for yet greater academic depth should consult the bibliography, and the Internet.

I should also add that I do not play the guitar; in this respect, much help has been sought and gained from those who do, and in one case from an ex-colleague of McLaughlin himself. Similarly, I apologise for my incomplete musical knowledge, and my lazy reluctance to improve it. No apologies, however, for any extra-musical input in terms of sociology, history and philosophy. Whilst I believe that English music journalism has been almost entirely consumed by the chimera of extra-musical criteria, it is true that some of the finest music in any genre is indissoluble from the social conditions which produced it. I believe that John McLaughlin's music, particularly at the crucial period of its maturing (around 1969-72), is particularly deeply informed by the times and society into which it emerged. McLaughlin's finest inspirations may imply the fiction of timelessness better than most popular musicians, but his music, like all other music, cannot ultimately be detached from its timeframe. No true understanding of the man's art can be arrived at without a true understanding of the man's times.

I believe that such analysis makes for a more rounded view. McLaughlin, an intellectual man who believes in the power of music to exalt the head and heart, would surely sympathise with any attempt at the impossible dream of liberating the 'real' glory of music. Social analysis alongside musical analysis can help do just that; the finest jazz biography ever written, and the book which most inspired this one, Ian Carr's *Miles Davis* (Quartet, 1982) is proof of that.

McLaughlin himself has said that if he has made one listener happier his life will not be in vain. Similarly, if my book makes one consumer of his music a more enlightened consumer; musically, socially or emotionally; then the writing of this book will not have been in vain either.

Go Ahead John owes its existence to many people. These include the inestimable and faithful Mick Fish and Dave Hallbery of SAF, Charles Alexander and Stephen Graham at *Jazzwise* magazine, Tony Herrington at *The Wire*, Big Jim Sullivan, Kevin, Rob and Andrew at PA, Christelle Chaigné, Pete Brown, Howard Riley, Danny Thompson, Dick Heckstall-Smith, Mike Carr, Bob Knapp, Phil Hirschi, Mike Barnes, Rod Sibley, Andres Didriks, Walter Kolosky, Emma, Rowan and Nicki Stump, everyone at the National Sound Archive (London), Jeffrey Frank, Becky Stevenson, SuperGeordie II John Bland and family. Finally, *besos grandes* – and as much thanks as anyone can carry – to Alquimia Saavedra.

Chapter One
Beginnings

Kirk Sandall was never much more than a hole in the hedge. Situated
north of the industrial town of Doncaster, where the southern half of
Yorkshire bottoms out into the marshes around the Humber Estuary, it
had neither much agriculture nor industry to justify its existence.

In 1942 it was home to the McLaughlins, a respectable middle-class
family of Scottish descent. On the 4th of January of that year, the family's fourth child and third son, John, was born.

The world McLaughlin entered on that winter day was a precarious
one. The Second World War was in full, depressing cry; despite the entry
of the USA after the "day that will live in infamy" at Pearl Harbor exactly four weeks previously. Britain and her Allies were tottering, battered
in the Atlantic and in the North African desert. The countryside in
Yorkshire was full of fatigues, convoys, evacuees and dark talk of defeat.

The McLaughlins lived a comfortable, if straitened existence. Mr
McLaughlin was a turbomotive engineer; his wife was a teacher. Culture
and education were highly valued; music was seen as particularly germane to that self-betterment although very strictly 'leisure' and not a
career option.

In 1949, though, the McLaughlins divorced and, in the custody of Mrs
McLaughlin, the family moved to a village near Berwick-on-Tweed, in
the topmost North-eastern corner of England, a caber's toss from
Scotland.

Interestingly, McLaughlin's adult accounts of his musical awareness have always returned to one indelible, central theme – an instinctual attachment to the mysteries of musical creativity inspired in him by the European classical tradition.

"My musical development started before I was aware of what was going on", McLaughlin recalls. "I remember when I was about eight, one of my brothers – an avid classical music listener – tuning into the BBC a lot. One night I heard something that was very beautiful which impressed me. We got a gramophone about that time, too, which was quite a rarity. Another distinct memory was listening to Beethoven's Ninth Symphony. It made my hair stand on end... it was the quartet at the end. I was aware of the effect it was having on me. The fact that something could have such an effect on me was very profound in my youthful mind. So when I was nine I asked if I could start studying piano which I did for about three years." McLaughlin also remembers "regularly putting a record on the player and getting one of my mother's knitting needles and waving my arms around in front of the mirror and 'conducting'."

McLaughlin studied "the usual, basic stuff" for those three years, by which time his elder brothers were moving on through high school to college. McLaughlin remembers that they "got into the blues. So from about eleven years of age onwards I was exposed to Muddy Waters, Leadbelly, Sonny Terry..."

McLaughlin's siblings were impressed by their little brother's passionate involvement in music, and more specifically in the blues, which, unlike symphonic music, was technically and physically easier to create as opposed to simply consuming. Instead of feeling loftily protective of their own adolescent musical tastes from a younger member of the family, they encouraged him. "There was a guitar in the house that had come down through the family," remembers McLaughlin. One brother took the time to show him how to play chords.

"Chicago blues – which I then thought was delta blues – was the first real big influence," McLaughlin told *Down Beat*. To another reporter he said; "I was really into Sonny Terry and the whole blues-harmonica-guitar-bottleneck thing. I didn't even know what a bottleneck was. For years I thought they were doing it with their fingers. I was trying to sing and play like Big Bill and Muddy."

Later, he again had his brothers to thank for transmitting to him the glories of flamenco music. "There was a sense of freedom, like that in blues and jazz. There was also improvisation. And there was a passion that hit a certain spot in me. I must have been about thirteen by then." If his own testimony is to be believed, McLaughlin also skipped school two days a week at this time to hitch-hike to a flamenco club in Manchester, some 150 miles away. At the age of 13, and boasting a respectable background such as his, it seems unlikely, but far from implausible.

The McLaughlins, like many lower middle-class families, regarded music as an exercise in self-improvement as well as a form of entertainment. Mrs McLaughlin was proficient on the violin, which meant that when John heard Stephane Grappelli and Django Rheinhardt on a gramophone record in his early teens it "touched a chord... sort of turned my head around."

"The music made my hair stand on end, but it wasn't like I said, 'Oh, that's it, I'm going to be a musician'...", McLaughlin recalls. "But it *was* a situation where music made everything else pale in comparison. My daydream world was immersed to the core in music. I used to spend all my time listening to records. Finally I found the *Voice Of America* coming from Frankfurt with Willis Conover through the static. I discovered American jazz..." He also assumed that Oscar Peterson, whose music was another early love, was Swedish.

McLaughlin, nonetheless, spent more and more time hunched over his guitar, listening less, playing more; active rather than passive. "After Django I was starting to play and using my fingernails to pick. I also picked with the little finger because of my studies in classical Spanish and flamenco music. But, it wasn't working. So, when I was about 14 or 15, I picked up the plectrum and tried to work with it. Then I heard a Tal Farlow LP in a record store in Newcastle. I couldn't believe him. He just knocked down my socks. I ran in to find who was making this incredible music. So Tal Farlow became my first real hero. His harmonic concept, even now, I think is stunning. He was quite a revolutionary. Actually I had the fortune of meeting him once at the Newport Jazz Festival when I was playing with Tony Williams. Just to see him was a thrill."

After leading a band in school – "my first and last band right up until the first Mahavishnu Orchestra" – McLaughlin turned professional when he was 15, his first gig being a pick-up member of Pete Deuchar's Professors of Ragtime in his native north-east. It was through their offices that he moved to London a year or so later. Around this time he encountered the next musical life change, after purchasing Miles Davis' 1957 landmark album, *Milestones*. "He turned my head around because of the simplicity of the concept and its beauty. But really, it was the concept of the rhythm section that in itself was a revolution to me."

McLaughlin quickly gained confidence – perhaps too much confidence. At 15, he asked a seasoned crew of local jazzmen in a nearby pub if he could sit in with them. They agreed, and promptly launched into "Cherokee" at breakneck speed. Initially humiliated, the young McLaughlin nevertheless learned the necessity of immediate and dedicated delivery – if you can't do anything on stage, at any time, don't bother. It certainly didn't diminish his love of jazz, now becoming all-encompassing, despite the squeaky appeal of a skiffle band his sister was putting together.

"If you go back in time you find that the drummers were swinging – but it was a more traditional kind of swinging," McLaughlin recalls. "With Philly Joe, instead of going 'chung-chunka-chung-chunka', it went 'ting-ting'. It was less but more intense. Another factor was the way Red Garland was playing suspensions."

Mingus became an icon too, and after *Kind Of Blue* came out in England in 1959, McLaughlin determined to follow the careers of all six musicians featured thereon. Coltrane, Davis and Bill Evans, in particular, wove threads into his musical mind that unravel in McLaughlin's music even today. Of Coltrane, the guitarist later commented that he "couldn't understand *A Love Supreme* when it came out... I couldn't get *Giant Steps* either... I couldn't really 'hear it'. Too high for me, I guess."

* * *

For many years, the literature about how and why popular music and popular culture interacted with each other and upon society at large in the 1960s was relatively thin. The sociology of the 1960s was inexhaustible; the musicology was non-existent. Only recently the reality of what happened in terms of musical inspiration in the socio-cultural matrix of the sixties has been adequately investigated and tentatively explained.

In a book such as this, only a précis of the dynamics of the 1960s in music and lifestyle is now necessary. The "Great Turn" of that decade, when pop music became popular culture and popular musical thought sought artistic legitimacy, is easily traduced by trivialization. For the issues that are germane to our discussion of McLaughlin and his music – it goes like this.

The abnormally prodigious constituency of youth in the 1960s, combined with the affluence of the post-war economic miracle, cracked open a fissure in the idea of what it was to be young. A general social libertarianism, inspired by the post-war triumph and subsequent unassailable moral sovereignty of the centre-left consensus in the western world, was changing the view that you could only be adventurous within limits proscribed by responsible adults – parent/teacher/cop/priest. This sliver of light illuminated limitless possibilities; economically, socially, sexually, artistically, chemically. The young of the 1960s viewed the consensus of their parents' generation – and the modest rewards it offered – and found it wanting. Kids wanted it all, and wanted it now; not merely as consumers, but as human beings. This ambition did not preclude music-making.

What helped the cause of the blues revival was that the values it represented to the revivalists were synonymous with the bohemian values that became identified with the 1960s. The latest flowering of jazz in 1950s/60s Britain, for example, oscillated between trad and New Orleans. Trad, in particular, was considered a monster of triviality by the hardcore British jazz audience, young and old. Something 'more real' was sought, something with cottonfield dirt under its fingernails. Given that pop in the early sixties had apparently finished with the kids, and had gone back to wooing Mom and Pop with diva torch singers and/or crooning weeds called Bobby; modern jazz, bebop, hard bop or r'n'b at least offered something ostensibly primal. Here was the soundtrack beyond suburbia – a world that a young rebellious spirit could call his own while he got quietly (or noisily) toasted on Watney's Red Barrel and a spliff or two. This was music, it was imagined, that came straight from the heart.

A blues boom of both Chicago and Delta varieties was well underway by the time McLaughlin reached London at the turn of the 1960s. Spearheaded by the unlikely figures of Alexis Korner (a London Jew of Greek origin), and the Welshman Cyril Davies, it took root at the Blues and Barrelhouse Club in Tottenham Court Road. In 1958, however, the B&B closed down when Korner returned to the fold of Chris Barber's traditional jazz orchestra to play piano. No matter; rhythm and blues was firmly entrenched in the bohemia of late fifties London alongside cool jazz. Both were consonant with the overriding concern of bohemia – a dedication to the purest liberation, and by extension, expression of the soul. Here was the High Romantic prescription propounded in the exponentially expanding milieu of the post-war British art school (for details, see Frith and Horne's *Art Into Pop*).

Korner and Davies stayed friendly, and by 1962 had their own band, Blues Incorporated. Korner and to a lesser extent Davies, as Nicholson points out in *Jazz Rock*, were living embodiments of the compromise essential to popular music's survival. Both men felt at home in jazz and blues; both men encouraged other musicians to feel at home in both camps, and found that few musicians of either persuasion needed encouraging to commute between the two. Charlie Watts was considered a trad man through and through (as was Jack Bruce) until they met Korner.

The extraordinary extent of the blues revival was immense. The devotion it attracted and the fluidity of the interaction between its participants, meant that those engaged were caught up in a missionary cause – not to forget the bonuses to the zealous of booze, dope and girls. Every night, jams and sittings-in would create music whose jazz and r'n'b roots became ever more densely intertwined.

"In those days," McLaughlin told the German author and jazz neophyte Ernst-Joachim Berendt, "there were two clubs, the Marquee and the Flamingo. They were great. Everybody met everybody there and the attitude was that everybody could play with everybody... I kept playing rhythm and blues and it was great because we were playing real jazz solos. It was blues but at the same time it was much more than the blues." McLaughlin had arrived in these clubs via a roundabout route, picking up sheaves of good notices, encouraging pats on the back and scores of friends, but precious little money.

The road to London opened up for him as a member of Pete Deuchar's band and would later feature refreshment stops as a jobber with the Marzipan Twisters and Al Wilson's backing group in 1961. The summer and autumn of 1962 saw a brief gig with Georgie Fame and the Blue Flames. On the jazz side, McLaughlin met and befriended a splendidly gifted young 18-year-old baritone saxophonist named Glenn Hughes. He also cut his teeth with Ray Ellington's quartet (a sometime provider of the music for the BBC's *Goon Show*) and briefly depped with pianist Howard Riley's trio.

In the end, Davies' missionary blues purism irked Korner, whose affinity with jazz never died. In 1962, after a fall-out with Davies (who, tragically, only had two years to live), Korner reconstituted an altogether more musically eclectic Blues Incorporated with drummer Peter 'Ginger' Baker and organist/altoist Graham Bond (the latter having been voted Britain's 'Brightest Jazz Hope' in 1961 for his work with the Don Rendell sextet). Recordings of the band, aficionados have declared, betray a distinct rock outcropping in jazz as early as 1962.

After McLaughlin left Korner – something that, as he related it to Berendt, he considered his first 'real' gig – he joined other Korner protégés, Jack Bruce, Graham Bond and Ginger Baker. Bond quickly became the leader and they toured, often in the company of jazz poet Pete Brown.

Baker took over the running of Bond's band because of the leader's infamous dissoluteness, and promptly fired McLaughlin. "He was a fucking moaner," growled the drummer during a TV documentary thirty years later. McLaughlin was perhaps fortunate not to experience the sharper end of Baker's questionable man-management; after a row with Jack Bruce in 1965, Baker forced him out of the band by pulling a knife on him. There was also a spell in a trio which McLaughlin convened along with his friend Glenn Hughes and included New Zealand expatriate bass player Rick Laird. Within a few months, Hughes would be found dead in his bed, overdosed at 25, one of the most unsung musical tragedies of the era. The three played Jim Hall/ Jimmy Giuffre numbers along with covers of Chico Hamilton, Miles Davis and Sonny Rollins' tunes.

Befriending a young contrabass player by the name of Dave Holland, McLaughlin moved into the latter's flat where the two lived in "in pretty abject poverty."

"It shouldn't have been that way, of course," says McLaughlin's friend and colleague, the session guitar legend 'Big' Jim Sullivan. "He was bloody good. He got work, but it should have been more, and he should have earned more." McLaughlin added, "It was driving me completely crazy... I had to do it in order to survive yet more things were happening musically that I wanted to do."

The sessions, which Pete Brown remembered as depressing McLaughlin almost to the point of despair, included a stint with ex-Shadows drummer Tony Meehan (October 1963). He also recorded two tracks in 1964, "Song of Mexico" and "King of All", alongside John Paul Jones on bass and Sullivan's mate Joe Moretti on lead guitar, as part of Brian Auger's quintet. There was also TV work, including playing in the house orchestra on *Ready Steady Go!*

Cracks were crossing the glass ceiling above McLaughlin's head. He got married, and bore a son, Julian. Work followed with Ian Carr, and crucially, the Rolling Stones. Playing on their 1964 album *Metamorphosis* did his CV no harm at all – simply being there announced his presence to many other, more exalted players. McLaughlin plays on three tracks; "Heart of Stone", "Some Things Just Stick In Your Mind" and "(Walkin' thru the) Sleepy City". Another youngster in the background was one Jimmy Page, who reputedly approached the Yorkshireman for lessons. "Not impossible – in fact, quite probably true. He was good enough for that, even then," declares Jim Sullivan.

Charles Alexander remembers, "McLaughlin, I think, had an idea of just how good he could be. And so did everyone else. Because he practised his instrument like nobody's business. He just put every waking hour into it. He was *serious* about what he was doing in a way that most British musicians aren't and most American musicians are. That's why, in the end, he made it so big. He worked."

One jazz musician of Alexander's acquaintance told him of a mid-'60s gig with McLaughlin when, having travelled hundreds of miles to play a gig, he collapsed exhausted in bed in the room he was sharing with the guitarist, only to be awoken at five in the morning by McLaughlin still practising the phrase he'd been working on four hours earlier.

In 1965 the band became the Graham Bond Organisation, and in doing so, had in the eyes of their hardcore jazz/blues bohemian following sold out to the Beat Boom. They even went as far as to feature in an eye-poppingly dire farrago of a '60s Britpop movie, *Gonks Go Beat*. Nonetheless, history has treated Bond more than kindly, and the affection one senses beneath the tributes and eulogies (Bond died under a train at Finsbury Park Station, London, in June 1974) suggest that the man wasn't only well-liked but was a fine musician. More importantly, at a time when bridges were being built in music, he was a facilitator for players to meet and mingle and make music they were unfamiliar with. "Graham was a crusader, a path-finder," summarised the drummer Jon Hiseman, "...playing music with an improvisatory element that we take for granted in jazz, but which of course had never existed in pop music."

Herbie Goins, one of the supernumerary r'n'b trudgers of the now exploding pop circuit in the UK, was a vocalist of valorous stamina whose musical prowess was judged less in technical merit or good taste than an ability to swing. He offered employment and a congenial jamming atmosphere to his fellow musicians. He was also a generous employer of talented youngsters that could be plundered from the fringes – or from the centre – of the scene. Recognising McLaughlin's potential, Goins secured his services for his band the Night-Timers from autumn 1965 onwards. The chief musicians in the band were Harry Beckett (trumpet and flugelhorn) and Mike Eve (tenor sax).

Despite the mouthwatering motivation of a Parlophone record contract, (McLaughlin's first two recorded tracks, "The Music Played On/Yield Not To Temptation" were released as a single on that label), The Night-Timers' entire *raison d'etre*, as with so many bands of its nature, was as much for the sustenance of like-minded and sympathetic musicians as for the entertainment of the public. Not that this prevented bids for stardom; one single from 1966 (McLaughlin left them in the spring of that year having stayed for about a year) features the guitarist's first recorded composition, a soul number entitled "Cruising".

McLaughlin stoically suffered poverty over pride. He strummed anonymously on a bizarre waste of vinyl recorded in February 1965 called *British Percussion* by the London All Stars. As an attempt at a British jazz percussion showcase, it had about as much relevance to current global jazz thinking as an album by the best percussionists in Tonga, and was all the more pointlessly naïve for the talents it wasted – not least Jimmy Page on lead guitar and McLaughlin on rhythm guitar.

Jim Sullivan, a few years McLaughlin's senior, was by now moving into the session big league. By 1966 he had played onstage and in the recording studio with just about every major British pop solo performer it was possible to name, and McLaughlin could now depend on having friends in high places to drop his name. With the phenomenal growth of pop recording at the time, the musicians' community in London had to survive together and friends getting work for each other was easier to facilitate. Within a few years McLaughlin was playing with employers of Sullivan, notably Tom Jones, Petula Clark and Engelbert Humperdinck. At the other end of the scale, he featured on two tracks, "Let Me Sleep Beside You" and "Karma Man", on the debut album of an edgy, effeminate youth from Beckenham, South London. The album was entitled *The World Of David Bowie*.

Even more outlandishly, McLaughlin helped confer some 'swinging' muscle on Euro-schlock bandmeister Biddu; again teaming up with Jimmy Page and John Paul Jones. Perhaps constraining more pure energy than on any other session in pop history, McLaughlin grooved dutifully along on "Daughter of Love" and "Look Out Here I Come". After a while the sessions got to McLaughlin and he cracked up, jumping into his car one night and driving non-stop the 350 miles to his mother's home just to be free of the pressure of London.

One collaboration with a pop singer who was neither on the way up or at the top, but who had dropped out of the rat race, came in the mid-sixties with the one-time Norrie Paramor protégé Duffy Power. Power hadn't achieved the crooning chart success of an Adam Faith or Cliff Richard and so had attempted to return to his blues roots. For his *Innovations* LP of 1966 he called upon Alexis Korner, who had worked with previously, as well as a host of UK jazz and blues luminaries, including drummer Phil Seaman, bassists Danny Thompson and Jack Bruce as well as pianist Terry Cox. McLaughlin had briefly been in a jazz trio with Thompson and Tony Roberts, a reed man far ahead of his time. BBC recordings of the line-up are reputed to exist, but due to the corporation's now notorious and near-criminal abuse of its own recorded heritage, are next to impossible to obtain.

Power had first crossed McLaughlin's path in June 1963 when the Graham Bond band had appeared on BBC Radio's Light Programme broadcast *Pop Go The Beatles*. "I Got A Woman" and "I Saw Her Standing There" feature Power's vocals; "Cabbage Greens" and "Spanish Blues" make up the sessions. There is little here of distinctive merit; McLaughlin is clearly a polished young player, absolutely in control of his instrument and utterly able to subsume himself to the beat and the drive of the songs. To dwell on his work here is superfluous; one might just as well analyse the rest of the instrumental input. It is functional and expedient. It's the sound of machinery making hit records – which, in this case, didn't actually hit.

Danny Thompson was friendly with a fellow North-easterner, the organist Mike Carr, who just happened to be the brother of McLaughlin's chum Ian Carr. By 1967 McLaughlin featured in Mike Carr's trio, having first encountered him during a Herbie Goins session, as well as appearing with Carr's Emcee Five, of which a summer 1967 live track, "Bell's Blues", from Newcastle on Tyne's New Orleans club, remains in boot-legged posterity.

Sillier things happened as they were wont to do in 1960's. The talented organist Howard Blake had thrown in his chips with the Jimmy Smith-led crusade for non-threatening instrumental jazz-pop. He had house-trained his Hammond to treat the new standards with just the right amount of crossover appeal that wouldn't turn off the kids or offend parents. Among the tracks on *That Hammond Sound* which McLaughlin tactfully accompanied in late summer 1966 were "Moon River", "Till There Was You" (a workaday, sentimental old tune resurrected from its slumber by the Beatles' splendid bossa-nova version) and Sonny Rollins' then-inescapably trendy ballad "Alfie" (from the film of the same name).

There was also the session pop band Twice As Much, a very early attempt by corporate music to 'manufacture' a Beat Boom sound using session musicians only and a shopfront of girl turn-ons as the public face of a 'pop act'. The Twice As Much gimmick was that their leaders, vocalist/pianist Dave Skinner (later to turn up as a temporary member of Roxy Music) and vocalist Stephen Rose were ex-public schoolboys. The uncredited stellar platoon was made up of McLaughlin, Moretti, Page and Sullivan on guitars, not to mention Nicky Hopkins on piano, drummers Eric Ford and Andy White, bassist Alan Weighall and other forgotten studio sloggers whose countless hours upholstering the pop soundtracks of a million childhoods have been long forgotten. The travesties churned out at the behest of Immediate in England's World Cup-winning summer of 1966 included versions of "Help", "Sha La La La Lee", "We Can Work It Out", "As Tears Go By", "Hey Girl", "Do You Wanna Dance" and "You'll Never Get To Heaven". Offhand, competently undertaken, they may just as well have been recorded for a time capsule marked 'Beat Boom' to be bundled into a deep-space probe, so ubiquitous and cynical was their emasculating of current popular songs.

Most of McLaughlin's session cohorts on this and many other dates were friendly with the indefatigable Pete Brown, one of the London underground's premier, moving-and-shaking 'faces'. Brown retains immense affection for his guitarist friend; "Those were funny times. Around the time we started working together I stopped taking drugs and drinking, and things got a lot clearer after that... I used to hang out at Ronnie [Scott]'s old place and I must have probably seen him, maybe once at Klook's, playing with Graham Bond's band. But I do remember seeing John playing with Herbie Goins' band at the Hornsey Art School, either '65 or early '66. I knew Dick [Heckstall-Smith, saxophonist with Bond and others] from 1960, '61... I probably came across John around that time. The main thing that happened was that I started my own little jazz-poetry group. Terry Smith was my guitarist. But I saw John playing then in Mike Carr's trio and being completely and utterly knocked out by what he was doing."

Carr was booked for a summer tour of Majorca. Brown recalls that McLaughlin was indifferent to the idea, so Brown "suggested that Mike take Terry, and I stepped in and offered John some work! John suited my band better than Terry, really."

Originally named The Huge Local Sun, Brown remembers that his ensemble "played together quite a lot, a good few gigs. John was locked into some nasty session work, which he hated because it restricted him. Listening to some of his stuff though, even then you can hear his style coming through. I think he liked playing with me because I let him do more or less what he wanted.

"I didn't know what the hell I was doing," Brown continues. "I was basically a poet, but I'm also a musician, although I didn't realise it at the time. In a way I felt incredibly inhibited by the brilliance of the players around me – of whom John was one! When I got John I knew he was going to be amazing and did all I could to encourage him. He needed encouraging, needed freedom. He was so far beyond anything I could even think of doing at the time, musically. But working with him and other great musicians, inhibited me – when I began singing, I went out and purposely got people who were nowhere near as good!"

Brown recalls that his band was "a little guitar-bass-drums line-up. Pete Bailey, who was Graham's ex-road manager, he'd play percussion. To start off with, Danny Thompson was on bass and Lawrie Allen on drums. I had a bit of a name at the start because, one, I'd done the Royal Albert Hall poetry gig in 1965 with Ginsberg, Ferlinghetti and the Beats, and, two, because of the work I did with Cream from '67 on. We worked together for a year, I'd say, but that work was nothing like regular. We had an on-off residency at the Middle Earth Club.

"We did a very weird psychedelic gig at Bristol Polytechnic. The support band came in, all dressed very straight; suits, short hair, like die-hard Mods. Then they brought in a hamper full of kaftans and wigs, put them on, went on and played "In The Midnight Hour". Totally bizarre, completely incongruous. They came back into the dressing room and changed back again. John was still doing TV sessions and had to drive down at breakneck speed with Binky McKenzie, who by then was playing bass for us. This was before the M4 motorway was built, remember.

"He drove so fast that the minute he got to the gig he ran straight to the bog and threw up. Then we had go on and we stood around like lemons onstage waiting for him. He came out eventually, very apologetic looking and said to me, 'sorry I'm late, Pete, but I've just been a bit Moby...'" [Cockney rhyming slang: Moby Dick = sick].

"John was really playing great," Jack Bruce told an interviewer of his days with the guitarist in the Graham Bond Organisation. "But he was getting very stoned, which was really saying something in those days. He actually fell off the stage at one gig in Coventry and played this death chord as he landed; kkkkrrruuuggggggg!" One well-known musician who saw the band several times at this time told the present author; "they were amazing live. But they were all totally wasted, it seemed to me, totally strung out."

McLaughlin, by all accounts, was a promiscuous experimenter with drugs. One friend later admitted that of all the people he knew who he would have expected to have killed themselves with narcotics, McLaughlin had been top of the list.

Pete Brown, once again; "He could get miserable, though, very depressed. It wasn't the drugs, it was just his situation. He just couldn't see any way of breaking through, and at one point I said to him, seriously, 'John, I honestly think you're one of the best guitar players in the world. You've got something that nobody else has got.' There was terrible snobbery among jazz listeners then. People would sit and listen to John playing his heart out at Ronnie's and they wouldn't get it, because *it wasn't just bebop* – there were other elements in it; Ernest Sumlin, Phil Upchurch. John was *very* into r'n'b. There was still a very great stigma even about the blues, and of course John has very great feeling for the blues."

Work was about, but in terms of expressing himself creatively, McLaughlin was coming to the end of his tether. He was getting on for thirty, and with no hope of a break in sight. At one session with Heckstall-Smith, Brown et al, whilst recording two of Brown's songs, an observer from the industry said sniffily of the band that they were little more than 'jazz hasbeens' – in a year McLaughlin would get the call to New York and help to make jazz history.

That break was partly due to the efforts of two of McLaughlin's old colleagues, Jack Bruce and Ginger Baker. Their elision of rock with jazz elements was emphatic and populist enough to make the phenomenon not only practicable, but sound historically inevitable. This was, as we shall see, the milieu in which McLaughlin's eclectic instincts could best be expressed for himself and for his public.

Baker and Bruce, of course, made up two-thirds of Cream, one of the prime movers in the late '60s assumption of an expressionist ethic by rock musicians, in which only the music, and how it conveyed the inspiration of the player, mattered.

These, of course, had been concerns of jazz musicians for some years. Eric Clapton told one interviewer in 1968 that on one visit to the US with Cream, that "a lot of people in New York, you know – *jazzers* [my italics] were amazed that a pop group was doing such things and that we could get away with it."

That we could get away with it. That was the key; the 1960s were all about getting away with things, but only because people tried them in the first place. By the middle of the decade, the urge to experiment, to confess through musical instruments, had become evangelical. "It is clear," writes Stuart Nicholson, "that as early as 1966 [Cream] were providing a working model of what a fusion between elements of jazz and rock might actually sound like."

Acknowledgement of virtuosity aside, Nicholson's most telling critique of Cream is of Baker's polyrhythmic and plainly Elvin Jones-inspired drumming, which conferred a sense of dramatic light and shade, contrast, and tension and release on the music, colouring it beyond measure – not only tonally, but structurally also.

Interestingly, after Cream, the one-way traffic of tribute between jazz and rock began to change. Beatles cover versions still found their way into the mainstream repertoire, but progressive pop and rock bands, secure in their commercial supremacy, felt the time had come to acknowledge past debts to jazz. Jethro Tull covered Roland Kirk's "Serenade to a Cuckoo" on their debut album, fair exchange for an entire repertoire of flute bravura and gimmickry that the band's leader Ian Anderson had purloined from the older man. Ten Years After romped through Woody Herman's "Woodchopper's Ball". Subsequently, many movers and shakers of Progressive rock, who had finally thrown off traces of r'n'b soloing in clubs up and down the land, shed their inhibitions and came out in sneakers and berets as closet and longtime practising jazzers. Many weren't aware of much differentiation between blues and jazz in the first place. Says Soft Machine drummer Robert Wyatt:

"We just played covers that we could play. We collected Don Covay and Solomon Burke records, and the simpler jazz things of the time – Cannonball Adderley doing soul tunes – there was some soul... you take Booker T and the MGs – it's very easy to move from that to Jimmy Smith and on into jazz."

The rock drummer Bill Bruford, who as a public schoolboy in Tonbridge, Kent, had seen Bond and McLaughlin performing in 1965, recalls them playing material from Ray Charles' LP *Genius + Soul = Jazz*. So fluid was the world of the pop musician becoming, and so vital the necessity to take work from wherever it came, that the distinction between the roots of blues, r'n'b, soul and jazz weren't only dissolving, they were seen not to matter very much any more.

Nicholson claims this was happening as early as 1965, in the shape of Mike Bloomfield's guitar work with Paul Butterfield's Blues Band, stating that "his clear tribute to Wes Montgomery in his use of octaves clearly shows how clearly rock was peering over the fence and looking at jazz."

When a player was fortunate enough to be commissioned to record an album, his (almost exclusively his) friends were often crammed into the recording studio to make some contribution that might enable them to stave off the landlord and his bully boys, or buy a few extra hours on the electricity meter. Better, it would enable them to earn money and play at least a semblance of what they had always wanted to play. It also gave them the sense of being really creative at last – the sense that this was what they'd learnt their chops and slogged around for all these years. Among these dates for McLaughlin was *Experiments With Pops* (Major Minor Records, 1968) by the pianist Gordon Beck, a comparably leftfield interpretation of the music from the hit show *Hair* (rejoicing under the truly fabulous title *Hair At Its Hairiest*) by Sandy Brown and his Gentlemen. His friend Jack Bruce naturally summoned him to work on his solo album, *Things We Like* in August and McLaughlin's last English session towards the end of 1968 was a distinctly strange album *Windmill Tilter* (1969) by the mercurial trumpeter Kenny Wheeler.

Wheeler, a highly talented if painfully introspective young trumpeter and flugelhornist, was one of British jazz's leading young lions in the 1960s. By the end of the decade he was in its vanguard. Concept albums, following the example of Ellington and Evans, were growing in popularity. *Windmill Tilter* was a Cervantes-inspired suite on the Don Quixote theme and sees Wheeler billed as playing "with the Johnny Dankworth Orchestra". Dankworth, himself keen on assuming classical pretentions for jazz composition, was a master arranger and motivator of young talent, and his own playing here is admirable. Wheeler's compositions are vital, fluid and lyrically memorable. One Michael Gibbs, later to surface as the arranger of McLaughlin's first venture into neo-classicism, *Apocalypse*, is numbered among the players as one of two trombonists. Tony Coe's tenor saxophone outdoes Dankworth's alto, and despite the sleevenotes presciently if overpolitely stating that McLaughlin is an 'inscrutable genius who could deserve his own LP soon', the guitarist still plays a largely chordal, traditionally jazzy accompanists' role, as does bassist Dave Holland.

McLaughlin actually appears only on five tracks, "Preamble", "Sweet Dulcinea Brown", "Sancho", "Propheticape" and "Altisidora". It is nonetheless a fine album, well worth investing in for any British and/or orchestral jazz follower. It seems implausible that McLaughlin, an inveterate magpie and indefatigable learner, didn't take some ideas away with him from this record about the integration of blues and classical harmony and the assumption of classical structure. However, it could hardly have been called a major staging post on McLaughlin's road, but is nonetheless important in that it remains one of his last purely in the role of accompanist.

Bruce's album is a marginally rockier affair. About to see the lucrative vehicle of Cream disintegrate under him, it was a chance for Bruce to revisit his love of modern post-bop jazz and also road-test ideas and potential partnerships for the future. Teaming the ebullient Scot with McLaughlin, saxist Dick Heckstall-Smith and drummer Jon Hiseman, it was in effect a blues-boom supergroup. Its accents, however, were singularly jazzy.

Heckstall-Smith, in his excellent memoir *The Safest Place In The World* (Quartet Books, London 1989) describes how McLaughlin turned up at Pete Brown's flat in London's Montague Square and the saxophonist reported his presence to Bruce and Hiseman. Bruce summoned McLaughlin to the sessions, "with a guitar and an incredibly minute, fucked-up amp that made an incredibly minute, fucked-up noise which, when recorded and played back loud, sounded out of this world.... John just joined in, without rehearsal."

The guitar's lines still lack authority; they unobtrusively integrate into the rhythm section's woodwork. Still shy of too many effects, McLaughlin sounds more like a jazz or blues player than a rock player, although his more experimental timbres betray a recent free-jazzing stint with Gunter Hampel (see below). His solo on "Sam Enchanted Dick" shows audacity, though, and the range of his musical thinking is beginning to make itself known.

It's probably only McLaughlin's presence that distinguishes the session from a full-on post-bop blow, although Hiseman's irresistibly busy bass drum and fondness for a foursquare rock beat shouldn't be discounted. "Hckkh Blues" is perhaps the most extreme example, with hurried full-ensemble ostinato themes and stop-start time-signatures. Bruce, who plays an acoustic bass throughout, is much more static on this track and more redolent of his his electric bass guitar playing with Cream.

By the late 1960s McLaughlin had just enough time and money to separate from his wife (and young son) and remarry. Eve McLaughlin had been a friend of Pete Brown's; "I'd met her at her art school when I did a gig there. She came to London and was actually Lawrie Allen's girlfriend but she broke up with him, bonded with John and they got married."

McLaughlin became increasingly anxious about the effect upon his creativity imposed by the constraining nature of session work. For instance, he had rejoined Georgie Fame, playing on the hit albums *Knock On Wood* and *Three Faces Of Fame* between spring 1967 and spring 1968. McLaughlin also actually played guitar on a BBC concert session featuring Fame's global smash "The Ballad of Bonnie and Clyde". Annoyed by

the limitations that even swinging London placed upon the kind of unfet-
tered Romantic musical creative endeavours he'd grown up with,
McLaughlin tried his luck in Europe with the German free-jazz vibra-
phonist and multi-intrumentalist Gunter Hampel, basing himself halfway
between Germany and England in the Belgian city of Antwerp, "so I
could go back to England every now and again."

There are no extant recordings with Hampel, but shortly afterwards
McLaughlin went into the studio under his own name for the first time.
He had been nurturing a "fantastic" little trio with his friend Dave
Holland and the fundamentalist free-jazz disciple Tony Oxley on drums.
McLaughlin meanwhile managed to wheedle a contract out of Polydor
subsidiary Marmalade on the strength of his performance on Gordon
Beck's LP the previous year – also a Marmalade product. Holland, meanwhile, had been summoned to the ranks of Miles Davis' band, so Oxley's
friend Brian Odgers stood in. The young phenomenon of the baritone
saxophone, John Surman, joined in the fun on January 16th 1969 for a
session – which would later be released to initial dismissal but growing
and then sustained raptures – for a solo LP release tentatively entitled
Extrapolation.

The album, while enjoying only modest sales in the UK and margin-
alised to a cult Progressive rock audience, immediately assumed the status of a minor classic, not only of its genre but in the repertoire of the
popular guitar. Saddled with poor distribution, McLaughlin should have
become a major guitar superstar overnight. At times the music was too
diffuse to overwhelm the public at large, but it nonetheless confounded
guitar aficionados everywhere with its sheer audacity of conception and
steel-nerved panache of execution. A star was born, no doubt about it.

Critics struggled to elucidate McLaughlin's quality. Listening to
Extrapolation today it's impossible to imagine what an impact it had on
the discerning jazz and rock guitar lover. Perhaps the most dazzling features were the harmonic arsenal at the group's disposal, and the leader's
quicksilver imagination when soloing. In the words of Jim Sullivan, one
of McLaughlin's greatest assets was his "speed of thought and action. It's
extraordinary. Not many people have that ability... the minute the idea
occurs it's down there on the fretboard".

The other stand-out was the ferocity of McLaughlin's tone, depth-
charging the genteel backwater of jazz guitar styling with extreme prejudice. The guitar was no longer a surrogate horn, but a noise machine in
itself. "I love the sound of distortion," McLaughlin would later tell an
interviewer, when reminiscing about his 1960s salad days. "In those days

you could get this Vox amp [with a] *bad* sound. I wanted a big amp. I found a circuit diagram for something – maybe a Fender. I knew this cabinet maker who would make me a really big speaker... Ginger [Baker] used to play so strongly, along with Jack [Bruce] and Graham [Bond]. I'll never forget the day I got this amp. We were on the gig and plugged it in. I found out that I could get feedback, but it was uncontrolled because I was playing a Gretsch guitar at the time, a hollowbody with pickups on it. But I noticed there were some notes I could get to really feed back on me. If I really pushed the amp, I could get it to distort which was, for me, quite a revelation. It was kind of scary at first... I didn't know how to handle distortion at the time, but I discovered with this amp if I got up to the amp with the guitar and it came out as screaming feedback because it didn't like it. I'd go up to it with one of the notes it never liked and the amp would go *grrowwwllll*."

This was pretty much unlike anything the jazz world had heard before. It was already to be heard from a young man named Larry Coryell in America. That was where the future was, and that was where McLaughlin was headed next.

Stuart Nicholson summarises the album's significance admirably; "rhythmically and harmonically fluid, *Extrapolation* made use both of modal harmonies and of the 'time, no changes' principle as a basis for improvisation in which the composition provides tempo, key and mood, leaving the choice of chord changes to the spontaneous interaction of improviser and accompanists... what is immediately striking is McLaughlin's technical facility... he also accented his notes evenly, rather than employing a 'jazz-swing' feeling, using relatively little syncopation in the construction of his phrases."

This abstract approach is heard to its best advantage on "Pete The Poet", dedicated to McLaughlin's friend, the poet and librettist Pete Brown. The guitar tone that so impressed was a fat, gutsy tone, as dirty, sweaty and downhome as a pair of standard-issue chain-gang dungarees, but allied to this was a jazzman's sense of fluid invention.

The whole album runs as a segued sequence of pieces, and to most ears it is far more jazz than rock, from the bebop-flavoured unison melody statements of the title track and opener to the fizzing and crackling top-kit work of drummer Oxley. Surman plays up a storm on baritone and soprano saxes, and for long stretches his personality seems the more dominant, although there's no question that McLaughlin's mediation of mood through choice of phrasing and chords dictates the feel of the album. It is as the record goes on that the guitarist comes more and more to the fore. There is little of the devastating speed heard later, but given Surman's own penchant for furious velocity of blowing that's hardly surprising. McLaughlin's wildly strummed solo on the riotous "Two For Two", the most prophetic number on the album, makes for riveting listening however. Even his acoustic work, on the Bill Evans-derived "Peace Piece" which ends the album, sounds new, spikily aggressive, with a brutal attack.

Two of the compositions also betray a genuinely original musical mind. These are "Arjen's Bag" (a tribute to Dutch bassist Arjen Gorter, later reworked as "Follow Your Heart") and "Binkie's Beam" (a tribute to British bassist Binkie Mackenzie, sometimes listed as "Binkie's Dream" and later to become the body of "Celestial Terrestrial Commuters" on the 1973 Mahavishnu Orchestra album *Birds of Fire*).

McLaughlin might have been hailed as a revolutionary, but it was plain that in London at least, the counterculture was being postponed. The dream had begun to disintegrate by the late sixties. In the words of Mick Farren, "the hippies... either died or went home [and]... gangs of skinheads began to invade." The casualties of the party began to mount – Cyril Davies, two Brians (Jones and Epstein), Joe Orton. Among the scores of other unheralded personal tragedies in bedsits where the headlines didn't reach, one of the most tragic of all, perhaps because of its neglect by historians – was Binky Mackenzie. McLaughlin's one-time colleague and friend, whom he had first recorded with during sessions for Duffy Power in late 1966, is at least alive today, but by some accounts may as well not be. Pete Brown recalls the story thus; "Binky was playing electric by then [1968], and I was gassed with him, I thought he was way ahead of his time. He had a bit of a chip on his shoulder, because at the time, black musicians had a hard time of it. But he was such an innovator on the bass, and he was a tremendous influence on Colin Hodgkinson from Back Door, whose technique in turn had an influence on Stanley Clarke.

"But the openings were so few, it didn't matter how good you were. And Binky had very weird parents, very straight, very religious. A lot of people couldn't get Binky's musicianship, but John saw it and in fact he recommended Binky to Miles.

"Binky did drugs. Who didn't? Not much, just personal use. Didn't deal. But his parents got very heavy about it and called the police in, and Binky did time. When he came out of the nick, he was one very, very angry young man indeed." The upshot was a domestic siege in which McKenzie killed one of his parents and injured the other. He is now serving life in a secure unit, but, as Brown points out, McLaughlin still visits him when in England. "He's about the only one of us that still does, I think," he adds, sombrely.

It was time for those who were going to profit from the counterculture to put up or shut up. McLaughlin put up. Or rather, someone else put up for him. "He deserved it," says one friend. "He'd been smashing his head against a brick wall for so long. He was so good, he deserved a break."

It came, and McLaughlin took it.

Chapter Two
A Bigger Apple

The origin of rock 'n' roll was primarily in the music of black America. The origin of jazz was almost entirely in the music of black America. But not quite.

Both musical forms only became themselves, only succeeded as cultural artefacts and business propositions, thanks to sometimes accidental, sometimes expedient, sometimes intentional collaborations with white musicians and white musical styles. Some went further, even claiming that the evolution of jazz was another case in point. "Jazz wouldn't even exist without America," drummer Art Blakey once commented.

Popular music, at nearly every level of creation, has always been about compromise, whether willed or otherwise. The Beat Boom, an Anglicised hybrid of r'n'b and rock 'n' roll, was a classic synthesising of two antitheses; the American tradition and parochial British traditions. The synthesising tendency inherent in British pop music in the 1960s is well documented above and elsewhere.

In the world of jazz, as Stuart Nicholson has perceptively pointed out, this raised several issues. The immense popularity accorded to rock 'n' roll served to diminish jazz in the popular cultural pantheon. It was off the dais. Hamstrung and leaderless, it faced another challenge, from within.

Society faced not only disquiet among youth, but among racial minorities. In the US, black militancy for civil rights was gaining ground. If the world could be changed in Selma or Watts, it could also be changed on the jazz platform. A new generation of musicians determined to search and locate the 'blackness' within jazz. Miles Davis, Ornette Coleman, Archie Shepp in their own diverse ways reconstituted the form and aligned its idiom decisively away from the white bourgeois marketplace, away from what they perceived to be the emasculated nature of the music at the hands of white consumers, managers and record labels.

Jazz rose manfully to the challenge; younger jazz musicians had to play rock or pop to survive, the net result being the opportunistic likes of Blood Sweat & Tears and Chicago, who fancied being neither underground freaks nor serious concert musicians. Elder statesmen and women of the genre tried to take the popsters on at their own game and, discreetly, the pop cover version slipped into the jazz repertoire (notably Duke Ellington's take on "I Want To Hold Your Hand" and, somewhat more shamelessly, Count Basie's *Basie's Beatle Bag*, both appearing in 1966).

"You've got to bend a little their way," commented Basie. "Meet them halfway at least – give a little of their flavour... just to let them know that we know they're alive." Most of these well-intentioned efforts (note the them-and-us terminology), in their attempts to 'tune into the kids' had about as much understanding of contemporary youth culture as an average episode of *Ironside*. The momentum of the embrace of pop and rock was irreversible. Wes Montgomery and Bud Shank both courted the symphonic light music market with 'tasteful' renderings of pop numbers, with jazz little more than a memory which distantly shaded their phrasing. Nicholson observes that a mere mention of Stan Getz's 1970 album, *Marrakesh Express,* "would probably make Getz spin in his grave like a lathe". Jazz still disdained pop; occasional *rapprochements*, such as Chuck Berry's playing with Jack Teagarden and Buck Clayton at the 1958 Newport Jazz Festival, remained rule-proving exceptions.

By the end of 1967, though, *Down Beat* magazine was proclaiming that rock 'n' roll had come of age (presumably something to do with justifying the pages of Fender and Gibson guitar adverts that broke up the vehemently anti-rock editorial and critical opinions). The result was that the Beatles strolled nonchalantly onto the cover of the magazine.

Young white jazz musicians had their own agenda; "everybody was dropping acid and the prevailing attitude was let's do something different." This was the guitarist Larry Coryell, who "loved Wes Montgomery... Bob Dylan... Coltrane... The Beatles. We wanted people to know we are very much part of the contemporary scene, but at the same time we had worked our butts off to learn this other music [jazz]. It was a very sincere thing."

Coryell couldn't have learned in any other way; the advent of the Beatles guaranteed a phenomenal increase in the ubiquity of pop music. The implications for youth lifestyles in the 1960s was immense, especially as America still trusted that its youth was malleably patriotic enough to lay everything aside for the good of the flag and society, specifically in Vietnam. The Beatles, as much for their rampage through popular culture as through the hysteria their music engendered, hinted that this reality need not be so. It would have been scarcely natural to not have succumbed.

In 19 Eldridge Street, New York City, in 1965, a score of young jazz-raised musicians lived, and loved the Beatles and James Brown. "When I first heard James Brown," noted the pianist Mike Nock, "it floored me." Reading any account of twenty-something New York City jazz life in the 1960s is not only to open a who's who of fusion greatness but to realise just how completely and simultaneously a generation was seduced by rock and what it seemed to embody. It was the transfiguration of the world (collective or individual) through music and self-expression that so appealed to young jazzers. They played non-jazz venues; they listened to Motown records; they wouldn't have been seen dead playing in a tuxedo even if they could have afforded one. Outside the Coryell ménage at 19 Eldridge Street was the Jeremy Steig circle, with the flautist assembling pianist Warren Bernhardt and bass prodigy Eddie Gomez into a performing unit, with Mike Mainieri on vibes also a contributor.

This was symptomatic. After the assassination of Kennedy and the Vietnam tragedy of errors, kicking out the jams had become a national sport among the under-25s. Barriers were there to be broken. "Psychedelic rock and avant-garde jazz are being fused into an orgasm of emotion and integral art-life totality," foamed the *East Village Other*. Suddenly here, quite incidentally, was a musical and cultural way back for young jazz musicians to communicate their love to their peers.

Those who took the plunge included vibist Gary Burton, whose *Duster* album (1967) gave the rock-oriented guitarist Larry Coryell his head. Coryell, who had already recorded with his own band the Free Spirits, was perhaps the first jazz-raised guitarist to dally with rock voicings and timbres with any kind of abandon. As Nicholson has said, listening to McLaughlin rehearse with Bob Cornford in 1968 – especially on the tune "Good Citizen Swallow" – is to realise how, even through the relatively poor distribution channels of jazz recordings, Coryell's playing had been broadcast and absorbed by those willing to listen. Importantly, it was assimilated by those who felt they could not only go so far, but moreover, wanted to go further.

Rock presented jazz with a fundamental problem. Jazz's appeal had less to do with the electronic reproduction of sound; for jazz musicians, musical artefacts were endlessly malleable, "Lush Life" or "My Foolish Heart" were inexhaustible sources of individual improvisational interpretation. Jazz listeners viewed music similarly. Most rock musicians and listeners valued an individual performance committed to disc as the Holy Grail. As Stuart Nicholson points out, Bud Shank's rendition of "The Sound Of Silence" sounds inauthentic because of the sheer insistence of the sonic image of Simon and Garfunkel's recording of it. Rock and pop music appropriated electronics as a means of manufacturing itself as a cultural artefact and thereby creating the definitive parameters of its own genre.

Electronics, in terms of amplification, also played a part in the development of rock instrumental technique. For Nicholson, a jazz trio attempting to cover a rock standard sounds trite when compared to the original. For example, Chuck Berry's "Maybellene" would not work because the music lacks the electrified drive and pulse for which its musical structure is best suited. This is not to condemn rock 'n' roll as musically simplistic, merely mutually dependent on electric amplification for its greatest musical effects. To older jazz musicians, rock was simply a rhythmical thing, like a bossa nova. They were, in Nicholson's words, "missing the point by a mile". If jazz was going to take on rock, it needed the instruments and the amplification too. It needed to assimilate its own syntax and vocabulary into that of rock. The shift of musical consciousness needed to be considerable. It needed to retain integrity, win new fans and earn a future.

For Nicholson, jazz had to match rock's sex appeal. This author prefers to (reluctantly) recruit the help of the French semiologist Roland Barthes. While much of what Barthes wrote about music is worthless, his concept of the 'grain' of a singing voice was sympathetic to those critics who attempted to put the strange majesty and compulsion of rock's soundworld into words. I would contend that this was what jazz needed to either colonise or assimilate into its own soundworlds. The resultant technocratic production and effects-heavy trends in jazz-rock seem to bear this out.

Jazz-rock became a national phenomenon in America with the rise of Blood Sweat & Tears and Chicago. Both combined rock energy and groovy psychedelia with lengthy instrumental extemporisations. But ultimately the sole vindicator of the jazz half of their generic rubric came down to the crude augmentation of their sound with brawnily soul-jazz fatback horn sections and garrulous, almost parodic attempts at big-band bop. The brusque shoehorning of these elements into otherwise straightforward rock numbers soon became recognised for the cheap gimmick that it was.

Others had a nobler aim; to integrate other musical influences to a degree that might best be articulated as a musical style, whereby both jazz and rock musicians could learn and add to their own generic vocabularies. Thus, the pioneers who outlined the concept of such a musical relationship in the US, were those musicians who opened negotiations between the two camps, or, to use a better analogy, introduced the prospective couple. The marriage still had to be consummated. And in Jimi Hendrix, Miles Davis, and eventually John McLaughlin, the marriage brokers were found. Davis and McLaughlin not only brokered the marriage, they arranged it down to the supply of contraceptives on the bridal pillow.

* * *

Davis' music, in the 1960s, was meditative, suggestive, allusive. The formation of his 1964 quintet – Tony Williams (drums), Ron Carter (bass), Wayne Shorter (saxes) and Herbie Hancock (piano)   seemed to suggest an ever-greater minimalisation and distillation of the beauties of jazz harmony and phrasing. Saxophonist Shorter's instantaneous compositional blossoming – perceived jazz wisdom still resists heralding his genius as player, composer and avatar – reified Davis' impressionist vision with originals from within the band line-up. Shorter's apparently bitty but elliptical compositions were exquisitely clever games with rhythm, melody and harmony that allowed the rhythm section to eschew old bop patterns. They also enabled the rhythm section to come to the fore by providing impressionistic spacing between phrases. Williams filled in with polyrhythms, only adding to the fleeting, liquid, impressionist nature of the whole. But Williams' drumming counted for more, for the future – it shaped jazz fusion drumming to come. The result was the rhythmic language of jazz fusion – sometimes proto-symphonic and with intimations of the polyrhythmic subtlety embodied in an African 'drum choir' effect. Alternatively, it also allowed the foregrounding of a rock rhythm. By the time of recording the title track of *Nefertiti* (1967), this could be a sixteen-bar theme repeated for ten minutes which, given the impressionistic nature of Williams' polyrhythms hitherto, were dutifully garnished with all manner of rhythmic grace notes. Streams of eighth-notes – a bop device – were substituted with fragmentary solo voices, epigrams rather than rhetoric. Complexity had become a means and an end, but so had a rock beat. The 'walking' bassline was out, and drum patterns, albeit sporadically, were becoming squarer and rockier by the month.

But music wasn't the only motivation in Davis' rockward move. As Ian Carr's biography outlines, Miles was increasingly dismayed by the way in which his record company, Columbia, were pouring larger and larger sums into the development of rock music. Carr's faultless musicological dialectics outline the organic progression of Davis' 1960s repertoire towards a collective harmonic/rhythmic group voice that was sympathetic to rock. Carr also outlines Davis' concerns that some critics were, by the time of *Miles In The Sky* (late 1967) inferring that Davis was missing the bus; that his music was straying farther and farther from the social and cultural hotspots of America. Riled at the thought he might be abandoning the ghetto, Davis plagued Columbia for more favourable PR and set to the task of understanding what was going on around him. The fact that he integrated rock voicings so slickly into his subsequent records vouches for not only his artistic integrity (he deplored the easy expediency of Chicago/BST-styled 'jazz-rock') and his idiosyncratic musical genius. As one of Carr's chapter titles suggests, Davis robustly proved that 'jazz into rock *will* go', at a cost to neither style.

Another, altogether wilder card in the deck was the guitarist Jimi Hendrix. A mainly blues practitioner for the years up until 1967, his outlandish and revolutionary technique, both as a utiliser of electronics and, simultaneously, as an improvising soloist, were greeted in jazz with equal parts dismay and messianic fervour.

Hendrix's drummer, Mitch Mitchell introduced him to Tony Williams, who hustled the guitarist some sessions with Larry Young. He also invited Hendrix to sit on embryonic sessions for Williams' new band Lifetime, although with conspicuous lack of success. The freeform Young/Hendrix sessions, however, were altogether more successful. Nicholson; "the guitarist uses sustained feedback and wah-wah effects in an improvisatory context, juxtaposed against the riffs of Young's organ. In these sessions, the possibilities of rock-jazz fusion emerge as something real, tangible and in places euphoric."

Hendrix fully realised the potential that volume and distortion could bring to improvisation, both melodically and timbrally. Hendrix was the first musician to treat electric guitar as *just that*, an electronic instrument per se and use it thus. "Nobody could doubt that Hendrix was a rock 'n' roll musician, yet to jazz musicians... he was also a jazz performer," eulogised *Rolling Stone* magazine.

Hendrix himself never openly espoused a jazz image or handle. He and his management were too aware of his chart potential for that. Although with time, had he lived, assuming jazz colours might have proved profitable – especially given the direction of jazz, rock, and its hybrids in the 1970s. Here was a young man with an instinctive understanding of the blues, not only as mythological chain-gang folkiness, but as potentially-complex harmonic improvisor's paradise. It was the most complete personal assimilation of blues harmony as a colouristic tool since Coltrane. Moreover, his understanding of electronics – of feedback, overtones, reverberation was quite peerless among musicians of the time. No one else was capable of deploying such sounds as agents of tension and release, both for individuals and amongst small group settings with such mastery.

The sheer bravura brilliance of Hendrix as a soloist was catalytic; given the fact that Larry Coryell in New York and McLaughlin in London, both voracious consumers of his work, were painstakingly mapping out their own routes from electric blues to jazz. As such, his influence in the electrification of jazz can never be overstated. Hendrix gave jazz guitar permission to take the turn it did. Without him, McLaughlin might never have been classed as anything more than a delicate, musicianly freak-show. McLaughlin could be as loud and brazen a player as Hendrix, but he never had the American's physical or musical charisma, the potency of which made the 'black Elvis' tag almost inevitable. Hendrix and Davis – who influenced each other – had the chutzpah to push jazz too far. They succeeded, partly thanks to the artistic climate of the age, and partly due to their own phenomenal abilities and mythologies.

On March 25th 1969, McLaughlin and Holland recorded with Hendrix in New York at Record Plant studios, with Buddy Miles sitting in on drums. It says something for the naivety of a rock industry then regarded as an implacable juggernaut of cultural capitalism that no contracts had been signed for the release of the results. Perhaps just as well, however; released as *Hell's Session* in bootleg form in 1988, McLaughlin said laconically and with a metaphorical shrug, "it was just a session... it was four o'clock in the morning and everyone was a bit tired." McLaughlin nonetheless testified also; "I loved Jimi... I was playing this hollow-bod-ied Hummingbird and it was feeding back all the time. It was so loud in there. But I didn't care... Jimi was killing." The sessions, involving but not engrossing, suggest otherwise.

McLaughlin's own ventures into Hendrix-like territory are amply and startlingly catalogued on *Devotion*, an album peculiarly occluded in the guitarist's output. This may be partly due to its rarity – it was initially hard to obtain in the UK and even harder in the US. This was thanks in no small part to the minimal distribution enjoyed by Alan Douglas, on whose eponymous label it appeared. Secondly, the record was often wrongly credited to "John McLaughlin and Buddy Miles", despite the fact that the input from the Band of Gypsies' drummer to the album is marginal, to say the least. As several critics pointed out, he was a poor substitute for Tony Williams' drumming in Lifetime. Thirdly, the album was almost disowned by McLaughlin for many years.

Having taped the LP in New York in March 1970, he went on the road with Williams' Lifetime to return two months later to find that the record had been mixed, produced and pressed without any input from him what-soever. McLaughlin was miffed; but after years of barrel-scraping penury, the contract waved under his nose by Alan Douglas – $2,000 for two LPs – was tempting, and he proceeded to embark on the second of the two, *My Goal's Beyond*, with only token complaint.

Alan Douglas has been dismissed by some as one of the most rapacious and musically venal leeches in the rock business. Others portray him as a hard-working preservationist of some of the electric guitar's richest her-itage. This dichotomy makes divination of his motives on many occa-sions problematic. How much did he care for the music? How much did he care for the musicians? On the evidence of *Devotion*, he cared for the music only slightly more than for eating hot rivets.

Devotion, while containing some fine music, was an abortion. It has the air of a flown kite; the presence of two of the Band of Gypsies, Buddy Miles and the bassist Billy Rich, indicate that Douglas may well have been testing the potential of a new guitar idol or at least comparing his chops to those of his most precious asset. There's no proof either way; the lavish gatefold sleeve and state-of-the-art psychedelic rubbish mas-querading as artwork (a nauseating aquatic distortion of an apparently-bearded McLaughlin and his classical guitar amidst garish foliage) sug-gests investment in a valuable new asset. But how far was Douglas play-ing McLaughlin off against Hendrix?

The music offers few clues. It wants for Hendrix's laterally-thought-out gift of surprise and heaven-storming audacity, as well as his gut feeling for the blues. How odd that here, in this context, McLaughlin's blues feeling should misfire. It often languishes, as though waiting impatiently for ignition. It's still a worthy effort, though. It's enjoyable and illuminating to contrast McLaughlin's western pop and classical tradition, with the musical summits Hendrix was scaling from the tradition of American blues and African tribalism.

McLaughlin was by now immersing himself ever deeper in Indian lore and learning, although the definitive conversion was some way off. India sings from every note of the music; the title track, dominated by the omnipresence of a two-note riff (reminiscent of "In My Life" from 1976's *Inner Worlds*) creates and sustains a drone-mood recalling a raga's opening. There's already a massive harmonic vocabulary quarter-backing McLaughlin's instincts, arising from the hectic variety and tone-coloration of his choice of notes in a solo. Already he is doing just about everything tonal (and polytonal) around chord progressions it's possible to imagine. Particularly notable are his solos on the opener and on "Siren", where a blues line is quirkily twisted at its end to set up another raga-like feel. This is obviously more European than Hendrix – ditto the orchestral thinking behind the playing on occasions. At the outset of "Don't Let The Dragon Eat Your Mother" his picking recalls tuned percussion. The climbing chords here, incidentally, would reappear as "Resolution" and "One Word" on later LPs. But there's also a soul-jazz feel; "Marbles" is almost like Motown in its perky pulse, built smartly from the guitar/drums interplay at the outset.

McLaughlin's solos are double-tracked with delightfully anarchic abandon, blisteringly fuzzed, distorted and fed back. Not only is he finding a rock accent here, but by the finale of "Purpose of When", the phraseology of his solo resembles later Mahavishnu Orchestra work. It's almost too tempting to concentrate on the album purely as a preamble to that band, and indicators of the future are left prominently lying around, with unisono accelerations of subtle and not so subtle kinds. The rhythmic ambiguity of the superb "Siren" is knocking on a door marked 'Billy Cobham'.

The real find, though, is organist Young. A spectacular talent, his revolutionising of the Hammond organ didn't only encompass jazz, it compared favourably to any rock practitioner, even the man described as "the Hendrix of the organ", Britain's Keith Emerson. But few organists ever developed the sheer tonal and textural iridescent beauty of the instrument while also appreciating its immense suggestive power as a rhythmic motor. The drummer Bill Bruford, when appreciatively appraising the talent of the young Rick Wakeman on his entry to Yes in 1971 said; "he had a burning organ sound. It cut." Young's organ burned and cut but also healed and painted and caressed.

But McLaughlin's album it was, and in truth Young's talent never did receive its due. McLaughlin, meanwhile, had built a little on a lot, and was ready to go into the studio again, this time with a quite different line-up for a record commissioned by England's Pye Records, *When Fortune Smiles*.

Whilst McLaughlin's guitar may have been the only 'electric' instrument on the record, *Fortune* is nonetheless important not only to his career, but to the jazz-rock trajectory he helped plot. The language is basically Coltraneian post-bop, with more notes and scales than anyone can count. To this end, analysis hardly seems worthwhile. What makes the album so important is the textural density of it, most notably that between saxophonist John Surman (a hangover from the *Extrapolation* sessions) and McLaughlin himself. At first Surman garners all the laurels, for speed if nothing else. On the formally conventional opener he simply goes berserk with floridity, while miraculously maintaining rhythmic thrust. It's like a goad to McLaughlin, who's slow to respond but by the album's end he has cranked up his guitar sound from relatively polite to as demonic as anything heard on *Devotion* or *Extrapolation*. Given the acoustic nature of the ensemble, this distorts balance and often gives a surreal effect. But it's a measure of his voicing and of the irresistible rhythmic pulse – even in the album's wildest moments of free jazz, of which there are plenty – that by the time *When Fortune Smiles* comes off the turntable all the elements seem to be in place for jazz-rock.

It would be wrong to leave it there, however. *When Fortune Smiles* is not simply a historical document, not simply a component of jazz teleology. It also contains moments of melting beauty, exemplified by two lengthy meditations which form the quiet heart of the record; "Earth Bound Hearts" and the title cut. On the former, McLaughlin's harmonies are austere and faintly forbidding, but his phrasing, though that of a rocker, is exquisite, poised and tender. "Where Fortune Smiles" is a duet with vibist Karl Berger, inhabiting however a quite different soundworld; wistful, almost sentimental. Again the emphasis is on establishing the mood of a raga-like tonality, which Berger and McLaughlin do with magnificent sensitivity and also kinetic mobility. All the loveliest chords that can arise do arise; the slow appearance of a chord sequence prefigures "A

Lotus On Irish Streams" and "Thousand Island Park" from later work, not to mention McLaughlin's meditations on Bill Evans' music. His touch here is as delicate as a pond-skater's; surely it is no coincidence that he was at the time studying the viña, a four-stringed Indian lute with legendary sensitivity of tone. A pity about the disgraceful recording, but taken with *Extrapolation* and *Devotion*, the album is the perfect finale to a triptych of development, not just in the life of one musician but of a whole musical style.

* * *

Miles Davis' *In A Silent Way* and Lifetime's *Emergency!* were released practically simultaneously; one of the biggest double whammies in recording history. Miles' LP was the velvet glove; Williams' very much the iron first. *Silent Way* is just as the title suggests – it tiptoes through its 38-minute length. *Emergency!* is similarly aptly named. It careers along like an invading army, and, given its 71-minute double-LP length, a big one at that.

Williams had been a child prodigy who, before he was seventeen, had played with Sam Rivers and Jackie McLean and jammed with Art Blakey and Max Roach. Then came the call from Davis. Having failed to persuade Davis to take the jazz-rock route in 1964, and having heard Charles Lloyd and Gary Burton bee-lining for the new stylistic grail, Williams determined to make a bid himself. He left Davis amicably – and after a failed attempt to woo the avant-garde electric guitarist Sonny Sharrock into a new unit, he chose McLaughlin.

It was not, contrary to popular opinion, a call from Miles Davis that took McLaughlin to the US, but that of Williams. Dave Holland had been meant to play on *Extrapolation* but Davis called him first. Already within the master's circle after playing on the sessions for *Filles de Kilimanjaro* and what would later become *Water Babies*, Holland called McLaughlin from Washington in November 1968 and asked, "Guess who I'm with?"

"Miles?", answered McLaughlin.

"No," replied Holland. "Tony Williams. And he wants to talk to you."

Holland had played Williams a tape that he and McLaughlin had cut in London the previous month – on October 28th, 1968, to be precise – with drummer Jack DeJohnette, visiting the British capital with Bill Evans.

Nicholson; "Two tracks are with an acoustic piano and are subdued, post-bop compositions using a tonal centre or 'time, no changes' as a basis for improvisation, creating moods of fluid introspection.

Rhythmically and harmonically, McLaughlin is at home in this challenging climate, responding to the ebb and flow of creative impulse yet subtly mediating the mood through the strength of his own musical personality.... the final track is constructed around a two-bar rock vamp, derived from the first two bars of 'Money'."

For Nicholson, evidently here was a musician with "much in reserve", playing just "technicolour flashes" of virtuosity. He terms the recordings a "glimpse of the future, a recording which demonstrates more than any other of the period a union between jazz and rock that confronts volume – electricity – as an important element in constructing a new dynamic... power and volume were central to the group's expressionism. As the music swirls and eddies around the collective energy of the moment, it leaps free of the traditional song forms associated with rock into open form, enabling the musicians to take the music wherever they want."

McLaughlin left London for New York on February 3rd 1969, Williams having called him a few days hitherto. His good fortune lasted; on his first day in the city he produced a blinding performance during a jam session, knocking out an audience at Basie's in Harlem which happened to include all of Cannonball Adderley's band, Larry Coryell and Miles Davis. Coryell was convinced after just thirty seconds of McLaughlin's first solo that this was the finest guitarist he'd heard in his life. This, rather than the Williams connection or any fabled phone call, was what convinced Davis to summon McLaughlin for the forthcoming *In A Silent Way* sessions.

McLaughlin could hardly have been surprised by the reception. He had been on autopilot for stardom for some time. The interest of Williams proved that. It was the presence of Miles Davis that overawed the guitarist. Davis had been until that day, McLaughlin later admitted, a "man who had lived inside of my imagination, inside my record player for so many years. Suddenly to be confronted with the actual reality... was quite disturbing emotionally, but not in an unpleasant way."

McLaughlin did not join Miles Davis' extant group; committed to Williams' project, he politely rebuffed Davis' enthusiastic overtures. "It was so important for me to go with Tony Williams. I had compositions and I realised with Tony I would have more of a chance to play them than with Miles." Moreover, McLaughlin had been a Williams fan for some time. The justly famed recording of Miles Davis' classic 1964 quintet recording at Carnegie Hall 'knocked out' McLaughlin. "When I heard Tony Williams," he told one reporter, "that was it. The guy was unbelievable."

When Davis tried a second time to entice McLaughlin in December 1970, the guitarist again gently rebuffed him. There had been too much 'invested' in Lifetime, he asserted, an investment that was to prove emotionally and financially costly – in the short term, in any case.

The third member of the (originally bass-less) band was organist Larry Young, who himself was also in Miles Davis' orbit. Born in 1940 in Newark, New Jersey, he had turned from piano to organ at 16 after having played the one installed on the bandstand at his father's jazz club. He was a seasoned recording player, with a string of solo efforts for Prestige and for Blue Note, all of which drew enthusiastic or bemused notices. Like McLaughlin he had also played with Hendrix during the late spring of 1969 and was much in-demand. He had transformed the jazz identity of the Hammond organ from the somewhat gospelly, rhetorical voice it had hitherto been in the hands of Jimmy Smith and others, and made it into a modally improvisatory monster after the fashion of Coltrane's saxophone. (Young had sat in with Coltrane shortly before the older man's death and hung out with him at his house, experimenting with mixing instrumental voices).

Emergency was recorded at Olmstead Studios, NYC, between 26th and 28th May 1969. The ludicrous quality of the recording couldn't disguise its importance. The album explodes like a police action. *No one* is going to argue until this thing is *over*. It's hard, though, to evaluate the album objectively now; hindsight has seen to that. Its novelty, perhaps its most jarring feature, is now history, but it's still a mammoth achievement. The music is predominantly tonal, and doesn't once approach the out-and-out shock value of the free jazz that McLaughlin was playing (see *Where Fortune Smiles*) but the whole has an authority, an almost tangible sense of its own manifest destiny as a trailblazing album. The *voicings* are what matters here.

This sounds undeniably like a rock band, not a jazz group playing rock. The volatility of the relationship between instruments force a blurring of timbre. Listen to the opening of "Where", with Young's organ and McLaughlin's guitar becoming each other – and the muscled volume of the whole is irresistible. There are jazz fingerprints – Williams' triple-time ride cymbal, for example – but also of rock (his inexhaustible, pumping hi-hat which would kick songs into action at the drop of a hat, as noted by the excellent liner notes by James Isaacs in the 1991 CD reissue of the album). Apart from a few places in which transitions from 'rock' to 'jazz' time signatures are a little telegraphed, as in "Sangria For

Three" there really is no point in trying to distinguish where the bound-
aries are drawn, and that is the achievement of this stunning record.

Williams' drumming is phenomenal. He takes the prototype of his
work with Davis – complex cross-rhythmic interpretation of a basic four-
pulse – and warns all around him to don ear protection. Brushes were
thrown aside in favour of heavy-duty military band parade-ground sticks;
he used a purposely small bass drum to "make it sound like he had a third
hand" (Isaacs) and also provide even greater propulsion. Williams told
Down Beat, "the rock musicians don't really consider us rock. You know,
we're not trying to be rock. They think we're trying to play up to them,
and we're not."

These were guys who understood that pop wasn't just another music. It
was an attitude, a sound quality, a cultural effect as much as an assem-
blage of notes. What Lifetime did was to perform as an elite corps of professional musicians and *still* rock, a feat that jazz traditionalists thought
oxymoronic. The pop and rock vulgarity of sound couldn't disguise the
musicianship on show, nor the gutsy swing.

Williams doesn't come off as a stainless hero – his decision to include
vocals is regrettable. They are usually delivered in a strained, husky
drawl, sounding not a little like John Shaft trying to do *sprechgesang*.
The words are dire too, for the most part; meliorist, countercultural
whimsy about 'being yourself' etc. etc., the sort of stuff that the produc-
ers of *The Mod Squad* might have included in a scene featuring hippie
performance art. "Where are you going... where are you from?", maun-
ders Williams on "Where". On "Via The Spectrum Road" he and
McLaughlin sound exactly like a stoned Four Freshmen.

The lack of a bassist isn't even noticed until a few minutes into the
opener. Young performs his anchor role in the bass well, especially on
"Vashkar" but his towering musicality and brute physicality at the organ
is the real quality he brings to the recording.

"Larry had a sense for voicings and a touch that had previously only
been thought possible on the piano," commented Williams. "Yet he was a
total organist... he literally redefined the organ without denying an iota of
its integrity." His invention is also admirable, with the chattering staccato
figures unleashed in the psychedelic cartoon the trio make of Carla
Bley's "Vashkar" a particular highlight.

The music itself is a chaos of riffs and rhythmic figures with little
adherence to verse/chorus structures. Indian scales, peeking into
McLaughlin's solo work at the time (see *Devotion)* aren't employed,
although the use of a basic riff or scale from which melodies are slowly

evolved does at least peer forward towards a musical future for McLaughlin. The hierarchy of voices has been dismantled; the order of voices haphazard, rather than pre-ordained. It's every man for himself; and every man takes his chance. McLaughlin has finally found the edge suggested on *Extrapolation*, unwittingly aided by the scrappy recording quality. His voicings are still predominantly bluesy – as on "Via The Spectrum Road", with its shit-eating tone – but his choice of notes, exploring the crevices around the body of the blues, hinted at something more.

McLaughlin also composed tracks for the album, unaccountably using the pseudonym A. Hall. "Spectrum" was very different from the version heard on *Extrapolation*, and leans even more towards its final incarnation as "Awakening" on *The Inner Mounting Flame,* albeit with very different emphases deployed in the riffs. McLaughlin veers further away from tonality. "Spectrum" is, indeed, the pivotal track between Lifetime and the Mahavishnu Orchestra, between the elemental brutality of the former and the drilled, controlled violence of the latter. By the finale, a brisk 6/8 romp through "Something Spiritual", McLaughlin's emotional range and more Romantic European harmony echoes even more a music from the future.

Despite an initial rash of gigs and ecstatic critical notices for *Emergency!* the Lifetime progress graph quickly nose-dived. "Everything about it, apart from the music, was bad," admitted McLaughlin later. Despite the acclaim, record companies were ambivalent. No less than Al Kooper, in his capacity as a Columbia A&R man, turned the band down, to McLaughlin's incredulous disgust; "I lost all respect for him... because we were burning." In the end Polydor Records stepped in; as yet a new player on the field, they had none of Columbia's clout or financial nous.

At first, both rock and jazz venues had clamoured for the group, although some rock listeners were uncertain – Lifetime were roundly booed by Who fans while on a support bill for the British band at the Tea Party Club, Boston. Among early admirers were the guitar prodigy Duane Allman (who McLaughlin sought out and briefly befriended until the younger man's death in 1970) and Janis Joplin, who would take time out to catch the band at the Gaslight Club in New York. Comedian and highly accomplished jazz pianist Bill Cosby was also an early convert, beginning a lifelong interest in McLaughlin's music. But outside the avant-jazz capital of New York and the progressive rock capitals of Los Angeles and San Francisco, listeners didn't want to know. The gigs dried up, despite prestigious engagements at high-profile events such as the

Monterey Jazz Festival in 1969, at blue-chip jazz venues (Village Gate, Shelly's Manne Hole) and rock clubs (Fillmore East and the Electric Circus). At one stage Williams was forced to drive the tour van himself.

On reflection, the abominable ill-luck that dogged the recording of *Emergency!* was a portent; McLaughlin's guitar pickups malfunctioned, the studio organ malfunctioned, and Williams' bass drum signal was hopelessly distorted (even today, admirers of the record are as quick to acknowledge its sonic limitations as its thrilling energy and musicality). Furthermore, Polydor's mix appalled the musicians. "Badly recorded and badly produced – whoever did that hadn't a clue what the band were about texturally," said one fan and friend of the band.

Management went from bad to worse. Williams recalled that, "They believed in us, but they didn't have the capability to keep the band working." When Williams invited Jack Bruce into the band in 1970, the exciting and immediate integration of his sound and personality into the unit was undermined by the hustling aggression of Bruce's manager Robert Stigwood, who demanded equal billing for his client with that of Williams himself.

"At this stage, I think," Pete Brown – now involved in the band as the lyricist to the songs Bruce brought with him – commented, "Lifetime had three managers – absolutely the kiss of death. It doesn't matter then how good you are."

Stigwood's intransigence was actually harmful to Bruce, who expressed the view that, "Ever since I heard Tony's *Emergency!* album I thought that's the band I'd like to play with", and that Lifetime were "without a doubt, the best band there ever was in the world... I've never experienced energy like that in a band," giving extra credence to Stuart Nicholson's assertion that the band were "an abstraction of Cream".

Even thirty years on, those present at this stage in McLaughlin's career are unanimous in their appreciation of Lifetime, "Just incredible. The best thing he ever did in a band," Pete Brown said. "The musical impact of that band was scary. It was beyond people at the time. They weren't fucking around. It wasn't just a dilettante, ooh-let's-see-how-far-out-we-can-go vibe, it was a natural evolution from where those guys had been already."

"They were really something else. Nobody had ever, ever heard anything like this before," commented the jazz writer Charles Alexander. "Lifetime was a misunderstood band. But no question about it, it was one of the greatest bands that ever existed."

Turn It Over, while a radically abbreviated musical statement when compared to the sprawling double LP which preceded it, was an even more outlandish statement. It was an album which was intended to incite people to 'turn over' society – a slightly fanciful idea, Williams later remarked. Nonetheless, it was a statement of musical radicalism that few acts, even within rock, could match.

Bruce's recruitment not only lent greater rhythmic flexibility and drive to the group, it also brought another texture to bear; Bruce's experience with Cream had tutored him in the use of fuzz, wah-wah, feedback, distortion, and a whole shelf of electronic tinkery. From the outset of *Turn It Over* the brutal miasma of bass guitar and electric guitar shading into and over each other are foregrounded.

Turn It Over featured some audacious cover versions. Chick Corea's two-part "To Whom It May Concern/ Them" and Coltrane's "Big Nick" simply didn't stand a chance. The latter was treated with some respect, the chorus and verse structure remaining at least recognisable. On the former the furious ensemble statement of the theme prefigures the wild unisono passages of the Mahavishnu Orchestra. It went as far as to enable the drummer to flail spectacularly around whilst these passages took place. Significantly, on this album, McLaughlin finally settles on his guitar tone for the Mahavishnu project; full-toned, sharp, shrill, aggressive, uncompromising.

The treatment of the Corea song is extreme; from a basic 3/4 pulse each instrumental voice extrapolates its own idea of the rhythm and riffs to be played thereon. Williams' bass drum seems to be tearing the heart out of the rhythm and yet is its chief custodian. On "Them", McLaughlin's darting, chaotic, yet almost wholly tonal solo seems like another Mahavishnu rehearsal. Larry Young's vampirically spooky legato organ lines provide the musical link between the furious bluesy workouts of the verses and the relaxed statements of Corea's characteristically whimsical main theme. There are other acts of wanton musical terrorism; notably Williams' unprovoked snare-drum attack on "Us". "Right On" is probably the strangest track of all; introduced by an alarm on Williams' bell-tree and snapping crackerjack sequence of snare shots, it roars into a fuzzy juggernaut of sound that would shame Sonic Youth. Only as a rabble-rousing organ solo by Young begins to darkly unfurl, does the music fade.

A single, "One Word" (later to reappear on the Mahavishnu Orchestra album *Birds of Fire* in radically refurbished form) was released in July 1970 and vanished without a trace. British tours drew astounded guitar fans from far and wide, but often to dingy gigs in venues wholly inadequate for the awesome spectacle of the band in action. "No two ways about it; their best stuff never made it onto any record. Live, nobody could touch them, ever," was Pete Brown's opinion.

Finally, the combined management's meddling got too much for McLaughlin. The band had been rehearsing new material, led by Bruce's vocals. "Very new, very revolutionary," said McLaughlin later. Polydor refused to issue it; management support was at best lukewarm and McLaughlin left in a rage.

Thus the initial incarnation of Lifetime broke up in April 1971. Tragically, McLaughlin was the only one to emerge into the light. Williams continued to play and record for two decades and more. Although subsequent Lifetime albums are cold fish compared to the debut discs, he remained, rightly, one of the most renowned of drummers both among the fusion and the straight-ahead post-bop jazz fraternity. He played again with McLaughlin at the end of the 1970s, appearing on the album *Electric Guitarist,* as well as in a live session with the imposingly-named Trio Of Doom with McLaughlin and Jaco Pastorius. He never attained the limelit fame of band-leadership conferred upon McLaughlin and other fusion stars, and died at the age of 52 – after what should have been a routine gallstone operation – at a San Francisco hospital in February 1997.

Larry Young – by now Khalid Yasin – appeared on the McLaughlin/Santana jam *Love Devotion Surrender* in 1973 but, increasingly dependent on the emotional narcosis of religion and the chemical narcosis of heroin, he began to fade from the scene like text on parchment. By 1978 he was dead, surprisingly unheralded. Only in subsequent years was the importance of his legacy to jazz-rock fully explored, and even then only intermittently and sometimes grudgingly. It took the re-emergence of the Hammond organ in the genre (ironically in McLaughlin's own 1990s trio, the Free Spirits, in the capable hands of the prodigy Joey de Francesco) for a full re-evaluation of Young's real abilities to be undertaken.

McLaughlin, meanwhile, had been paying his bills as a serial guest star performer; notably on Wayne Shorter's *Super Nova* and the hyper-rare *Moto Grosso Feio* from 1969 and 1970 respectively. From those sessions came work on *Infinite Search* (aka *Mountain In The Clouds*) by the electric bass phenomenon from Czechoslovakia, Miroslav Vitous, who had played on the Shorter albums and would later gratefully follow him into the first incarnation of Weather Report. Additionally, and most explosively, there were sessions for his friend Larry Coryell on the latter's two 1970 albums, the ferocious *Spaces* and *Planet End*. Saxophonist Joe Farrell also used him on his *Song Of The Wind*. McLaughlin was, as he had been in London, once again the busy sessioneer, the trailblazing jobber. This time, however, his employers didn't want unquestioning adherence to commercial rules. They had little respect for the rules themselves, and they wanted like minds; the intellectually curious, the mercurial, the magical. Herbie Goins had been pie and chips; this was *nouvelle cuisine*.

Beginning with Shorter, these sessions were largely outcrops of Miles Davis recordings. Shorter decided to use these to record his own takes on his many successful 1960s compositions which had been so distinctively rendered by Davis' quintet. *Super Nova* and *Moto Grosso Feio* were recorded in New York within months of each other, both utilising present and recently-past members of Davis' ensembles. The victim of Blue Note's financial difficulties and contractual wrangling within the label, *Feio* lay unreleased until 1975, and remains one of the great lost recordings of the jazz-rock era. Details of its creation are sketchy; even the recording date has been disputed, and the phenomenal drumming on display, credited to one Michelin Prell, supposedly a 19-year-old female, has been attributed with a nudge and a wink by some cynics as a Tony Williams incognito to sidestep contractual hassles.

To fans of Davis' great '60s quintet and Shorter's sometimes pithy, sometimes elliptical, always engrossing compositions, *Super Nova* often comes like a dose of cod liver oil. It is barrelling, head-on, steely-eyed post-bop and free jazz in which the leader has only a nominal role and takes it with aplomb (Shorter plays like his life depends on it), all reckless expressionism upon a stark and dense sound-coloration provided by a furiously-concentrating band. Ironically, McLaughlin's contribution is little more important than those he made to Duffy Power or Tony Meehan, although his random squirts of chords and rhythmic spurs do at least lend him more distinction than most of the ensemble.

Elsewhere he is less constrained. On the classic LP *Mountain In The Clouds* by the sensational young Czech émigré bassist Miroslav Vitous, he is complicit in a hair-raising crusade across the bumpy territory of Eddie Harris' "Freedom Jazz Dance", and does his share of leadership with flying and freakish colours. His interplay with drummer Jack DeJohnette, having already established its volatility and dynamism with Davis and Shorter, again crackles appetisingly – how unfortunate that the two men would later play so seldom together.

Joe Farrell's album *Song Of The Wind* was, astonishingly, recorded just several weeks after this. Another miracle of invention, it suggests that all musicians had to do in New York in 1970 was tap into genius like a soda fountain, so torrentially inextinguishable was its supply. This is a splendid LP, full of vigour and lyrical singularities as well as truculent hardcore blowing half a universe away from the all-smiles "fusion muzak" or "Fuzak" that Farrell and sidekick Chick Corea would syndicate later on in the '70s. The title track alone is worth the investment, Farrell and Corea indulging in winds-and-piano impressionism with sinews showing beneath the velvety flesh of the music. Fortunately, it displays none of the smug and snooty whimsy their later profitability imposed on their music-making. McLaughlin, though only present on two tracks plays possum here, and chameleon too. He chimes bell-like as chordal, Montgomery-esque accompanist here and taking no prisoners with chromatic, fretting, slashing solos elsewhere. His "Follow Your Heart" opens proceedings, and few other versions better highlight the harmonic sophistication of the song. The sad, contrary downward motion of what seems to be an ordinary blues progression is emphasised by Farrell's poignant wind playing. The rhythm section seems to drag the melody down while Farrell tries to keep it aloft; lovely.

* * *

Also, of course, there was Miles Davis.

McLaughlin's first stint with Davis lasted three and-a-half years. At the beginning of his association with the master, McLaughlin had been a next-most-likely-to, a guitar demigod with a zealous cult following. By the end (his last sessions were for the 1972 *On The Corner* album, cut in June of that year in New York City), he was an international star, possibly even more recognisable in the popular music marketplace than his illustrious employer.

McLaughlin became a star thanks to Davis. Irrespective of his talent, only through his association with the master could he have hoped to have been chosen as a star soloist in a supergroup put together for the 1970 Randall's Island Jazz Festival in New York. Featured as part of a jam opposite Eric Clapton, Davis, Larry Young, Jack Bruce and Tony Williams, the bill never actually happened after Davis suddenly announced his decision to play the festival with his own band instead.

McLaughlin and Davis got on well; both men respected each other's ability – although it is true to say that McLaughlin's was by far the deeper respect, bordering at times on fanatical adulation. Of the first day he spent in Davis' and producer Teo Macero's recording studio during the *In A Silent Way* sessions, McLaughlin, even in the mid-'90s, would gush, "I remember that day. It will stay engraved in my memory. It was one of the most beautiful days of my life, maybe the most beautiful day." Similarly, in another interview, "Playing with Miles in Harlem was a high that I've never really come down from."

There also seems to have been a personal bond between them. Certainly few musicians in the 1970s lasted as members of Davis' circle, and, the saxophonist Dave Liebman aside, no white man ever earned so much admiration from Davis as John McLaughlin. At a time when racial pride was a tinderbox, and his own profile as a leader closely scrutinised by black radicals, Davis gruffly dismissed those who criticised his recruitment of McLaughlin (and his friend Dave Holland) for cutting black musicians out of the action. Joe Zawinul tells of overhearing Davis' laconic putdown of some persistent questions as to his black integrity; "Shit! Nobody plays as good as him [McLaughlin]. You give me one of them niggers and I'll hire him *and* McLaughlin."

Davis' own writings and comments, whose brimming machismo prevent much real evidence of the depth of friendships with men, nonetheless draw McLaughlin sympathetically. Despite rumours that murmurings of jealousy escaped from the master when he regarded the astronomical success his (white, with the exception of Herbie Hancock) protégés would win at his expense in the 1970s, Davis' friendship with McLaughlin stayed firm until the trumpeter's death in 1991. McLaughlin surfaces on two 1980s Davis recordings and in a historic 1991 concert staged in Paris to celebrate Davis' receiving the Chevalier de la Legion d'Honneur from the French government.

In A Silent Way was the first of ten Davis albums to feature McLaughlin (eight between 1969-72 and two between 1985 and 1989). McLaughlin confessed then and on innumerable later occasions of the awe and respect he felt, but also of the way those emotions relaxed him in the apparently offhand company of the master.

"I grew up listening to what Miles did with Trane, and then *ESP*, *Nefertiti*, *Live in Berlin*, some 'out' things, straight-ahead, but crazy. And here, what we played wasn't like that at all," McLaughlin opined. "Right off, I was nervous. Miles wasn't into that other stuff; well, he was into it, but he was looking for something else and since he didn't really know what he was looking for, I didn't know, nobody knew, and so when he started giving me these obscure suggestions like, play the guitar like you don't know how to play... well, he cooled me out when he said that. I just started to do the thing in E, 'In A Silent Way,' and I played the whole thing very open in E major. Miles didn't even wait, he had the recording light on and I just started playing these real simple things, and then Wayne came in with the melody and then Miles and Wayne together. But when Miles had Teo Macero (the producer) play the take back, I was really in shock at how Miles had made me play in a way that I had not been aware of. He had a way of pulling something out of me that I would have never figured out myself, which is uncanny. Of course in subsequent sessions with him I could see that Miles had an incredible gift. Sometimes he'd come in and not have a clear idea of what he wanted himself, not even a concept. Or maybe just a concept and no notes. So we'd go in there and he'd write something on a bag on the way over in a taxi and at the session, he just sang something. Just a sound."

In A Silent Way is not for McLaughlin fans *per se*, save as a definitive statement of one of the guitarist's premier musical avatars at a crucial developmental stage. It is, of course, an ageless LP, although time has not diminished its diffuseness, certainly when compared with its immediate predecessors, *Filles de Kilimanjaro* and *Water Babies* (the latter was unreleased until 1977).

At his first concert with Davis, the trumpeter had swivelled on the bandstand and without warning cued McLaughlin in. He was then still featuring recognisable themes in his music; on this particular occasion it was "Round Midnight". "He pointed at me to start playing 'Round Midnight' at breakneck speed. It was like going back to when I was 15 years of age and it was 'do it or don't bother'."

McLaughlin, under Davis, was transformed from merely a jazz guitarist with an accompanist's voicings and phrasing, to an integral soloing voice in a jazz unit, responsible for a major share of the melodic and rhythmic interplay, as well as distinction as a solo voice in a manner still new in the genre.

From the start, on *In A Silent Way,* McLaughlin is used more for his input into Davis' rhythm section than a soloist. But he was playing as part of a rhythm section that helped revolutionise the genre and was often spurred to considerable creativity even within the apparently constrained role of rhythm guitarist. Of course, there are the solos, too. Nobody became a solo star *in* Miles Davis' orbit; they only hinted at what they could achieve *outside* it, and of course many went on to fulfil their promise.

Davis' rhythm sections were, according to Ian Carr, charged with a twofold mission; to underline the return to a squarer, rock pulse on the drums (highlighted in the mix) and also to create a soundstream of rhythmic and melodic fragments and solos around these square figures. This, for Carr, "reworked the traditional New Orleans jazz idea of collective improvisation behind a leading/solo melody voice".

On *Jack Johnson*, McLaughlin remembers his part in one of Davis' strongest and most intensely concentrated sessions. "We were in the studio: Herbie Hancock, Michael Henderson, Billy Cobham and me. Miles was talking with Teo Macero in the control room for a long time. I got a little bored and I started to play this shuffle, a kind of boogie in F with some funny chords. The others picked it up and locked in. The next thing, the door opened, and Miles runs in with his trumpet and we played for about twenty minutes. It was a large part of that record. It came out of nowhere."

Jack Johnson, as with most of Davis' studio recordings since 1968, was heavily doctored by producer Teo Macero, and each piece is little more than a collage of takes, brilliantly patched together by the producer. In "Yesternow" for example, a snatch of "Shhh/Peaceful" (from *In A Silent Way*, recorded a year earlier and with different musicians!) is heard.

McLaughlin's solo on "Right Off" is mainly chordal. It modulates with brilliant timing to ratchet up excitement to fever pitch for Davis' entry, hard as a Joe Frazier right hook.

The Davis period also saw McLaughlin's choice of guitar change from a hollow-body round-hole Gibson Hummingbird ('a folk guitar!'), used at the *In A Silent Way* sessions, to a Gibson Les Paul classic. Although, he is pictured on the sleeve of *Devotion* bearing an eye-burningly psychedelic Fender Stratocaster. The Gibson would remain with him throughout the consolidation years of 1970-71, before giving way to the trophies of fame, and the grander scale of a Gibson double-neck guitar. But while McLaughlin retained faith in his Gibson guitars, other convictions were undergoing severe strain, and in some cases being shed entirely.

Chapter Three
'Greetings, O People Of
(Insert City Name Here)...'

"Just before I went to America I started to do yoga exercises in the morning. [When] I arrived in Manhattan, I thought I had to get myself more together, so I did more exercises. I was doing an hour and a half in the morning and an hour and a half in the evening. Just yoga. So after a year of doing this I felt great physically, but I thought I was missing the interior thing."

McLaughlin had been raised as he put it, "Without any religious instruction apart from the dust they serve you up at school... by the time I was about 19 or 20, I'd taken some acid. And I'd been getting high for quite a while, you know, just smoking regular old marijuana. Graham Bond, however, opened up my eyes to a side of myself I was unaware of... I knew there was something magical about life, although I didn't know what it was. But I knew that it was there, and that it was something that connected everybody together". According to later Mahavishnu alumnus Philip Hirschi, McLaughlin's interest in the subcontinent had been cued by adolescent contests with friends in north-eastern England as to who could consume the hottest curry at the local Indian restaurant; by now, however, chillis were assuming less interest than chakras. "One night in 1963," he told one reporter, "after reading about Tarot, playing with Brian Auger, I felt the spirit enter me and it was no longer me playing." With the already occult-besotted Graham Bond and Jim Sullivan,

McLaughlin joined the Theosophical Society, whose library soon provided him with an extensive lens into any number of Eastern philosophies and traditions. In New York, McLaughlin sought out the words of various yogis before settling with a man on the verge of imagined immortality and social notoriety, Sri Chinmoy. This introduction was thanks to Danny Weiss, manager of Larry Coryell and producer of his album *Spaces* on which McLaughlin had performed.

Sri Chinmoy Kumar Ghose moved to New York from India in 1965. He moved to the district of Queens, not far from where John and Eve McLaughlin set up home in the spring of 1969. McLaughlin was ripe for the plucking given his background and a degree of intellectual curiosity. This, combined with the spiritual void in the wake of the abandonment of drugs and dope, not to forget a naturally Romantic inclination to the fragrantly vivid visions of eternity, the lexically-voluble Chinmoy could spin the impressionable. Chimnoy did the trick. "Immediately, I felt good about him, he said some important things to me." McLaughlin developed his yoga, and got into the writings of Hazrat Inayat Khan. "Every musician should read the second volume of *The Sufi Message Books* which deals with music and is called *The Mysticism of Sound, Music, The Power of the Word and the Cosmic Language.*"

"Manhattan is a tough town," McLaughlin told *Melody Maker*'s Richard Williams. "I've never seen so many people derelict, destroyed... to me, Manhattan ate people for breakfast just to start the day. It destroyed a few people. But what it does is, you either become strong, or you become weaker and leave." What may have helped McLaughlin adapt was less Chinmoy than the very real nature of his acceptance in the community there. Other refugees from Europe had not been so lucky. Ernst-Joachim Berendt, in particular, has written movingly on the initial hells endured by the Europeans Joe Zawinul, Karl Berger (both, coincidentally, playing with McLaughlin during his first eighteen months in New York) and Attila Zoller.

But McLaughlin's fondness for the Orient was far from merely superficial gorging on the mind-candy of Panglossian faith. Spiritual awareness, even if only of the eclectic hotch-potch of idealism inherent in Chinmoy's 'teachings', was a mutual cousin of a serious and searching curiosity in the music of the Indian subcontinent. It was a curiosity which would bring forth innumerable riches in his later repertoire and, through its shaping of his own composition and performance techniques, bring him greater long-lasting satisfaction than Chimnoy ever would or could.

"As time passed by I was exposed to Indian music by being involved with the culture. Again, it was something I couldn't hear. I couldn't grasp it. But there was something about it. In particular, there was a sitar. As I remember, I think it was Ravi Shankar... I pursued it and listened to it. Finally, I 'heard it' and it had a devastating effect on me."

Of course, jazz as a genre had been experiencing eastward impulses for some time. Interestingly, one of the pioneer fusions of Indian musics and jazz was alto saxophonist Joe Harriott's 1966 *Indo-Jazz Suite*, featuring a jazz quintet with four Indian musicians. McLaughlin was definitely aware of that recording, and it seems inconceivable that a musician of such catholic inclinations – abject poverty or not – should have not been in possession of the work of Don Ellis' Hindustani Jazz Sextet, formed by the eccentric bandleader with Hari Har Rao, a former student of Ravi Shankar. Ellis' recordings, however, used Indian music as inspiration for rhythmic complexity rather than tonal diversity – initially, at least.

More recently, John Coltrane's own dalliance with Orientalism had flowered into a full-blown infatuation in the music of his widow Alice and disciple Pharaoh Sanders. Critic Ralph J. Gleason went so far as to say that "John Coltrane moved the centre of musical consciousness from the USA to Asia, and by this he opened up a musical horizon for a whole new generation". This was a slight over-simplification. Partly inspired by the total revolution of lifestyle and self-proposed by the counterculture and also by the shadowy ascent of Black Muslim militancy in the US in the mid-'60s, the East was seen as a prophylactic at first and later as a panacea.

If Chinmoy, like so many other gurus, was flying a kite and hoping to snag the spiritually-bereft in the turmoil of the late 1960s, his flew higher and carried more than most. By 1973, meditation centres had been set up worldwide. High-profile adherents dotted the newspaper gossip columns.

All he may have needed was love, but for McLaughlin, the Lifetime experience had left a bad taste. McLaughlin discussed the problem with Miles Davis. "Go see Nat Weiss if you want to make some money", suggested the trumpeter. McLaughlin rang Weiss, a galvanic New York Jew then managing James Taylor among other heavyweights and quickly formed a partnership. In the meantime Weiss and Davis advised the guitarist to form his own band, and fast.

Alan Douglas, also, was making noises as to solo work; McLaughlin had yet to complete the second album of his two-album deal. The result, *My Goal's Beyond*, is astonishing, given that in the hands of many musicians it may have been seen merely as a kiss-off for an aggressive and possibly greedy producer and impresario. It is perhaps the most personal statement of McLaughlin's career, albeit one which freezes in time a moment of intense transitoriness in the player's life. It reeks of incense, temple and shrine, yet it still commands devotion even amongst those otherwise unkindly disposed to McLaughlin. Alongside *Extrapolation* and *The Inner Mounting Flame* it is probably the album which has proved most durable amongst critics. Given the backlash against the hippie mysticism its every pore exudes, this is no mean achievement.

Its two albums; the electric side one and acoustic side two are sufficiently distinguished and distinctive to warrant analysis whilst standing alone. There is occasional accompaniment from Billy Cobham's suspended cymbals to add extra grandeur to the soundstage on side two, but such is the incandescence of McLaughlin's virtuosity, it's scarcely worth it. This is a guy in a hurry. Come on, give me the prize *now.* The good thing about this is, one is never sure if money's the only prize he's after.

Mingus' "Goodbye Pork Pie Hat" starts off bluesily, unassumingly. It would be easy to comment, "yeah, a *guitarist's* album, we've heard it all before" – except that such criteria only applies to the late-1990s. In 1971 nobody had heard anything quite like this. There are enough lines for a fingerstyle picker, whether the music was overdubbed or not. Even without overdubbing, the Rheinhardt-styled blues picking at absurd speed, as bass line and as solo, shows an amazing sense of drama, as does the flurry of notes into the top register. The influence of Rheinhardt returns with the gold-leaf delicate playing on "Something Spiritual". The notes on the upper-strings are almost engraved, which contrasts nicely with the deep-throated delta blues belches from the bass end of the guitar. The piece picks up speed with a furious momentum signposting the exponential gas-pedalling of the Mahavishnu Orchestra.

McLaughlin warms to his theme in the flamenco-like contrast of chordal strumming with close pickwork on "Song For My Mother". "Something Spiritual" and "Blue In Green" reveal him as a dauntless harmonic adventurer, as does the original "Follow Your Heart". "Something Spiritual" shows harmonic chutzpah around basic chords, falling seamlessly into an effortless *accelererando.* His subtle attack on Bob Cornford's tender "Hearts and Flowers" is like that of a practised seducer – carrying tenderness before it, but never besmirching or degrading it.

Revealed as a picker, amidst this hailstorm of notes, the guy either had to be a fraud or a sensation. History, consumerism, and the judgement of his peers, elected him as a 24-carat sensation.

* * *

There was probably little to persuade McLaughlin in the spring of 1971 that in the wake of the Lifetime fiasco with its bitter disappointments, a new group project would offer much in the way of rewards. But, spiritually recharged by his association with Chinmoy and buoyed by ever more gurglingly appreciative encomia, McLaughlin set out on the road again with a new bunch of musicians, this time with himself as chief, not Indian. What might have happened had he decided to accept Miroslav Vitous' offer of a place in Joe Zawinul's and Wayne Shorter's embryonic band Weather Report is best left to the imagination.

Instead, the Mahavishnu Orchestra debuted at New York's Club-A-Go-Go in July 1971. The name was taken directly from McLaughlin's own nom d'esprit, Mahavishnu (Maha=creator, Vishnu=spirit). On drums, McLaughlin had already struck up a rapport with Billy Cobham, a young, black Panama-born American whose path he'd crossed briefly at Miles Davis sessions in 1970. He had featured, sporadically, on *Bitches Brew* and had played drums – impressively – on McLaughlin's *My Goal's Beyond*. Hitherto he'd played with Joe Tex, the Sam & Dave Revue, and Horace Silver, with whom an entranced McLaughlin had seen him perform at Ronnie Scott's in London. The guitarist knew he had his Mahavishnu Orchestra drummer, although Cobham already had a jazz-rock gig with the epigonic outfit Dreams.

"Dreams wasn't really a commercial band," said the vibist Mike Mainieri many years later... "[they] didn't have a lead singer like Blood, Sweat & Tears or put on an obvious show like they did." This was in response to the band's first album (1970), which some felt was compromised by concessions to the corporate judgement of CBS. The band also featured guitarist John Abercrombie and a young trumpeter named Randy Brecker. Cobham's first engagement with McLaughlin, on *My Goal's Beyond*, was comparatively introspective and helped establish Cobham as something more than a rapid-fire master of heavy-ordnance percussion.

The recruitment of Jerry Goodman on violin was less clear-cut. McLaughlin originally signed the young American for *My Goal's Beyond*, having failed to entice Jean-Luc Ponty, an astonishing technician trained at the Paris Conservatoire, whose natural inheritance of Stephane Grappelli's laurels as premier French jazz violinist inaugurated a modern French jazz tradition. Ponty's *King Kong* (an electric violin tribute to

Frank Zappa) was essential avant-jazz listening at the end of the 1960s. McLaughlin would, of course, later get his man (and lose him), but in the meantime he checked out contemporary records featuring violin and set-tled for a player living on a farm in Wisconsin. Goodman fiddled, played occasional guitar for the journeyman jazz-rock outfit, the underrated and much-lamented Flock. He even did a little roadying with them.

Miroslav Vitous put him in touch with the keyboard player Jan Hammer, a Czech émigré who'd performed in the same band as the bassist in Prague in the early 1960s during the years of the Dubcek cul-tural thaw. Hammer was then in the US and playing with Sarah Vaughan. On bass, Vitous came under consideration for the briefest of spells before committing once and for all to Zawinul and Shorter. McLaughlin, having tried and failed to coax Tony Levin away from Gary Burton's band, called upon his old colleague Rick Laird, who had shared a bandstand with McLaughlin in Brian Auger's quintet in the early '60s. Laird had also studied for two years at Berklee and toured with Buddy Rich. Of the band's inaugural gig, *Rolling Stone* opined, "their music is as loud and raucous as The Who's, as subtle and precise as the MJQ's."

On reflection, the music is not wildly dissimilar to Lifetime's, at least not at first glance; the instruments have similar places in the soundstage, and their hierarchy (guitar nominally on top) is much the same. But the chaotic speed with which the hierarchy breaks down, marked this as something else. Also, there was the spectacular ability of the players to remain together through the tightest and most head-spinning *unisono* pas-sages over strange time signatures at maximum (and, as their career pro-gressed, ever-increasing) speed. Summarily, self-evident from the first pile-driving chord was the winning combination of a raucous, shit-kick-ing energy and abrasive snarl with passages of almost unbelievable tech-nical facility. It sounded, in short, like a garage band touched by an angel.

Nicholson states that *Flame* was a perfect distillation and précis of the "turgid and congested" moments of stasis in *Bitches Brew* with its "dis-cursive melodies and soloing." In contrast, *Flame* "...remains an impres-sive statement that turned out to be more influential [than the Davis album] ...*Flame* represents the next decisive step in the evolution of jazz-rock fusion. The music was more focused in structure and rhythm."

"Meeting Of The Spirits", the opener, buckets frenetically along, set-ting a rubber-burning pace which scarcely lets up throughout the album's entire 46-minute span. The initial riff of "Spirits" is, harmonically, pure rhythm and blues, but in the context of the time signature, with Cobham's snare and ride cymbals crackling away like rain on a hot tin roof and Hammer's searing Hammond organ chords, all context is removed. It sounds wholly new, wholly effective, as though these harmonies had been meant for this music since the beginning of time. Solos are swapped with feverish regularity, and the music twice descends into a sort of counter-riff, as though the musicians are frantically searching for a point of calm in the storm with which to regroup and begin improvising again on those initial, sensual, captivating chords and McLaughlin's menacing arpeggios.

"Dawn" is comparatively tranquil, but also deceptively so. Its baroque, impressionistic introduction of drawling violin and pearly Fender Rhodes notes only serves to give the leader a breather before he unleashes a solo out of the introductory chords and cues in a biff-bang explosion from Cobham – 7/4 becoming 14/8. Then Goodman joins the hoedown gleefully with a new violin riff.

Cobham's gradual muscling of himself and his instrument to the foreground on the album is fascinating. He's first out of the blocks on "The Noonward Race", snare brashly, snappily sharp as a jockey's whip, the ride cymbals harshly metallic. He plays first against one riff and then *unisono* with another. As Cobham fatbacks off again into the distance, Hammer's first opportunity to solo at length is greedily grabbed, although his Moog solo, complete with distortion is as nasty as nails on a blackboard. His jazz antecedents are less well-defined; his soloing style owes more to European piano tradition, but also to rock 'n' roll, and at times here he is Jerry Lee Lewis produced by Beaver and Krause. It's Hammer's finest studio moment with McLaughlin, and it's maybe a shame that the leader's solo thereafter is miraculously musicianly but also gobsmackingly dextrous, and is one of his best Mahavishnu Orchestra moments, thereby overshadowing the Czech's superb contribution.

The side, maybe the finest side in McLaughlin's catalogue, ends on the only truly relaxed note of the whole album, but probably its most unarguably musically satisfying and beautiful. "A Lotus On Irish Streams" has McLaughlin rescuing his acoustic 6-string for a ravishing and delightful piece of impressionistic chamber-ensemble tone painting with Goodman, while Hammer displays a seraph's touch on acoustic piano. McLaughlin's melody is characteristically convoluted and chromatic, but is harmonised with inexhaustible invention and lyrical sensitivity. Sometimes with halting, hesitant individual notes, or with tinkling arabesques fluttering like dragonflies, and at other times with rolling, stormy arpeggios. It was an inspirational stroke which, sadly, McLaughlin referred back to all too infrequently, although "Thousand Island Park" from *Birds of Fire* would make an honourable stab at it. Goodman and Hammer have never sounded better anywhere, ever.

Side two needs less analysis; the blueprint merely expands further into even more mind-boggling realms, but keeps its basic shape. The guitar broadens its agonised repertoire, Goodman saws grimly, Hammer's Fender Rhodes flings clusters of chords and notes indiscriminately around the soundstage, Laird remains stonily immovable amidst the pyrotechnics, and Cobham sounds like a syncopated car-crusher. "Vital Transformation" is a more bombastic, more through-composed piece, for the first time really teasing the listener by deconstructing time-signatures and introducing the first remotely Latinate percussive element into the band's music. For Nicholson, the theme resembles "Baby Be Good To Me", an old Graham Bond number. Cobham employs more crash cymbals on this side, scuzzing the soundstage up even further, and quite often the precision of the ensemble begins to fray at the edges. But such is the almost angry abrasion of sound and the sheer exhilaration of the delivery that it hardly mattered – "like sticking your head out of a train window at 200kmh", one fan later said.

"The Dance Of Maya" was, from its growling opening, enough to transfix a generation of music students. As drummer Danny Gottlieb, who found fame first with Pat Metheny and with the reconstituted Mahavishnu Orchestra in the 1980s, later noted, "that was what changed everything. We all started trying to play 'The Dance Of Maya'. Drummers especially, with Billy's cross-rhythm."

"Maya" is distinguished by the insistent integration into the texture of a 17/8 time signature, into which the whole band eventually falls, despite the fact that even McLaughlin's main solo maintains the illusion of being rooted in the original time signature of 20/4.

The energy burns volcanically until the very last second of the album, when the final note blinks out with a strangled squawk as though an angry landlord had pulled the plug on a bunch of noisy hippies in his attic. This final track, "Awakening", sports a rollercoastering, 40-note riff played at breakneck speed by all five instruments, and would have been an alarm call second only to Judgement Day itself.

The most stunning aspect of this amazing album is the miraculous coherence of the ensemble, and most of all, the relationship between McLaughlin and Cobham, who could play the most ferociously difficult lines in perfect ensemble at ridiculous speeds and also duel with each other's rhythmic sensibilities within the music itself. Later McLaughlin would tell one writer that he had "a lot of fun interacting directly with the drummer". On this occasion he was talking about the drummer Dennis Chambers, with whom he was working in the organ-blues trio the Free Spirits in 1993, but it could equally apply to Cobham, Michael Walden, Trilok Gurtu and almost every drummer McLaughlin has directed or worked with. McLaughlin went on; "Allan [Holdsworth] is absolutely phenomenal, but I wouldn't want to play that way because I'd miss the impact, where I'm able to directly interact with the drummer, for example. But that's my way, that's the only way I can go, I can't go against my nature." McLaughlin's unaccompanied duets with Cobham became such a showstopper that he began to consciously develop such musical relationships with his drummers; Michael Walden in particular, with whom he recorded long drums/guitar passages.

Flame surprised McLaughlin by reaching number 89 on the *Billboard* album chart. The acclaim for the Mahavishnu Orchestra was immediate and prolonged. McLaughlin was inundated with offers of sessions and gigs, and the workload which would eventually drive all five members to each other's throats a little less than three years later was already piling up. McLaughlin, unsurprisingly, turned most of the offers down.

The gigs continued; torrents of them. Starting at campuses – they played Syracuse University in New Jersey twice in six months, packing out two different venues. At Easter 1972 they journeyed to Puerto Rico's Mar y Sol festival for a gig on 3rd April. As supporting band, they intimidated the headliners. As headliners, they intimidated the supporting bands. At a few gigs they were supported by an embryonic Aerosmith, stoking already hyped audiences into rumbustious hysteria by the time the eagerly anticipated Mahavishnu Orchestra arrived. Later, the then-Aerosmith manager bragged that his band had the measure of McLaughlin's act and had 'blown him offstage'. He made his judgement on the guitarist's plea to a frenzied audience for a moment of quiet before the Mahavishnu Orchestra set began. The truth was more prosaic; by this time McLaughlin *always* asked for a moment of contemplation before the music began. A better assessment of the professional differential between the two bands was that of Aerosmith drummer Joey Kramer, who confessed to sitting behind Billy Cobham at those same gigs and being so awe-struck by the man's technique that it almost drove him out of the business in despair of ever matching such achievements.

Henceforward Europe beckoned, with a headlining appearance at the Munich Jazz Festival held to commemorate that city's hosting of the

1972 summer Olympic Games. The band brought the house down and became a sensation throughout the Continent. McLaughlin also made a short solo appearance at the same festival. Britain welcomed its prodigal son back with ecstatic notices, he took the Crystal Palace Garden Party open air gig by storm in mid-August. A BBC television concert was also arranged and broadcast live on BBC2 on the 25th August. McLaughlin was becoming a star, and increased his luminosity with his cavalier handling of a massive double-neck Gibson guitar, an instrument that would become his signature. It was his cipher in rock's pantheon of images; Elvis had his rhinestone suit, Michael Jackson his white glove, McLaughlin his double-neck. It seemed to confer an extra authority on a man rapidly becoming the most celebrated non-classical guitar player in the world. He'd used his favourite instrument, a Gibson Les Paul custom, for most of the early months of the Mahavishnu Orchestra, but after finding the constant switching of six- and twelve-string guitars a drag, he acted when seeing the Gibson in a catalogue. "I did go look at a Mosrite double-neck, too," he confessed.

McLaughlin always enthused about the sheer practicality of the double-neck, despite its heftiness (30lb). "Full utilisation of both necks comes fastest through working," he noted. "When you're up there on stage and you've got to play the thing, you do it. I tend to do... arpeggiated chords on the twelve-string. And it's sonorous, it's sweet, it's clear, and it's bell-like, which you can't get on a 6-string. I do play melody on the 12-string sometimes, though, and then I hit both of the paired strings when I solo."

Back in the USA, sessions began for the band's second LP, *Birds Of Fire*, but McLaughlin was now also preoccupied with the first major extra-curricular project since the launch of the Mahavishnu Orchestra.

McLaughlin's decision to enter into a collaboration with fellow-guitarist Carlos Santana in 1972 has polarised opinions amongst critics, fans and even sidemen of the two guitarists ever since it was first mooted. For every critic who uses adjectives like 'explosive' and 'ecstatic', two will use 'vapid' and 'spiritually-obsessed'.

It made sense at the time – McLaughlin's only serious rival as a guitarist in popular music (discounting wholly rock-based performers like Clapton, Page and Beck) was the wiry Mexican. He had arrived destitute in the USA from Tijuana in 1966 with a few pesos and a caseful of blues licks. He opened at the Fillmore West the following year and stormed the Woodstock Festival, *The Ed Sullivan Show* and the *Billboard* charts within eighteen months. With a chewily physical, seductive, chilli-hot concoction of foot-tapping Chicano rhythm, soulful melodies and achingly lyrical guitar intonation, he also had improvisatory skills to die for.

His and McLaughlin's paths would have inevitably crossed; by the summer of 1971 Santana was headlining over Miles Davis and natural curiosity would have led the Englishman to check out the hype and what, if any, justification it had. Whether he was impressed or worried, McLaughlin didn't let on, but liked what he heard. What followed was inevitable; McLaughlin/Santana, not duelling, but dispensing smiles, flowers and wisdom in the spiritual quest of the electric guitar. He told the press that he'd, "woken up one morning and wanted to do an album with Santana", only for his manager to ring and tell him that Columbia chief Davis had been onto him with the selfsame idea. Whatever, the result was predictable; everybody happy – both musicians, Chinmoy and very definitely the pair's employers, Columbia Records.

A little too happy, some critics might say. *Love Devotion Surrender* was recorded in two sessions (October 1972 and March 1973) and McLaughlin reported himself pleased with the results, as did Santana. At least McLaughlin's appearance on the hyperactive Santana's next LP, *Welcome*, gave the lie to this simply being happy shiny Chinmoy gloss on a botch job. Santana, once a renowned rock 'n' roll rake, was mellowing; he expressed an interest in Chinmoy to McLaughlin, and that was enough. McLaughlin took him along to one of the weekly prayer meetings Chinmoy had set up for staff at the United Nations building and the guru blessed Santana there and then, bestowing the name Devadip on him. Both men, if contemporary accounts and interviews were anything to go by, became utterly infatuated with the Chinmoy path, even going so far as to collaborate on the music to an American television documentary on the guru in April 1973.

McLaughlin, in particular, was a believer to his core. Charles Alexander recalls watching the band play at Glasgow's Kelvin Hall in 1973. "The whole two front rows were entirely taken up with Chinmoy's people – these massed ranks of white shirts! And then the band appeared – Goodman and Hammer and Cobham, conspicuously lacking the white numbers, Laird, who wore a white shirt, and then John who wore white all over. They go into the first number. And it's great, but then they finish and John comes to the apron and does a little bow with hands clasped and goes, 'Greetings, O people of Glasgow'. It was a little hard to take the gig seriously after that, no matter how good he was."

Ernst-Joachim Berendt, who interviewed and befriended the guitarist during his triumphal visit to Munich in the summer of 1972, was rather nonplussed and recounted how McLaughlin asked for some fruit and flowers to place before the tiny altar which Chinmoy had given him to carry with him everywhere.

Love Devotion Surrender chooses to use the more mystical inspirations of John Coltrane as a kind of legitimizer. Formerly, McLaughlin had lifted the saxophonist's secular compositions. Here, "Naima" and "A Love Supreme" got the treatment.

The problem with the Santana recordings lay in a very subtle but crucial difference in style. Santana, despite possessing a highly exploratory musical mind as evidenced on the 1972 album *Caravanserai*, was at heart a man rooted in western harmony. Despite his skills, he was prone to constrain those gifts within a fairly regular, recognizable blues- and Latin-based language for guitar soloists.

Both men liked to unleash torrents of notes crowned by mercilessly triumphant stabs of feedbacky sustain. But even a first-time listener should discern one guitarist from the other. McLaughlin's tone is also richer and fuller.

Love Devotion Surrender was, in retrospect, a spiritually-hobbled album. "Naima" was zonked rather than serene, the contrast of acoustic guitar styles lacking everything when compared to Coryell and McLaughlin's duel on "Rene's Theme" from the former's *Spaces* album of 1970. The Belgian virtuoso, Philip Catherine, would record a no less introspective but much more harmonically ambiguous version of "Naima" on his *September Man* album in 1974. "A Love Supreme" quickly settles down into a plink-plonk conga-heavy foursquare vamp all too typical of Santana, which even Larry Young's ghostly tone can't redeem. McLaughlin's solo contains a series of uncontrolled triplets which he attempts to echo on his 1978 reunion with Santana, the track "Friendship" from the *Electric Guitarist* album. The bovine chanting of the title is echoed on "The Life Divine", a promising McLaughlin composition whose maniacal charge down through the opening chord sequence is one of the few things to remind the listener of his Mahavishnu Orchestra achievements. Santana probably plays the more fluidly, and McLaughlin's technophiliac tendencies are manifesting themselves in the electronic gimmickry that would soon inundate the finer points of his playing.

By "Let Us Go Into The House Of The Lord" it's hard to care who is playing which solo. The long sequence of chords which forms the basis of the piece is hard to pin down to one particular traditional provenance although 'trad' is the compositional credit. It has hymnal, gospelly, vaguely European overtones but also a harmonic ecstasy familiar from McLaughlin's European transposition of Indian scales. Young's organ playing here, incidentally, with its overlapping flurries of triplets, is a moment of pure genius, worthy of mention in its own right, a musical equivalent of a swarm of surreally coloured butterflies.

The European symphonic tradition, again hinted at in the 1973 Mahavishnu live set *Between Nothingness And Eternity* crops up in the finale, the sedate "Meditation". McLaughlin, playing portentious if contemplative grand piano chords, provides the sonic universe for the mystic neophyte, Santana, to engrave his humble musical signature upon.

McLaughlin's and Santana's next meeting, the duel on the Santana album *Welcome* is its highpoint. The eleven-and-a-half minute "Flame Sky "is a remorselessly energetic guitar battle. Unfortunately, while Santana plays some of the fastest guitar on record during the piece, the insufferable phasing of his sound from channel to channel does the music no favours at all. Again, the harmonic progressions of both band and frontman are disappointingly mundane. One cannot doubt the tightness of the act, which often spills into infectiously chaotic melodrama – and there is a spookily dark flamenco feel about much of the action – but an attempted four-part contrapuntal duel between the two guitars, bass and organ, however, doesn't quite come off. The piece, it was said, was inspired by the pillars of spiritual light which reach into the heavens when the 'true believer' prays.

If McLaughlin was in danger of overdoing the almost effeminate delicacy and meliorism of Chinmoy's spirituality, it wasn't showing in the character of the Mahavishnu Orchestra's music. *Birds of Fire*, recorded in September 1972 and released the following March, is perhaps the most satisfying of all the Mahavishnu Orchestra's output, and shows a musical mind not fuddled by contemplation and meditation but grimly, almost manically focused.

Birds of Fire burns at phosphoric heat but without the same intensity as the debut. It is, if you like, ignited by the incandescence of *The Inner Mounting Flame*. There is more light and shade; this is not the express to hell that might have been evoked by some of the more extreme passages of "Vital Transformation" or "Awakening". The overall sound is broader and clearer, for starters, although Cobham, crash cymbals by now dominating his textures, ensures that the Orchestra does not as yet sound too immaculately 'orchestral'.

It was maybe a bit disingenuous of McLaughlin to claim at the time that *Birds of Fire* contained "no solos". There are three on the opening, title track alone, although the solos are sparer and shorter and, certainly in McLaughlin's case, less obviously rock-inspired. On *Flame*, many of his solos adhere closely to the tempo he is playing over, whereas on *Birds of Fire* there is a more erratic, haphazard delivery more in keeping with the formal flexibility of his idol Coltrane. There are also retreads – the title track recalls, in form and harmony, "Meeting Of The Spirits" and, as we've noted, there are throwbacks to "A Lotus On Irish Streams" and "Dawn" ("Thousand Island Park" and "Open Country Joy" especially) – McLaughlin's penchant for poetic titles reaches its zenith on this album. "Thousand Island Park" should be mentioned both for its fidelity to its spiritual sister piece, "Lotus", and for a strong and distinct autonomy from it. The music is altogether more severe, the soundstage more economical and the notes sterner. The spirits of Keith Jarrett and the contemporary Chick Corea (of the Circle and initial Return To Forever line-ups) stalk this ethereal, mist-laden, watery parkland.

Free jazz, or at least a fully electrified version, is hinted at on "Sapphire Bullets Of Pure Love", a wholly atonal, twenty-one second freak-out heavily fogged by white noise from Hammer's synthesiser. This, surely, represents something of a cop-out; even those antipathetic to free jazz would have found McLaughlin's electric interpretation of it worthy of a little more exposure.

The album *feels* rockier. "Celestial Terrestrial Commuters" has a rustic, galumphingly danceable gait; Goodman and McLaughlin swapping solos like they were playing a rock 'n' roll revival festival. "One Word", a juggernaut of a track, crashes along on a distinctly rocky time-signature and has the menacing dark glint of modern musical technology. There is a definite domestication of the Mahavishnu Orchestra's sound here. This is not to imply criticism; the integration of more conventional rock and funk devices is as yet subtle and subordinate to the whole. It was an even more individualised blending of styles from Latin to jazz to heavy metal, more assured even than *The Inner Mounting Flame*. The very facility with which more accessible forms could be grafted onto the original led many lazier musicians later in the decade to reverse the process. The result was to give the world the syndicated jazz-funk by numbers which acted like a concrete waistcoat on late-seventies and eighties fusion.

Another discomfiting portent was the sub-Symbolist doggerel of Sri Chinmoy's poetry reverentially reproduced on the reverse sleeve. Little more than a jumble of strophic spiritualisms and acidhead ecstasies, it was a kind of cross between Stefan George and Patience Strong, the stuff of a cultic greetings card. This febrile imagery had been appropriated rather well thus far by McLaughlin to append (presumably) arbitrary titles to his pieces but when applied to formalised poetry, it hung heavy on the mind of any sane reader. Worse would follow on *Apocalypse*, and McLaughlin himself would have a stab at using it as the basis of song lyrics on that same album, one of the moments in his career when he perhaps best needed a friend to step in and say "no". This, perhaps, was McLaughlin's most glaring lapse of critical good taste.

To return to the music of *Birds Of Fire*, relationships within the band were clearly changing. Hammer solos even less, and Goodman often sounds sulky and diffident, only bursting into form on the warmly lyrical and sunny "Open Country Joy". With its Mid-Western cod-folksiness, a kind of scruffy elder brother to Pat Metheny's later mom 'n' apple-pie impressionism, the man is clearly having a ball. Cobham and Laird, however, are all of a piece, and Cobham's star has clearly risen. His sound punches through with far greater muscle, and his textures, strengthened and broadened by tom-toms and cymbals are more daring, with fills scuttering all around an augmented kit.

The energy is phenomenal; but energy is finite, and Mahavishnu's was running low. 200 one-nighters in the US in 1972 and 250 days on the road in 1973 took their toll and eventually told their own story.

The strain got to Jan Hammer first; he gave a less than complimentary character profile of his boss during an interview with *Crawdaddy* magazine. An attempt at recording an album in London comprising originals from all band members and not just McLaughlin's own numbers was a well-intentioned attempt at mollification by the leader that failed. "It was a disaster," said Rick Laird, matter-of-factly. McLaughlin left some of the sessions in tears. This didn't preclude one last flailing, blazing musical document, *Between Nothingness And Eternity*, recorded live in New York's Central Park on 17 August 1973.

Between Nothingness and Eternity is commonly regarded as an afterthought of a great band, a kind of wan distillation of the more potent energies of its two predecessors. There was, it was whispered, as with the concurrent *Love Devotion Surrender* collection, the complacent atmosphere of white-boy jamming in the narcotically Olympian reserve of a festival stage in America in summer. It's true that it's more traditionally bluesy and rocky than other recordings of the Mk I Orchestra – the sauntering funk metres of "Trilogy" and "Sister Andrea" bear this out. (Less swaying, hot-panted female buttocks than the funk-created musical *idea* of swaying, hot-panted female buttocks which is evoked by the combination of fatback swagger and undercurrent of harmonic wistfulness).

There's also the feel that the band are leaping through hoops with a calculated choreography; the twenty-one minute "Dreams" for example, which occupies side two of the album, features most if not all of the band's tricks condensed into one handily side-length whole. But the LP also contains some furiously committed and inventive playing, not all of it fast and loud. "Dreams" (whose episodic character might be a nod towards the musical modus-operandi of Goodman and Cobham's similarly titled pre-Mahvishnu Orchestra band) contains haphazard if intermittently thrilling ruminations on a six-note theme at the outset. The music suddenly turns all European, with a vague punt at symphonic structure (and most definitely European symphonic harmony) placing it more in the field of progressive rock than jazz rock.

Nonetheless, the heart of the piece develops from a raga-tinged dialogue between McLaughlin and a revitalised Hammer. At the outset McLaughlin's scurrying, muted electric six-string lines echo tabla notation and voicings while Hammer creates impressionist filigrees. From this beginning, several blues figures are developed, often foursquare with Cobham agile inbetween the bar lines. When the riff from "Sunshine Of Your Love" emerges seemlessly from the texture, its appearance is so ungratuitous that the synthesizing achievement of McLaughlin and his chums in this band becomes most apparent. It's corny, but it's a two-fisted affirmation to the dullest of listeners just how harmonically and melodically flexible and eclectic this music could be. An impressionistic guitar extemporisation on a blues figure influenced by North Indian percussion voicings bearing forth a funk riff, which in turn produces, conjurous-style, one of the alltime great rock themes. Crazy, but crazily logical.

The highlights for spectacle freaks and rubber neckers of musical athletics, ironically, were thin. Hammer has a ball throughout, yet never gets an extended solo, save for his unhinged attack which brings "Sister Andrea" to a crazed conclusion. McLaughlin's astonishing solo in the middle of "Dreams" can really only be described as the sort of playing that made the legend in the first place and confirms it to be pretty much true.

* * *

All of Mahavishnu Mark I's music relates cleverly to India and to the blues, mostly through McLaughlin's deep interest in modes. McLaughlin staunchly defended his bluesman's faith; and wasn't shy in advancing intellectual proof thereof. "The Dance of Maya" from *The Inner Mounting Flame* was one example he used. He told an interviewer that the piece was inextricably connected to the blues. The basic chords were E, A and B; the first chord, E7, rises from low E to G#/A♭, then B. Then came G#/A♭ with a D on top. "In spite of the fact," McLaughlin continued, "that [in chordal terms] it ends up an A♭ major. You give me that and I'll play a blues on it, in spite of the fact that it's a very angular chord." It could be argued, of course, that this testified more to McLaughlin's harmonic resourcefulness than the flexibility of the music (he also talks about the possibilities of blues-based harmony at length below, discussing the much more obviously blues-inflected 1993 album, *Free Spirits Live In Tokyo*).

Then there were the modes; "Meeting Of The Spirits", he has pointed out, has the feel of a phrygian mode, or a combination of pentatonic minor and phrygian modes, with their roots in the blues and in the music of Coltrane, "who did a lot with minor pentatonic scales". "What I like to do," McLaughlin told one reporter, "is to stack modes sometimes; you can just stack a minor third on top of [them]." He has also talked, even a tad immodestly, of creating his own modes. He discovered the Super Locrian mode himself, he said, but also in trying to create his own scales he found ones that were musicologically obsolete, e.g. the Enigmatic, Neapolitan and Hungarian major scales.

The music was predominantly modal, as opposed to playing over changes and producing a clean, western harmonic movement which makes melody almost secondary. In Indian classical music, conversely, melody dominated harmony. Modes, noted McLaughlin, were related to raga, where a raga's scales could be played around and endlessly developed each time the melody is repeated.

As Ravi Shankar wrote in his sleeve notes to the 1956 album *Ravi Shankar Plays Three Classical Ragas,* "Indian music is modal by nature, and though harmony may be present in its simplest form, it is inherent, rather than deliberate. For the better and finer enjoyment of Indian music, Western audiences should forget about harmony and counterpoint or the mixed tone colours which may be considered the prime essentials of a symphonic or similar work. It would be much better to relax in the rich melody and rhythm, with the exquisitely subtle inflections through which the atmosphere of a Raga is built up."

The trumpeter Phil Scarff, a longtime expert on subcontinental music and in particular its relevance to jazz, hints at some of the Mahavishnu Orchestra's early music when he claims that in Indian music, "rhythmic tension and resolution is created by the use of rhythmic patterns such as tihais, nauhais, and chakradhars, that typically resolve to sam (beat one of the rhythmic cycle). These ideas can also be used in [American] jazz and in Indo-jazz. In jazz, tension and resolution is achieved by harmonic movement; melodic movement, by moving from dissonance to consonance against the underlying harmony... Indian classical music and Indo-jazz are very compatible with these melodic and rhythmic ideas; harmonic movement can be applied in Indo-jazz."

The resolution of the apparent contradiction – western harmonic movement with the linear harmony of Indian classical music where the rhythm and melody were everything – was one of the greatest achievements of jazz-rock. This is audible both in the music of the Mahavishnu Orchestra and their use of manifold rhythmic structures resolving onto the first beat of melodic cycles.

But all the intellectual credibility in the world couldn't save a band falling out of love with each other. The tension grew; McLaughlin pleaded with his sidemen one evening to tell him what was wrong, and when he left the silent room, an angry Laird turned on his colleagues and asked them, "Why didn't you tell him what you really think, eh? You don't mind telling people when he's not listening."

The band played its last gig on 30 December 1973 in Detroit, Michigan. McLaughlin told the press wearily, but not without a whiff of self-righteousness, "maybe they found it too hard, too demanding, but I demand as much from myself as I do from anybody... maybe the tension was there because I wasn't hanging out with the boys, as it were, and goofing off."

McLaughlin, hard on himself, was as hard on others, first in terms of group discipline, and then, gradually, in terms of ensemble discipline whilst actually playing, a tendency which swung further and further towards conventional western symphonic practise. By *Apocalypse*, the first album made by the second incarnation of the Mahavishnu Orchestra, this discipline threatened to straitjacket the music altogether.

Chapter Four
Planetary Citizenship

What had animated critics for some time was whether or not the slight hints at greater consonance in *Birds of Fire* prefigured a move towards more western, classical modes of expression, and on *Apocalypse* they got their answer.

In retrospect the arrival in jazz-rock of the group/orchestral project was overdue. In rock, the concept had long been discredited. The increasing substitution of western classical/folk/avant-garde compositional and improvisational devices by post-Beatles rock musicians for traditional blues-based Afro-American expression in the late 1960s had led to the inevitable and horribly mismatched textural miscegenation of electric group and (acoustic) symphony orchestra. One of the earliest of these shotgun marriages was the one that backfired most grotesquely, Deep Purple's notorious *Concerto For Group And Orchestra* of which one critic perceptively observed, "Its structure was clumsy, its instrumentation banal, its invention feeble and its claim to serious composition derisory". Other exercises in hubris included *The Five Bridges Suite* by The Nice and *Atom Heart Mother* by Pink Floyd. The latter integrated the textures of symphonic and electric instruments (solo and in ensemble) somewhat better, and the Floyd's keyboard player Rick Wright astutely observed that Deep Purple had simply not adequately understood the differentiation between the two soundworlds and how to bridge it. That was a little rich considering the manifold deficiencies of Wright's own work, but it highlighted the principal shortfall in the inspiration of rock-based musicians working with orchestral players.

Apocalypse had been premiered in Buffalo in January 1974, or at least one section of it was. It was hurriedly programmed to make up for the sudden indisposition of violinist Isaac Stern. McLaughlin had, apparently, had the idea for an orchestral work in his mind since mid-1972, and, encouraged by Chinmoy, and the (classical) Masterworks department of Columbia Records, trudged on through it from conception to completion. Finding a musical soulmate in the fast-rising young American conductor Michael Tilson Thomas, then music director of the Buffalo Philharmonic Orchestra and a specialist in the American and European impressionist repertoire which so inspired McLaughlin, he arranged a premiere of the work. "He's a guy," said McLaughlin at the time, "that I'm really happy to work with because he's had a total classical background but he likes Martha and the Vandellas as much as he likes any of the principal Western composers."

The premiere was simultaneously a preview of Mahavishnu mark II; here, it appeared as if McLaughlin was assuming the patriarchal role of Davis, assembling as he did musicians much younger than himself. Youth wasn't the only issue; orchestralism was. In the new Mahavishnu Orchestra ("the real Mahavishnu Orchestra" McLaughlin rather intemperately called it) personnel would number eight basic players, eleven maximum, and picked up through extensive consultation at local Chinmoy centres and at the McLaughlin's own Chinmoy restaurant in Queens. On drums there was the prodigy Michael Walden, just 17. On bass, the chunkily genial Ralphe Armstrong, 19. On keyboards, an ethereal, beautiful young New Yorker, Gayle Moran, 23, who had a light touch on the piano and a singing voice that angels would have squabbled over. The twenty-something string trio featured another Chinmoy follower, violinist Carol Shive, late of the Honolulu Philharmonic, also a piercingly wonderful vocalist. Chinmoy convert and cello whiz Phil Hirschi and willowy, lyrical violist Marsha Westbrook completed the line-up. One later recruit commented wryly, "They all got a big kick out of wearing tuxes and tails for the concert, something the first Mahavishnu Orchestra would never consent to, especially Jerry Goodman."

At the premiere though, McLaughlin kept his powder dry. His trump card came later – violinist Jean-Luc Ponty, who he'd tried and failed to snare for *My Goal's Beyond* and the original Mahavishnu Orchestra lineup after hearing the Frenchman's extraordinary transcriptions of Frank

Zappa's *King Kong*. Ponty, who doubled on electric and acoustic violins, was undisputed king of his instrument.

Bob Knapp, who with trumpeter Steve Frankovitch was required to play an entire brass section's transcriptions when McLaughlin took his Mahavishnu mark II out on tour, takes up the story; "I was recruited for touring by Michael Walden, an old friend who'd gone to my high school in Kalamazoo, Michigan. He called to tell me that he was playing with John McLaughlin, and that they were looking for some brass players to join the band, and asked if I was interested in playing with the group. I was stunned, and then he put John on the phone and we spoke for a few minutes. John said that he had reformed the band and the new group was going to be recording a new album in London during February with the London Symphony Orchestra. On their return they would be playing a tour of the US and wanted to know if I would be available to come down to do the tour. I naturally agreed and met up with them in New York around the end of March or the beginning of April. My position was to play the LSO brass and woodwind section parts that had been originally scored for the *Apocalypse* recording and had been rewritten for the smaller ensemble."

Walden also knew Armstrong, Moran and Russell Tubbs, who filled in brass/reed parts on the follow-up album, *Visions Of The Emerald Beyond* (1975). Testimony to Moran is almost embarrassingly positive. Originally a keyboard and cornet player in a gospel group, Bob Knapp remembers her as "a sweet voice and a sweet person", and Hirschi goes further; "Gayle had a beautiful apartment somewhere on the upper west side, and of course she sings beautifully, and she herself is beautiful. Pretty good combination, don't you think? Rhythmically the Mahavishnu Orchestra was a stretch for her (as it was for me, not having had weird 11's [3,3,2,3 time signatures] hammered into me during all those cello lessons!)"

Hirschi goes on, "I knew the other disciples: Carol Shive, Bob Knapp, Mike Walden. For a while we hoped that Mahavishnu would ask Louis Kahn, a lovely guy and a disciple who played trombone with the Fania All Stars... a Jew in the Fania All Stars! Only in New York City!... he also played some fiddle. But it didn't happen."

McLaughlin brought in Michael Gibbs to orchestrate his project. Incidentally, he had already seen his composition "Birds Of Fire" re-arranged for orchestra by the conductor and arranger Don Sebesky and segued with an excerpt from Stravinsky's *Firebird* suite on Sebesky's 1973 album *Giant Box*. Gibbs was a long-time alumnus of the London jazz scene, and a fellow-sideman on Kenny Wheeler's *Windmill Tilter* project, as well as an expert arranger. McLaughlin, while a student and lover of western classical music, wasn't going to stray where he felt less than confident, in among the brambled thickets of cors anglais and contrabass trombones. Gibbs, however, was a musician with an exceptional ear for timbre and was (and remains) one of the best arrangers in the world.

True, Gibbs' gifts were often in radiant evidence on the album, and on the magnificent "Wings of Karma" produces as glitteringly precise a pastiche of *Firebird/Petrushka*-era Stravinsky as it's possible to hear. But again the thorny problem of timbral integration intrudes painfully. The orchestra and group are usually kept apart, with only the odd swathe of plush upholstery of ensemble chords by the strings. Occasionally the two entities swap phrases with almost embarrassing crudity, as on the penultimate section of the epic finale, "Hymn To Him", and the juxtapositions seem to be made with little more than pink string and sealing wax. Transitions are anything but seamless and at times laughably arbitrary.

Ponty takes advantage of the greater space afforded to the violin soloist with some invigorating playing, tight-roping along between farcical self-indulgence and showstopping lyrical bravura. Indeed, the effects used by him and McLaughlin often make their instruments sound all but indistinguishable, Ponty sometimes identified merely by his bowing.

The recording of *Apocalypse*, according to producer George Martin, bordered at times on farce. On "Vision Is A Naked Sword", Martin later wrote about how the entry of the band, even at a fairly low level, had utterly swamped the entire forces of the LSO. McLaughlin later breezily informed journalists that the experience had been one of the greatest of his life. It must be conceded that Martin eventually came round, and in several interviews has cited *Apocalypse* as his most satisfactory project outside of the Beatle nexus.

The prelude opens with seven solemn, tolling downward chords on low strings, piano (Tilson Thomas, uncredited) and bells, a foundation for the first theme picked out on McLaughlin's acoustic guitar, around which Ponty's violin lines shimmer and sashay seductively. The raga-like Romanticism pervades almost throughout, with interjections of somewhat flatfooted *sturm und drang*, as with the introduction to "Vision Is A Naked Sword" which gave George Martin such headaches.

The music is, as befits its high-born accomplices, altogether tidier and more disciplined, but it also loses much of its dynamic penchant for chaos. As Brian Eno once memorably remarked of Roxy Music after his departure, his worry about the band was that without the element of chaos, they would fall into "just thoroughly-rehearsed performances with bits for the band to fiddle around in". This might be a direct reference to the evolution in McLaughlin's style which makes possible the sound-world of *Apocalypse*; certainly the band reformation makes itself vividly clear.

The rhythm section of Armstrong and Walden slot into funk grooves with much less fuss than Laird and Cobham, but the sophisticated slink they lock the band's pulse into wears thin at times, not least its humdrum domination of the two main tracks, "Vision Is A Naked Sword" and "Hymn To Him". Gayle Moran's electric piano style also anchors the band in a more mainstream, familiarly consonant sound. Walden, however, still a mere stripling, often is a little too fond of exhibitionism for its own good, his six-tom, double bass-drum freakouts sometimes add obstrusively to the pulse. On "Vision Is A Naked Sword", for example, his ringing up the curtain on the band as the low-string and heavy brass chords tumble around him seems little more than showing his mom and dad he's arrived and that all that investment in twenty-odd crash cymbals was money well-spent.

McLaughlin is curiously recessed in the music. This may have something to do with the often-excessive use of effects pedals on his sound, blunting its piercing edge, especially in the upper registers. His only extended solo of note is a dark-hued, chilling, cyclonic affair in the finale, often accompanied solely by Walden. But this too churns relentlessly around too few chords and lacks the manic, scale-hopping fervour of some of his more exciting runs on *Birds* and *Flame*. "Wings Of Karma", however, does have short salvos of McLaughlin at his best.

The sessions, aside of balancing difficulties, were hobbled in other ways. Union restrictions practically nullified McLaughlin's intention of using his own string section. Phil Hirschi recalls, "The big screw-up for me was that the LSO's union reps refused to let Carol, Marsha and me play with the LSO. John just couldn't do anything about it. After a couple of days of rehearsal with me sitting at the back of the cello section, talking to some bored, distracted guy reading a book between takes, I never got to sit in with them again. So what John did, was throw together something for the string trio to do by itself during "Smile". We got to sing, with male and female choruses answering each other on "*blessed are the pure at heart*" ["Smile Of The Beyond'] between Jean Luc and John riffing. In the same cut there are brief sections of the string trio playing the same parts that the vocals sing; that's Carol, me and Marsha, the only time we play on the album."

The band toured extensively, garnering mixed reviews, mostly harping on the balance differentials between the chamber ensembles used in the act and those which upholstered the original music on *Apocalypse*. Here, Knapp and Frankovitch came into their own. Frankovitch was another youngster, just 19, who had played with Lionel Hampton and Frankie Valli And The Four Seasons, leading some to muse that McLaughlin was attempting to recruit a core of pop-based young technicians to mould to his own ends. Knapp says that, "he was an outstanding trumpet player who had been referred to John from another New York studio trumpet player, Joe Shepley."

Visions Of The Emerald Beyond is not nearly so bad an album as a retrospective of its reviews at the time would indicate. In many ways, it's a better bet than *Apocalypse*. *Emerald* reforms the raw material of its immediate predecessor into a more cohesive and approachable whole. While *Flame* might be said to be ultimately a more thrilling listen than its successor, *Emerald* probably outdoes *Apocalypse*. There isn't the grandeur, for many that will be a plus; but the repertoire of gestures is all there, only more concisely put. The longueurs of the 1974 album are commensurately reduced. McLaughlin had also risked Ponty's wrath by signing a brilliant young violinist, the Seattle-based Steve Kindler, to turn his string trio into a quartet. Kindler, according to Hirschi, could "play Jerry Goodman riffs like they were written for him". Armstrong too plays manfully, although hampered by an unfriendly mix. Despite his age, band members recall a considerable confidence on the young man's part. "John gave him solos as he was never shy. Ralphe is so fast – and he always played fretless bass", Hirschi remembers.

Visions has its low points (some very low), though. The narcoleptic "Earth Ship" is a mantric piece of musical genuflection at the feet of Chinmoy. The same poetic syntax is, unfortunately, much more in evidence on no less than three songs. McLaughlin, however, seems less beatific, and at times thoroughly pissed-off, and produces his best playing for some time. "Eternity's Breath", the two-part curtain-raiser, divides opinion. Some, like the present author, believe it to be one of McLaughlin's most convincing and satisfying compositions; others, to be the acme of the guitarist's infatuation with cosmic grandiosity. Certainly its finely-wrought and rigorously-structured framework outdo *Apocalypse*'s ambition. The track tilts the band's rhythmic language and compositional orientation more than ever towards the wannabe-

Stravinskys of the Progressive rock mainstream, but with a harmonic richness and tightness of the whole. There is a seamless logic about the piece, best exemplified by how quickly the second part justifies its apparently random juxtaposition with the first. Its complexities are formidable; the piece is dominated by an anthemic figure which is counterpointed with two quite different figures. The first doubles up as the bassline to the central, up-tempo "Part 2", which features one of McLaughlin's finest solos.

The strength of the album is, undeniably, its greater success at coherently assimilating the European symphonic tradition into McLaughlin's music than *Apocalypse*. The ensemble writing is more mature and cleverer, even if the commitment to dazzlement often outweighs musical taste. McLaughlin had learnt his lessons from Mike Gibbs, and while the string and brass sections could be used more extensively and more subtly, the arrangements on the whole are good.

Unfortunately, while Walden's drumming is never less than sensational, the music-student-bedsit game of name-the-time-signature seemed to be the rule throughout, often at the expense of melodic felicity, harmonic innovation and experiment. For the record, the self-consciously guess-this-one-sucker time-signature trickiness of "Can't Stand Your Funk" is in 10/8. Walden's deconstruction of fatback snare (often cleverly holding back the downbeats), cymbal and bass drum work on "Cosmic Strut" and "If I Could See" had drummers puzzling for months over their tapes and eight-tracks. Precision choreography was how the Mahavishnu world worked now; awesomely, heartstoppingly impressive, but as with a touring Bolshoi ballet company, what left the punters gasping in the stalls was not necessarily where the impulse for newer and greater things was born.

Too many tricks had had their day. "If I Could See" on side two, casually aborts one of McLaughlin's loveliest melodies at the altar of preposterous grandiosity, utilising B-movie reverb deep enough to simulate an orchestra that isn't there and wasn't affordable. It mutates, pointlessly, into a jazz-rock romp which not only sounds imitative of *Inner Mounting Flame*, but of that album's epigones. Only Walden's irrepressible invention saves the day on many occasions.

McLaughlin's classical aspirations, savaged by the many, were appreciated by the few. "Pastoral" and its sister piece, "Faith", on side one, are intricately-plotted meditations around the key which, tellingly, contain enough detail, either from Ponty, McLaughlin or the string quartet never to slide into torpor (despite the taped birdsong). The thoroughly odd

"Faith", builds through the now familiar reverb-heavy and tom-roll gar-landed chordal ascent. It ends with a furious unaccompanied electric 12-string freakout from McLaughlin (sounding like a good ol' boy after too much acid and Jack Daniels). It is a headlong ensemble plummet through a polytonal 44-note raga-riff down to a plagal cadence and Carol Shive's hysterical laughter. This crazed, almost surreal piece was a double wham-my of Mahavishnu ethics; a climbing orgasm of harmonic dissolution in cod-religiosity and an athletic time-trial for the fastest ensemble playing in history. "Carol was laughing at how damn difficult the piece was. John liked it, thought it was funny, and kept it in", Phil Hirschi recalls.

Reviewers were growing impatient too, but McLaughlin's star was still in the ascendant. 1974 had been termed by lazy *Rolling Stone* staffers as 'the year of jazz-rock'; and why not? All the stars in the columns of rock comics like the NME were being earned by technocratic mergers of rock and jazz virtuosity. On TV, Quincy Jones and Tom Scott ruled the roost, scoring *Ironside* and *The Streets Of San Francisco* respectively with a funk swagger and a polyrhythmic shuffle. The rock guitarist's wah-wah gave an extra contemporaneousness to the time-expired orchestral tex-tures of TV and film scoring (Herbie Hancock had already accepted the commission for Charles Bronson/Michael Winner's 1975 epic of gutter vengeance, *Death Wish)*. In the uncertainly liberal USA of the mid-70s, when TV moguls sought to render the streets both as entertainment and as shock value, the mediation of funk via white musicians plainly schooled in the big bands had become a white middle-class consumer commodity. The result was a wild mix of rock and funk pouring into the living rooms of Everytown, USA. It might best have been brand-named 'Sofistifunk' (although the source of that brand name, a track penned by Return To Forever drummer Lenny White for their 1975 LP *No Mystery* is anything but sophisticated or funky).

Listening to the development of the *Ironside* theme is especially instructive of the way that serious musical study had changed in America in the post-war decades. When the show debuted in 1967, its memorable title sequence, written by Quincy Jones, was arranged directly in the big-band tradition, with only a few concessions to metric or timbral complex-ity, or to contemporary developments thereof. By 1971, however, it had been funked and rocked up almost out of all recognition. Such was the pre-eminence of musical cross-pollination in jazz at the time.

With the voracious appetite of the media – film, radio, TV – it had proved a necessity to write racily for the kids in Peoria. Be creative, and sell... the coming of rock music allowed a generation to study the selling points of rock close at hand and apply their own instinctive musical talents to it. The result was that the street scene in America became as synonymous with a funky jazz-rock soundtrack as a rutted high street in Dodge City had been with a harmonica-led orchestra thirty years previously. Randolph Scott's theme was Strauss trying to think of how to score a banjo or glassharp concerto, while the themes to accompany Steve McGarrett, Starsky and McCloud were Miles Davis hungover with a Beatles album jamming with Sly Stone in 17/11 time. This was musical postmodernism *avant la lettre* and among its founding fathers was John McLaughlin. He was all set for heroism.

He certainly cut a dash; his stage presence was now among the most commanding in popular music, and respect bordering on awe came from all quarters. McLaughlin was quite simply king of the hill. "Oh my God," Andrès Segovia is reputed (possibly apochryphally) to have said on hearing McLaughlin, "the fastest guitarist in the world." Joachim-Ernst Berendt called him "*the* musician of the 1970s". It might have irked McLaughlin to hear that more than it pleased him, but it oiled the publicity mill wonderfully. Guitarist Steve Howe, of the rock band Yes, widely regarded in the 1970s as one of the top two or three guitar technicians in his field, went so far as to say; "It's only when you play with super musicians like John McLaughlin that you start to worry; 'Is our music really good enough to stand up to his?'"

McLaughlin's sovereignty was symbolised not by a crown but by his double-neck guitar, most especially the new custom-made model he unveiled in 1974. Made by Californian Rex Bogue, it was a sensationally beautiful instrument. The fingerboards were engraved with mother-of-pearl vines and flowers inspired by the art-nouveau designs of Mucha and bearing the words 'Guru Alo'. The double-neck electric was so synonymous with McLaughlin that when Ponty quit the Mahavishnu Orchestra in high dudgeon, he forbade Daryl Steurmer, a phenomenal young guitarist whom he had chosen for his band, from using a Gibson double-neck in concert in case it led to comparisons (probably odious) with Ponty's former employer. (Steurmer wasn't to have the best of luck. His best known gig, taken on after he left Ponty in 1978, was with Genesis, and one assumes he was similarly barred from using a double-neck there because of the signature aspect that the double-neck bass/12-string guitar used by that band's bassist, Mike Rutherford, had assumed in the band's iconography).

McLaughlin, a poet amongst polyglots in this crude testbed of 20th century musical Esperanto, was worthy of acclaim as one of the creators of the Ur-text. The way seemed open for Grammys, further classical commissions, and maybe a civic role in the futuristic worlds of Bri-Nylon and Teflon that in the mid-'70s were still on offer to humankind and in which jazz rock might figure as a sensual and intellectual stimulus.

It never happened.

Pete Brown; "I visited John in New York in '75. He invited me to a party thrown by Sri Chinmoy to celebrate 'the master's' doing 5,000 paintings in three days due to what I thought I heard called 'a rush of spiritual power'. And it was full of people with what William Burroughs called 'cancelled eyes', just staring at you, nothing there. And there's Sri Chinmoy sitting cross-legged and beaming with people putting grapes into his mouth and I thought, 'oh, fuck'. Everyone was very nice and very holy, everyone in white. Chinmoy was supposed to be in this state of spiritual exhaustion and fulfilment – the paintings, of course, were absolute shit."

Such indulgence, presumably, had originally suggested to McLaughlin that it might be a good idea to make *Visions Of The Emerald Beyond* a double album, with disc 2 given over to a spiritual set of meditations for McLaughlin's acoustic guitar and his wife Eve/Mahalakshmi's vocals. This never transpired, although McLaughlin and Carlos Santana were involved in backing and arranging music for Chinmoy's recording debut in 1975, *Songs Of The Soul*.

Then it all went wrong. The Rex Bogue guitar fell off a bench and split irreparably up the middle. "Very strange circumstances, nobody was around it at the time", reported McLaughlin, who reverted to a Gibson double neck along with his trusty Gibson Les Paul and ES345. Ponty split amidst a welter of recriminations. The Frenchman was livid over the trivial matter of a composition credit for a piece on *Visions Of The Emerald Beyond* called "Opus One" which lasted less than twenty seconds. An electric violin/violectra solo with Echoplex, it ushers in the final segment of the album. Despite Ponty's authorship of the track it was credited to McLaughlin. "I left earlier than I thought I would," grumbled the violinist. "Mostly because of an incident which occurred over a copyright matter which upset me. McLaughlin asked me to perform a solo with Echoplex which was quite personal... I didn't realise it would become a separate track... this is what made me finally decide to leave, although I had other personal grievances... if I could have found a space within this band to make my own personal statements..." and so on.

Egos had clearly struck a few sparks too many off one another, although Ponty and McLaughlin had, for a few precious months shared a valuable musical bond. Philip Hirschi remembers, "Once on the bus in northern France Jean Luc and John started in on Django/Stephane Grappelli stuff. Oh my god, oh my god. Musical heaven right there on that Mercedes bus. They both, of course, knew the stuff cold. Jean-Luc once talked about how he and Stephane would force each other to practice together. Being raised classical but going jazz, they had both in their systems, and the jazz part of them didn't want to practice and the classical part of them insisted on it. One night in New York, when we were off the road, John drove Carol [Shive] and Bob [Knapp] and me downtown to catch Stephane playing at a club somewhere. Too crowded, couldn't get in! But we could hear outside on the steps. John said, 'you can hear what a master he is.'"

Mahavishnu mark II soldiered on. In Phil Hirschi's words, "When Jean Luc left, Kindler got to stand up and take some solos, and he killed! Kindler had a stronger rock sensibility than Jean Luc, and that came through strongly. You could hear the Jean Luc influence on his playing... Kindler emphasised the rock/blues scale more than the patrician Jean Luc did. Kindler was of course in awe of Jean Luc, but was glad to have the chance to stand out more when he left."

Shortly afterwards Moran left also, and the string quartet were soon in limbo. A last US tour saw them given a little extra leeway. Phil Hirschi remembers, "Toward the end, on stage John would give us a couple of minutes by ourselves, riffing on a simple two-chord deal that Kindler composed. I sure liked doing that, as it made me feel like I was finally contributing something significant to the overall concert. John originally scored lots of stuff for us in unison, lightning riffs travelling up two or three octaves. The kind of stuff a good fiddle player can play."

For the next tours, in the summer of 1975, Frankovitch and Russell Tubbs were unavailable, and Bob Knapp was replaced by one Norma Jean Bell, a saxophonist who, according to Pete Brown was, "fantastic... a great player and an incredibly attractive woman". Others say that none of the band was satisfied with her playing.

Pete Brown again, "They were double billing with Jeff Beck's band. And they went into this groove with Ralphe Armstrong playing bass and Walden behind this massive kit, about six toms and two floor toms and bell trees and cymbals and what have you, doing a kind of post-Elvin Jones thing, a great wave of sound. Which was fine in itself. But... when Beck came on, he had [Bernard] Pretty Purdie playing a four-piece kit and just laying down this incredible groove, plonk-plonk-plonk-plonka-plonk, it was total magic and the crowd loved it, and on that occasion, I'm afraid, in terms of reaching the crowd, the Jeff Beck Band won hands down."

Inner Worlds, witheringly rated as a one-star effort by the previously worshipful *Down Beat*, just doesn't hang together. McLaughlin, bare-shouldered, stares out levelly from the sleeve and this time the LP is credited to him and the Orchestra. On the reverse sleeve the band was listed as a quartet and it became obvious that the redundancy notices had been flying. The string section had gone completely. Armstrong and Walden hung in there, while the New York keyboard virtuoso Stu Goldberg replaced the inestimable Gayle Moran who had by now been wooed into the arms, and the band, of Chick Corea (not to mention the spell of Corea's new spiritual godfather, L.Ron Hubbard).

McLaughlin chose well. Goldberg was a formidable technician who could reproduce Hammer's schizoid burblings as well as Moran's space-princess chromatic arabesques on Fender Rhodes. He also added a pass-ably original timbre and soloing style of his own whose volume and use of scales closely matched that of McLaughlin himself. Certainly he was the most assertive keyboard player McLaughlin employed until the organ prodigy Joey de Francesco joined his enterprise in 1992.

Walden, who practically can claim to have co-created the album, opens it up like a pro at a percussion workshop, all double-bassdrum paddling and tumbling rack tom-toms. It sounds not unlike a very fast train cross-ing a set of points and blazes away at a very fast triple-time rhythm as though challenging the rest of the musicians to catch him. It sounds high-ly promising, but what follows is not. To say it was rock-inspired would demean inspiration. When the rest of the band do catch Walden up, instead of launching into a free-for-all as they might have done with Cobham, charging the music with impending confrontation, they merely perform immaculate solos (each note slavishly adherent to tempo) around a not terribly interesting riff.

McLaughlin's dabbling in effects and sound synthesis had now become all-pervasive, and the sound of the band is often an unsettlingly harsh and dissonant one. The place of each instrument in the arrangement is con-ventional and rarely disturbed. Regular metres are rarely disrupted.

Simultaneous extemporisation is as out of place as a whoopee cushion under Chinmoy's chair. And the Lord of Creation pops up again here like a cosmic jack-in-the-box, but unfortunately with all the gravity of one. "Gita" is perhaps the lousiest piece McLaughlin ever recorded – the excessive reverb lends it not grandeur but an emperor's new wardrobe of pomposity. "Lead me," the band ululate, "from death to immortality... lead me, from darkness to light". Or in this case, lead me to the secure ward.

Ironically, the rockiest track on the album, the strongly Progressive-flavoured "The Way Of The Pilgrim" (authored entirely by Walden, the first Mahavishnu track not to be written or co-written by the band's leader) is a winner. It's bombastic (not helped by Walden's elephantine timpani strokes) but has a kitsch sense of wonder and a winning chord progression, not to mention one of McLaughlin's most passionate and beautifully musicianly electric solos. It's worth noting that the synthesiser and the indigestibly-named 360 Systems Frequency Shifter go out of the window here in favour of an ear-sockingly sweet and sharp-toned Gibson Les Paul and the notes McLaughlin chooses to pilot his way through Walden's perfumed chords are enthrallingly lovely.

All too often, though, *Inner Worlds* flounders in sonic gimmickry (on "Miles Out" McLaughlin's new toys merely sound unintentionally comic, the way a bad-tempered Gibson Les Paul might behave with Daffy Duck). The two-part title track wants it all ways and still doesn't get anywhere. Intended, presumably, as a kind of hybrid of all McLaughlin's demonic duets with drummers from "Awakening" to "On The Way Home To Earth" from the previous LP, it merely sounds like an irritant. McLaughlin, while technically as accomplished as ever, plays little more than a conventional rock solo. Unusually, in spite of the flashy synthesis it was a solo that almost anyone else could have played. McLaughlin would later ruefully admit that these initial experiments in guitar synthesis were an unmitigated disaster, requiring him to attach a Mini Moog module to each string. The whole set-up was, he later said, "like an elephant."

"Lotus Feet" might be imagined to showcase both bliss-out and gimmickry, but doesn't; it's a hypnotic rondo dominated by the odd, creamy sound of Goldberg's modified mini-moog. It would prove a rewarding place for McLaughlin to revisit with his acoustic guitar (and those of buddies Larry Coryell and Paco De Lucia) when the trio played it on their *Meeting Of The Spirits* world tour in 1978-79.

For all his reputation as an icon of young musicologists and guitarists and wannabe musicians in the rock hack camp, McLaughlin was still far from financial and emotional security. The British music weekly *Sounds* reported on the Hilversum Festival of 27th July 1974 when the Mahavishnu Orchestra supported Van Morrison. Having been warned to be clear of the backstage set for Morrison's arrival by agents of the journeyman troubadour of expat Irishmen, McLaughlin and Co piled into their ancient bus to avoid the curmudgeon as he swept up in a chauffeured Mercedes.

The Mahavishnu Orchestra finally officially disintegrated in spring 1976. The quixotic mission – to reconcile European symphonics, blues, jazz and fatback – had floundered. It is possible even to fall in with the sceptics and cynics of McLaughlin's work and say that over-elaboration was the problem.

Even when the Mahavishnu Orchestra gave way to the populist tendencies in jazz-rock, personified by Chick Corea's Return To Forever and Herbie Hancock's Headhunters and settled into a streetcorner groove – as, for example, on 1975's "Cosmic Strut" and "Can't Stand Your Funk" – the music always dodged ahead of the consumer, always evaded easy comprehension. That extra drop-beat had to be added; that extra snare downbeat had to be integrated. What made these adumbrations seem all the more gratuitous was the perfectly adequate nature of their base. McLaughlin's material was always melodically and harmonically fresh. "Can't Stand Your Funk", if it had been played by the Headhunters for example, would have been a global hit on the strength of its playful bassline. In McLaughlin's hands, however, musicianly fundamentalism reduced it to a fretwork of metric cleverness for the sake of it. In the work of a band such as Gentle Giant, whose earnest stock-in-trade was to experiment with the European counterpoint and rhythm in a rock context, the elements of the jazz experience were subsidiary. However mythologised the jazz/blues iconography may be, it wasn't up to standing as decent material for an academic exercise in rhythmic flexibility, as much later Mahavishnu material came to be.

McLaughlin cannot be castigated for his relentless ambition; only the hubris that began to dominate that ambition. Ultimately, he sublimated and eventually degraded the individual characteristics of musical styles to service a personal, misguided vision of a musical fusion. Five years hitherto, it had been the stuff of dreams for jazz musicians, a topic for discussion for underground and campus music magazines; the stuff of spliff-stoked bedsit talk. After *Birds Of Fire* and *Headhunters* it was now potentially an internationally viable money machine. McLaughlin, for one, assumed the process of synthesis, with his own generation assuming control of the process. History, so far, had proven the rightness of this synthesis; why hold back? McLaughlin had grown up in a generation that had been told by post-war society that they were the agents of their own future. McLaughlin would see that through, come what may.

Then, suddenly, Chinmoy wasn't there anymore.

* * *

As we've seen, the fascination with the East that Graham Bond's interest in the occult and theosophy had triggered in McLaughlin hadn't just manifested itself spiritually and socially, in terms of the guitarist's choice of faith and lifestyle. Inevitably, it permeated his music also.

Shortly after arriving in the US, McLaughlin enrolled in music classes at Wesleyan University. One of his courses was in the two-stringed Indian lute, the vina, and McLaughlin was immediately smitten. He worked closely with one of the resident tutors and began immersing himself in the music of the (northern) subcontinent.

In Connecticut one day McLaughlin met an Indian percussionist who he discovered was uncle to a young violin prodigy named L.Shankar. "You must meet my nephew," this guy said. "He's a wonderful violinist." Shankar was brought around to McLaughlin's house and "we just sat down and played. We almost composed a piece right there and then."

Not long afterwards, in the fall of 1971, the Mahavishnu Orchestra played a benefit concert at Los Angeles' Dorothy Chandler Pavilion. Columbia president Clive Davis had offered McLaughlin his own choice of beneficiary, and McLaughlin, after little consideration, instructed that the proceeds be donated to the Ali Akbar Khan School of Music in San Francisco. Sarod-player Khan was the brother-in-law of Ravi Shankar, the two being disciples of the same teacher. Khan moved to California in 1965, relocated his school to Marin County some years later and has since taught traditional Indian music. His method was, and is, principally vocal (all serious students of Indian classical music study vocal technique) as well as sarod, sitar, violin, flute, guitar, sarangi or the instrument of the disciple's choice.

The next time McLaughlin was in the city, a grateful Khan invited him to dinner. Taking along a guitar, McLaughlin met another prodigious young talent, the tabla-player Zakir Hussain, who had by chance brought along his own instrument. They played together for their illustrious host, and whilst in conversation Hussain admitted he and Shankar were great friends and often played together.

Over the course of the next few years, the entity later known as Shakti took shape. After a while, Raghavan, Shankar's uncle, joined the group on mridangam (clay pot). The band picked up for the odd gig – churches, community centres – and recorded a little, although a dismayed CBS quietly shelved the tapes. When McLaughlin asked why, they replied, "It'll confuse people, John." McLaughlin, one of their most priceless assets was marketable, they assumed, solely as a fusion icon, and could function in public only when plugged into mains electricity.

McLaughlin later told one interviewer that by 1975 he had a premonition of a "great Shakti gig" approaching, and he demanded that CBS be there with an eight-track tape recorder. CBS vacillated; okay, they said, just get *Inner Worlds* finished first. Fortunately, McLaughlin's premonition extended beyond the sessions for that album at Chateau d'Herouville, and fixed on a date at Southampton College, Long Island, on 5th July 1975.

Shakti spares nobody. Side one is a furious jam entitled "Joy", which hurtles along at an unremitting pace for a full eighteen minutes and more. Initial hearings might hint that McLaughlin had completely gone native, so eastern does the soundstage seem. But manifold roots are strong, and the form quickly becomes apparent, with an insistent riff or scale dominant and with a style of ensemble voicing that hints at the Mahavishnu Orchestra of old. The opening of "Joy" in fact, played on electric instruments, would fit neatly onto *The Inner Mounting Flame*. The basic pulse is foursquare, albeit with all manner of polyrhythms developed by Hussain, Vinayakram and Raghavan. McLaughlin's understanding with Shankar – whose playing blew Ponty away when the two first met in 1975 – is very similar in nature to that heard on Mahavishnu Orchestra albums. Conventional harmony is lacking, of course – as we shall see, melody, improvisation and rhythm were all that counted, although shades and ghosts of chords briefly suggest their presence, as in Shankar's second long solo. This might have hampered McLaughlin's style, given his harmonic sense, yet the choice of notes is as wide-ranging as ever.

Shakti was in effect the culmination of seven years' study and dedication on McLaughlin's part, made all the more remarkable for the fact that it was effectively conducted part-time as a sideline to his stewardship of the Mahavishnu Orchestras marks I and II. In truth, though, as McLaughlin was often at pains to explain, the two projects were mutually compatible and mutually nourishing. The scalloped fingerboards that McLaughlin so loved in all his work in the 1970s, for example, derived from his love of the vina. As he explained to one interviewer; "...it has very big brass frets embedded in beeswax, very high... so there's nothing underneath, nothing in between the frets... the vina's articulation was so much more satisfying."

It led him firstly to alter the fingerboards of his guitars, "to at least satisfy my own self in terms of nuance and expression". It also led to the pioneering use of a unique 13-string guitar, with seven accompanying 'drone' strings stretched diagonally across the six normal strings covering the sound-hole in the guitar's body. This was inspired directly by the vina's configuration – four playing strings, three accompanying strings. Mark Whitebrook, a Californian luthier who had built McLaughlin's first acoustic guitar in the US, was prevented by illness from building the instrument, but eventually Gibson got around to the commission. The result, constructed from the flat-top body of a Gibson J200 was, according to McLaughlin, "more like an autoharp than a sitar". Involved in its construction was a luthier new to McLaughlin, named Abraham Wechter, of whom more later.

In one exceptionally long and enlightening interview, McLaughlin extemporised at length about the guitar and its deployment in the music of Shakti. When talking tunings, McLaughlin said, "[Tuning the guitar] varies with the piece. The music was exclusively linear. And so what was important to me was to extract the chord that was the most expressive of the emotion I felt was most embodied inside the scale or mode or the raga of whatever we were playing. Like the mode on 'Joy' was an invention of our own, E, F, G#, A, B, D. But that's just one. I would tune the accompanying strings in various ways so they might even come down and go back up like a waveform, no matter if you're going from the bottom to the top... I found this technique was very useful. Sometimes I would spend hours trying different tunings just looking for the right one."

McLaughlin waxed lyrical about the relationship of the raga to the blues. Side two of *Shakti*, he proudly reported, opened, "with a drone that was really a blues mode in E... the first time I used this blues mode as a raga."

Once again McLaughlin seemed to be almost challenging his critics and detractors to follow him and offer any kind of authoritative comment. How could any but the brave, the intellectually-equipped, present any valid criticisms of this new music? Sure, it had novelty value on its side (it wasn't the Mahavishnu Orchestra, it was clever and it was different). But was McLaughlin really on the level? Or simply turning his immense gifts to exploiting another musical style into which possibly bad-tempered critics might feel loath to follow him?

A little research suggests McLaughlin was simply following his heart, albeit with maybe one eye on the audience. He was merely practising the naturally Romantic eclecticism that his personal harmonic vision had presented with him since his first exposure to music. His desire to hybridise first, then play, then intellectualise was first exposed on *The Inner Mounting Flame* and his subsequent analyses of it. In the music of Shakti he simply explores still further the harmonic relationships between different musics and the joy that can be had from hard study of them and concentrated expression of them.

He wasn't prepared to go all out for obscurity; for example, his mixing and matching of Northern and Southern Indian music, with choices often weighted in favour of musical effect, suggest that. But he at least delved deeper into aspects of his musical personality before delving deep into his bank account.

Put very basically, and with the help of Adrienne Redd's essay *EastJazz; Intricate Connections, Cultural Contradictions and Coming Home, the Influence of Indian Music in World Music Genres*, the following description may clarify and rationalise McLaughlin's decision to form and perform with Shakti. At the time it was seen as contrary; this may prove otherwise.

Music from the Indian subcontinent, in popular or classical form, often shares an improvisatory paradigm with jazz and with the music of North and South America. In trumpeter Phil Scarff's words, "Both musics (Indian and jazz) are deep and expressive, and are based on improvisation. Both employ improvisation that can derive from an underlying composition. Concepts from both idioms can increase the musical vocabulary of the musician and composer, and can be used as resources for improvisation and composition."

Of Hindustani (North Indian) music, the legendary trumpeter and world music pioneer Don Cherry also recognised that the 36-note octave in Hindustani music gave rise to the possibility of playing microtonally ("between the notes" to western ears), suggesting a clear, if coincidental affinity with free jazz.

Northern Indian music, with its sustained notes, is a more natural partner for the musics of North and South America. Its aristocratic origins have allowed it to become cosmopolitanized, more receptive to foreign influences. "Another reason that Hindustani music may adapt to and blend with other influences," continues Redd, "is that Persian influences were grafted onto the rootstock of Hindustani music during the Mughal empire (1526-1857) when Islamic law was not tolerant of praising other than Allah, so the creative energy of the music had to be malleable." But as we shall see, South Indian (Karnatic) music, with deeper roots in the everyday folk music of the subcontinent's southern peoples, also played a vital role in Shakti's success.

What was most important was not arrival but travel. Perhaps the most charming thing about Shakti in retrospect, is that McLaughlin sought (it seems) no massive new 'definitive' musical personality, no new commercial identity through its agency. He merely sought a relatively unobtrusive musical workshop in which to figure the endless, and borderless ecstasies of musical complexity.

The Shakti experience, most notably the practical changes it forced on McLaughlin's thought processes and execution, were heard elsewhere; the scalloped fingerboards found their way onto McLaughlin's electric instruments. McLaughlin admitted the quirkiness of the experiment, but defended himself robustly. "You don't get the shifts, subtleties or nuances on the notes by pressing the strings down so you do it through pulling or pushing. Most contemporary guitar players push the string; sitar technique is a pulling technique. You're pulling the strings down towards the floor." McLaughlin enthused about the range of emotional effects he was now capable of, "much more glide, portamento, sliding, bending". It is certainly apparent on such albums as *Electric Guitarist* and *Electric Dreams*, where often sheer speed of articulation is substituted by sharp, stabbing, pitch-bent wails. It also introduced him to the idea of crosspicking; whereas hitherto McLaughlin's picking had been flat, up-and-down, with each note picked (with plectra cut from old plastic apple pie cartons) and not fingered. Crosspicking was something different. A development of an Indian concept, it meant for McLaughlin fiendishly demanding work in mathematical groupings of notes within an overarching eight-bar structure.

In the lifetime of Shakti, however, McLaughlin endured some tough times. 1975 was, for McLaughlin, an *annus horribilis*. He split with his wife Eve (who continued to follow Chinmoy, and according to Pete Brown is a disciple to this day). The remaining Mahavishnu Orchestra members, following the departure of Ponty, were coming to the end of their tethers, as *Inner Worlds* grimly indicated. Disillusioned musically and spiritually, McLaughlin abandoned his spiritual name, and symbolically broke up the band also after several final gigs in the summer of 1975. Their last British appearance was at the Reading Festival on 24th August 1975, and their last-ever gig in Toledo, Ohio, on 29 November the same year. McLaughlin cited a "lack of cohesion" as the reason for the break.

"I got to the point where I was in such an artistic and spiritual upheaval that I had to sever every tie I had to everything. I didn't play for many months", McLaughlin recalled. It was almost a year. And then *Shakti* came out and was met with a tremendous burst of indifference. He found the attitude of CBS to the project "unhelpful" and was "horrified" by the way it was "treated merely as an accounting exercise." McLaughlin took a sabbatical in India, returned to New York, took up booze and cigarettes once again, gave up the Queens' vegetarian restaurant he'd co-run with his wife, and moved into an upper West Side apartment where *People* magazine found him enjoying life in mid-1976. "I love [Chinmoy] very much, but I must assume responsibility for my own actions. When my sweet wife walked out on me, that catalyzed everything," McLaughlin explained. Mysticism was now confined to coffee table books and a bronze of Buddha's wife nestling in the midst of half a dozen trees, forming a meditation area. McLaughlin, the readers of *People* magazine were informed, "took a simple delight in watering his plants," but loved to win at the ping-pong table he'd set up and over which he hung his washing, when he wasn't cooking Indian or Italian meals for himself. As for romantic association, "I like to have a pretty woman about me – who doesn't?"

McLaughlin had cathartically got out from under the Chinmoy yoke, but, almost as remarkably as his rejection of narcotic in the late 1960s, had retained a wholly-formed spirituality and not succumbed to the backlash of naked cynicism.

No critics, or fans, have ever doubted the immense value of Shakti not only to McLaughlin's career but also his well-being. The guitarist has never spoken with anything but unqualified affection for his involvement with the band, in spite of the very real financial and commercial dangers it entailed. It could have short-circuited McLaughlin's career, and it is testimony to the sheer class of his inspiration and the high esteem in which his professional colleagues held him that he avoided either spiritual or musical bankruptcy. As we have seen, musical and economic elements were about to render fusion as it was, redundant. McLaughlin managed to survive with his reputation intact, and, by and large, musically enriched as a person and as a player.

The critical reaction was one of dazzled surprise; the 13-string Gibson monster which McLaughlin deployed with Shakti was, given the contemporary fascination with rock self-promotion, relatively overlooked. In an

era when the technological determinism of greater and greater rock compositional ambition demanded greater and greater technical backup,
McLaughlin's acoustic quartet was regarded as a sideshow. After five
minutes listening, however, it was clear that the rhythmic and harmonic
language and, above all, the suggestive locomotion of the music was
something special. Shakti took the BBC by storm after a May 1977
appearance on John Peel's Radio 1 show, and it was perhaps only the
whiff of dilettantism lingering around McLaughlin's membership that
prevented embryonic English-Asian groups from gaining greater mainstream cultural acceptance in the 1970s.

Shankar was, according to McLaughlin, "very interested in the theoretical and practical side of jazz." He taught jazz harmony to the youngster
and ways of perceiving the mobility of harmonic progressions, while the
pupil returned the compliment and gave lessons to his master in the theory and practise of melody and rhythm which formed the core of the
Indian repertoire Shakti and its constituent musicians concentrated upon.
In 1978, *Down Beat* asked McLaughlin what Shakti meant to him musically, and what directions in his own conception had been oriented by his
experiences therein. McLaughlin replied that, "the directions are articulated as accurately as possible on the records. I couldn't even speak about
it except to say that Shakti and my great love of Indian culture and music
helped me pursue my researches into the theoretical side."

A Handful Of Beauty (recorded in London in August 1976) and *Natural
Elements* (Geneva, autumn 1977) lacked the sheer audacity of the debut,
and made distinctly more concessions to western listeners. The resources
of the recording studio were brought to bear, notably on "Mind Ecology",
whose reverb is a little too gratuitous for the music's own good. This
sounds suspiciously like a concession to Columbia Records, who were
still tearing their hair out over McLaughlin's decision to go acoustic in
the first place. More of the music is conventionally harmonised
("Happiness Is Being Together") and far more eclectic. "Together" had
an almost Latin feel, and the vocal contributions are wholly western,
uncomfortably redolent of Crosby, Stills and Nash's "Marrakesh
Express". There had been elements of music from the nearer east on
Shakti, especially during the faster music when suggestions of Balkan
and Turkish rustic-wedding music are apparent. Oddly, for all his breadth
of reading and experience of global musical styles, McLaughlin has
never mentioned the oud, the Arabic stringed instrument, whose ringing,
barbed tone often comes to mind more often than vinas or sitars when listening to his playing with Shakti. On "Isis" McLaughlin is particularly

persuasive; as with all his best work, he wears the hybridity of inspiration on his sleeve; wandering and wondering wide-eyed between the Mississippi Delta, Morocco and Madras.

"India", from *A Handful Of Beauty,* is ironically one of the most western-sounding pieces; an episodic, suite-like composition. "Come On Baby Dance With Me" from *Natural Elements* was, on the other hand, pure South Indian Karnatic classical music, with a time signature McLaughlin claimed was the most complex and difficult he'd ever had to play. Phil Senders has gone on record as claiming that some of the pieces were in fact adaptations of traditional Karnatic pieces for which McLaughlin and Shankar took composer credit. "Isis", too, is faithful to Indian influences, merely a scale upon which solos are played and textures accumulate around – notably Hussain's incredible tablas. The tabla and claypot lines relentlessly drive the melody, and the melody drives the soloists. On "Isis", Hussain suggests rock timekeeping from time to time – McLaughlin's rhythm-guitar playing is too rocky for this not to be the case. His very long solo at the close of the piece also reveals just how deeply tabla soloists and their choice of tones has influenced McLaughlin's guitar soloing. Indeed, we also hear the first example of *khayal* singing in the guitarist's output (of which more later).

The virtuosity continues to bewilder, although some of the time signatures are on the over-elaborate side. Shankar is more often than not the hero – quite how this episode did not make him an international fusion star is hard to fathom. He puts Ponty and Goodman to shame with an individual, ripe, joyful tone. His gift for portamenti between extremely unlikely notes, made (and makes) him one of the world's great violinists. His shrieking, rollercoastering arabesques on "La Danse du Bonheur" are among the most amazing examples of musicianship on any McLaughlin album.

The last word on Shakti should maybe go to an authority – once again, the musicologist Senders. For him, Shakti produced "records [that] by and large have weathered well." He adds, "The music was acoustic, well balanced and highly virtuoso. Its downside was that it was if anything too much a virtuoso high-wire act that showcased more the dazzling technique of the participants than any particular innovations of structure or concept." This is hard to refute; "Joy" for example is an almost exhausting listen, so prodigious is the musical dexterity on show, although unusually this is often in the service of physical excitement rather than awed reverence; sometimes the music is goaded to speeds almost beyond the capabilities of the players.

Chapter Five
Electric Guitarist, Acoustic Guitarist

McLaughlin, ever the seeker and trufflehound in the blues-seeded land of pop and rock, couldn't ever be entirely disentangled from his musical heritage. In 1977 Columbia were making waves to renew McLaughlin's hitherto comfortable contract, and buoyed by the public ubiquity of jazz-rock and funk, saw little reason to sell it but to the biggest market available. McLaughlin's return to electric jazz-rock in 1977-78 was interpreted by some as a purely commercial decision, given the losses made by the critically-acclaimed but unfashionable Shakti.

McLaughlin contended that the Mahavishnu Orchestra mark II would have made more money than Shakti, but given the phenomenal costs of equipment rental in the wake of the futuristic, electronically-driven *Visions Of The Emerald Beyond* and *Inner Worlds*, that was maybe debatable. Shakti's overheads were negligible, after all.

But the possibility of returning to an electric guitar with a scalloped fingerboard may have proved too much of a temptation (in this case, a Gibson ES345). "I see possibilities for the execution of ideas with greater clarity now," declared McLaughlin, "given the qualities the electric guitar has that the acoustic guitar doesn't".

Columbia's accountants breathed a heavy sigh of relief at McLaughlin's decision to act on his jazzward impulses and strap on his electric guitar again. Jazz-rock and fusion was still lucrative, and this looked like a big payday. McLaughlin was to assemble a gang of friends old and new and, it was greedily assumed, would be supersessioning his way back into profitability.

Most of those old friends answered the call, but Jan Hammer, still sulking after the Mahavishnu debacle, wouldn't play on *Electric Guitarist* in spite of McLaughlin's invitation. "It might taint his rock image," chuckled McLaughlin, although Billy Cobham and Jerry Goodman heeded the call (later sources suggest that McLaughlin several times tried to reconvene the original Mahavishnu Orchestra for charity purposes, only to be rebuffed by Hammer. Originally, Goodman's friendship with Hammer kept him at a distance from McLaughlin but when they fell out, Goodman buddied up with the guitarist once again).

The front cover was naively charming – a cherubic McLaughlin in blazer and school tie grins grainily from a school photograph. McLaughlin later told an interviewer that this had been the only photograph taken of him during childhood; "I was the least photographed child in the world." The calling card (*Johnny McLaughlin – Electric Guitarist)* had been kept as a memento by a long-standing friend over fifteen years.

The eight tracks are introduced by "Do You Hear The Voices You Have Left Behind?", a tenderly-titled and affectionately conceived Coltrane tribute, the first overt tribute of any kind made in McLaughlin's music. It is a deceptively languid opener; featuring bassist Stanley Clarke with Chick Corea on keyboards and another fellow-traveller from the Miles era, Jack DeJohnette, on drums. McLaughlin, in the depths of post-Chinmoy and post-divorce angst had played acoustic guitar on two swishly competent Clarke workouts, the original "Song To John" and Coltrane's "Desert Song" which formed the centrepieces of the bassist's solo albums *Journey To Love* and *School Days* (1975 and 1976 respectively).

McLaughlin, playing a Gibson Birdland, drawls out one of his most poignant melodies in subtly fuzzed accents over a copybook Corea-Clarke polychrome haze of legato/arco bass and tinkling Fender Rhodes. DeJohnette's ride and crash cymbals kick the music into double time – upping the tempo revealing the theme's sly nod to "Giant Steps". McLaughlin's solo, all offbeat salvos of notes and piercing squalls, either tossed in handfuls or sandblasted in hundreds, scurries maniacally around the scale. The aggressive roar of his guitar tone contrasts nicely with the delicate filigree of cymbals, snare, Fender Rhodes chords and Clarke's exemplary bass. DeJohnette's increasingly complicated drop beats and syncopations on snare – he scarcely touches his toms – gradually winds up the tension. Corea's solos (somewhat gratingly, on mini-moog) are instructive. His greater adherence to the piece's home key sharply demonstrates the difference between Corea's bebop-derived approach, all Parker and Peterson, and McLaughlin's possessed, heaven-storming devotion to Coltrane's method, right down to the dominance of minor third chords.

"Are You The One? Are You The One?" is a rather lukewarm reheating of Lifetime, in places little more than an insult to the band's memory. Tony Williams fiddles around somewhere between the fuzzed meanderings of Bruce and McLaughlin. The question asked in the piece's (neat) title is only too well illustrated by the incoherence of the music. McLaughlin hadn't quite shaken the technophilia of *Inner Worlds*, going overboard with a Mu-Tron envelope filter for the effects heard here. Nobody seems to be able to decide if this is ever going to become a free improvisation or a piece of mindless funk jamming, although repeated listenings suggest the latter was winning out. "Phenomenon: Compulsion" is more appetising, a free workout on a 6/8 blues riff between Cobham and McLaughlin, with just the right degree of incipient chaos threatening to overbalance the music into self-indulgence. The piece, clearly an attempt to revisit the astonishing unisono lines of *The Inner Mounting Flame* is a creditable piece of time-travel, diminished only by a relatively genteel guitar sound and Cobham insisting on trying out every inch of what is now a substantially augmented drum kit. Despite the non-tonal freak-out at the end, this sounds like "Evolution" with a bow-tie on. It's just grandstanding; "look, we can still do this, too".

"My Foolish Heart" completes the side. It's McLaughlin's only entirely solo electric piece, played with melting tenderness and true romantic ardour. Generous use of sustain and tone-arm distortion blurs the passage between notes. The pulse and pacing of the original disappears, although the melodic top line is played whole and uninterrupted. It is indulgent and somewhat silly, but the emphasis on the piece's disjointed delivery lends the whole a distracted, impressionist air. The result is a warm ethereality that entirely befits the song's lyrical musings on the bittersweetness of the act of falling in love. McLaughlin called it his tribute to his first guitar idol, Tal Farlow. It's a genuinely lovely, and unusual, piece of musicianship, and an avenue McLaughlin could have done worse than pursue further. At the very end there is the suggestion of an improvisation taking hold, which is then abruptly cut off. A shame. McLaughlin told reporters later that he played plenty of chords with open strings and of his own invention, with his thumb only. Played on an old Les Paul

Above and below: John McLaughlin - Electric Guitarist
Top photo: David Redfern. Bottom photo: Glenn A Baker Archives

Above: The Mahavishnu Orchestra Mark I (l-r) Jerry Goodman, John McLaughlin, Billy Cobham, Rick Laird, Jan Hammer. *Photo: David Redfern*
Below: McLaughlin playing the trademark Gibson SG doubleneck. *Photo: David Redfern*
Right: McLaughlin with his Abraham Wechter-adapted Gibson J200 13-string custom acoustic guitar. *Photo: Andrew Putler*

Above: Jean Luc Ponty and John McLaughlin in Mahavishnu Orchestra Mark II.
Photo: David Redfern

Below: Shakti. (l-r) Vikku Vinayakram, McLaughlin, L Shankar, Eileen, Zakir Hussain
Photo: Andrew Putler

Above: The first incarnation of the acoustic guitar trio, 1979.
(l-r) Larry Coryell, John McLaughlin, Paco De Lucia. *Photo: Max Redfern*

Below: Do I know you? The second trio, 1996. Note the distance between the performers.
(l-r) Al DiMeola, Paco De Lucia, John McLaughlin. *Photo: Robin Little*

Opposite page (top): John McLaughlin. *Photo: James Dittiger*

Opposite page (bottom): John McLaughlin and bass prodigy Jonas Hellborg on tour in Germany. *Photo: Thomas Meyer*

Above: The dapper dresser, John McLaughlin on stage. *Photo: David Redfern*

Next page: John McLaughlin at the Vienne Jazz Festival, 1995. *Photo: David Redfern*

Deluxe and run through a Leslie Speaker cabinet for a sensuous approximation of Farlow's soundworld, the piece sounds, as McLaughlin has said, like a duet for bass and electric guitar. This effect was achieved by tuning the low E string down to low A, an octave below the open A of the fifth string.

On side two, "New York On My Mind" is often cited as Mahavishnu mark III and a half; two incarnations are represented, and it sometimes sounds like a glorified tribute band. But the number is so beautifully composed and contains so much lyrical glory that this scarcely matters. Personnel-wise, Cobham drums, Goodman fiddles, Stu Goldberg plays keyboards; only bassist Fernando Saunders is not an alumni. The two main, loosely funky riffs open proceedings, and the main melody is long and tortuous but more than usually romantic and virile. Apart from a recurring bridge-passage device requiring fast *unisono* playing from Goodman, McLaughlin and Cobham, what helps is the exquisite subtlety of the soloists. Goldberg is a particular delight, a birdsong of synthesiser arabesques in a wonderfully pungent and yearning interpretation of the piece's harmonic progressions. The leader is, by comparison, relatively economical in expression, preferring to wrench out warped squeals of emoting melodrama from the scalloped fingerboard.

McLaughlin's heart was rarely worn on his sleeve so explicitly. At times the music here, as on the succeeding *Electric Dreams* shades into the cadences of European Progressive rock with its aspirations to late-Romantic orchestral music. In other places, the harmonic language on these two albums verges on the Hollywoodian. McLaughlin seems to be angling for recognition of his European roots, while unable to distance himself from the demands of American radio playlists (a process he would get right in 1981-82 with his *Belo Horizonte* and *Music Spoken Here* albums).

This schizophrenia is never more apparent than on the anthemic "Friendship", whose irresistible melody suffers only from a distinct kinship (possibly intentional) with Lennon and McCartney's "With A Little Help From My Friends" (an effect augmented by Tom Coster's wheezy acid-rock Hammond organ chords). Carlos Santana, who also guests on the track, had himself spent the previous five years since *Love Devotion Surrender* becoming a flypaper for critical brickbats. As with McLaughlin, cognoscenti had been for some time writing eulogies for the death of a talent which had in the words of one perceptive critic, "vanished off the edge of a spiritual cliff". Certainly Santana's 1977 album, *Festival,* bears little comparison with the inextinguishable beauty and adventure of 1972's *Caravanserai*. McLaughlin, at least, had explored other avenues with Mahavishnu II and Shakti, even if some of them had become dead-ends, but Santana, it was considered, kept on plunk-plunk-plunking his way through the same crowd-pleasing, cod-Latino rhythmic measures but with ever more threadbare textural meat on the bones. But here, at least, his sweet-toned soloing abilities are allowed to shine in a freer and more ambitious musical environment. McLaughlin's composition may be simple but its scope for chromatic improvisation and the grand romantic gesture offer Santana space in which to play the sugary stuff and not sound hackneyed.

Anthony Allen Smith, the drummer on "Every Tear" would follow McLaughlin into the One Truth Band, as would Fernando Saunders and Stu Goldberg. Saunders had played and recorded with ex-Mahavishnu keyboardist and McLaughlin nemesis Jan Hammer as well as with McLaughlin's old friend Jeff Beck. The Mahavishnu comparisons would be considerably enhanced by McLaughlin's decision to include a violinist in the line-up, and he plumped immediately for Shakti's L.Shankar. Perhaps reflecting his experience with Vinayakram and Hussain in Shakti, percussion was for the first time provided by a specialist player, in this instance the in-demand Brazilian, Alyrio Lima, who had played for some years with Weather Report and starred on their 1975 album *Tale Spinnin'*.

Electric Dreams is one of the least heralded of McLaughlin's output, mostly due to its location therein; it belongs neither to the Mahavishnu years of the 1970s or to the acoustic decade of the 1980s, although close study of it reveals an interesting transition between the two. It was recorded, as per usual, in New York in the icy January of 1979 and won no friends with its risible packaging (McLaughlin brooding alone in a proletarian kitchen whilst electrical appliances drift around in thin air).

The album was received with studied indifference or numbskulled hostility in the case of the British press. While it lacks the devil-may-care bravado of *Electric Guitarist*, it inevitably hangs together better as a group effort, and is a distinct improvement on *Inner Worlds*. It is, however, impossible to dispel the impression that McLaughlin is attempting to placate his record company by hastily throwing together another electric project to maintain his profile at a time when the genre which had sustained him was becoming increasingly costive to a recession-hit record label.

There is indecision aplenty here, and while it may diminish the album, it is a useful benchmark as to McLaughlin's musical development. The beautiful acoustic-led opening track "Guardian Angel", for example, points forward to the DiMeola/De Lucia trios and, with Shankar's violin accompaniment, back to Shakti.

Song titles, as ever, are exquisite: "The Dark Prince", "Desire And The Comforter", "The Unknown Dissident". Perhaps feeling the mortality and ageing of jazz, McLaughlin throws in a direct titular tribute, "Miles Davis". At the time, Davis was a recluse, four years in retirement, and a full year away from his sensational and revolutionary return to the jazz-rock field he had helped plot in the first place. The track seems to have less to do with Davis' own most recent music – the monsters of space-funk riffing *Agharta* and *Pangaea*, recorded in Japan in 1975, and more to do with what McLaughlin may have wanted him to sound like. It's a subtle piece, however, incorporating three tempi which seamlessly integrate into one another, with sparse instrumental lines from all corners of the soundstage contributing. Only McLaughlin solos at any length, and sounds distracted and circumspect. "Leave me alone," the notes say, "I'm busy."

"Electric Dreams, Electric Sighs" draws seven splendid minutes from a series of chords and a complementary soul riff of phenomenal emotional import. Shankar solos first, more pyrotechnically than Goodman; the textures become thicker and the tempo more syncopated and dramatic. Goldberg solos above a newly-hatched riff, which only adds to the tension. Next up, McLaughlin solos, splendidly, on banjo and then on electric guitar as the third riff is reintroduced. Of his banjo playing, McLaughlin opined, "It's very percussive, and I love percussion and banjo. There's something haunting about that sound." Promises to acquire an instrument with sympathetic strings for further explorations sadly never materialised.

Goldberg is as forward in the mix as he was on *Inner Worlds*, and equally as complementary ("Miles Davis"). On "Electric Dreams, Electric Sighs" he can be overweening, edging towards Prog rock excess. "Desire And The Comforter" flatters to deceive. The trills of Fender Rhodes and rilling cascades of percussion and cymbals at the start prefigure the preoccupation with French impressionism that would inform much of McLaughlin's harmonic language in the 1980s. But from the chords at the start, a seamless transition is made to a funk pulse of disappointing staleness. The textures are boilerplate too. The solos are of a piece, though, spare and to the point, as the chords used encourage flexibility and freedom. An intermittent riff squawks out. Then the initial texture returns and McLaughlin solos at length – prefiguring *Belo Horizonte*

(1981). Using electric as opposed to acoustic guitar, the tempo is once again varied, for no very good reason, to a smooth come-on for FM programmers in Los Angeles. The raga-like, opening measures of "Love And Understanding", superbly played by Shankar, also suggest what's to come in later years. What's to come more immediately, however, is a rather embarrassing and plodding hymn to 'love' and 'understanding', two feelings this song is unlikely to evoke.

"Singing Earth", thirty-seven seconds of what sound suspiciously like treated tape-hum, is basically the prelude to the furious post-bop gallop of "The Dark Prince". The latter is a more concentrated and demonic extension of the inspiration which was first given explicit compositional voice in McLaughlin's ouevre with "Do You Hear The Voices That You Left Behind". This inspires him to even more extreme and dissonant virtuosity; rarely, if anywhere, does he pick notes as fast as on this insanely high-velocity track. Here, finally, Lima's percussion comes into its own, spurring on the action with well-placed clanks and rattles and shrieks. Goldberg's riotous Fender Rhodes solo compares well with Corea's on the earlier track as another mix-and-match of Parker-vs-Coltrane soloing styles, Goldberg's customised mini-Moog again laying down more notes than is strictly decent. Ultimately, however, the track falls over its own feet in its desire for balls-out bravura, and at times things become so frenetic that owners of the LP had to check their equipment hadn't surreptitiously readjusted itself to 45 rpm. Speed, unfortunately, sometimes substitutes for sincerity, although "The Dark Prince" is an astonishing feat of collective work.

The track wasn't cited as a specific instance – but could well have been – in an increasingly heated debate about the role of the soloist in fusion and how the desire for showmanship had terminated any humanity the music might once have pretended to possess. Certainly, "The Dark Prince" tends to overshadow the brawny and beautifully soulful finale, "The Unknown Dissident", whose harmonic progressions and use of David Sanborn's alto saxophone playing, produce a rather lovely hybrid of the *Electric Guitarist* tracks "New York On My Mind" and "Every Tear From Every Eye".

But the knives were out for McLaughlin even as he reconvened the One Truth Band in a wholly different format for a summer 1979 tour (which would also include an ill-fated, Columbia-inspired marriage with Tony Williams and Jaco Pastorius as the Trio Of Doom). The line-up consisted of Shankar, McLaughlin, Goldberg with the support of Sun Ship Theus (drums) and T.M. Stevens (bass), but McLaughlin was already being written off (again) as a relic of another era. Then, alas, McLaughlin would embark on an ill-advised golden goose-killing extravaganza of egotism, playing in an all-star band featuring himself, Stu Goldberg, Jack Bruce and Billy Cobham. This band became refugees of every three-ring festival circus in the world as well as a host of arenas packed with audiences wholly out of tune with the times, for whom it was eternally 1971. The result was often deadening. Pete Brown; "I saw John at the Rainbow with Jack and Billy. It was awful. The atmosphere was so bad, like they hated being onstage with one another. Just too much competition, and what for?"

The Trio Of Doom was another case in point. In March 1979, at the Karl Marx Theatre in downtown Havana, a motley crew of US jazz and rock musicians broke a twenty year cultural blockade and took part in the Havana Jam, a sudden intrusion of a banner event into the burgeoning jazz festival calendar. Prime movers and stars were Joe Zawinul's Weather Report, but along for the ride were McLaughlin and Tony Williams, earmarked to jam with Weather Report bassist Jaco Pastorius as a prelude to a possible all-star trio session later in the year.

McLaughlin had been aware of the mind-boggling abilities of Pastorius for some years. In 1973, Pastorius had newly-arrived in New York City from his home state of Florida, when McLaughlin, then rehearsing Ralphe Armstrong for Mahavishnu II, politely declined the 19-year-old Pastorius' offer of, "I wanna play." According to the guitarist, he gave Pastorius money, with extra to fix his car, a loan paid back 11 years later. McLaughlin called Tony Williams with an endorsement, "this guy is amazing". In the interim, Pastorius fetched up again on home turf in Florida, but had hustled his chops into the hearts of Weather Report's co-leaders, Wayne Shorter and Joe Zawinul. In the succeeding three years, Pastorius' astounding technique, part orchestral, part Hendrix, made him one of popular music's biggest instrumental draws (posthumous rose-lensing has lionized a talent which often over-indulged itself to a level of theatrics not even Spinal Tap would have entertained).

Pastorius, therefore, was one of the newest bankers in town for keeping the market for jazz-rock virtuosity alive. Surely only his irksomely-public addictions to coke and booze could stop him making the Trio Of Doom the biggest and best-publicized jazz act in history? Unfortunately substance abuse won the day. McLaughlin took the bandstand to play "The Dark Prince" on acoustic guitar with Williams and Pastorius. The latter, however, was not so much reading from a different score as a different grammar. Blasted to the gills, Pastorius' performance (immortalized on Columbia's own *Havana Jam* LPs) is never less than mesmerising, but given the tonal nature of the piece, it is a pitiful mess. On reaching the wings, the usually placid McLaughlin lost his rag. "Yeah man, that was the shit," slurred Pastorius. He wasn't kidding. McLaughlin, in retrospect, glosses the disaster as "The Bay of Gigs".

"The Dark Prince", a C-minor blues with altered changes, had Pastorius blasting out high-volume A-major chords. "I have never been more ashamed in my life to be onstage with somebody," bellowed McLaughlin to Pastorius afterwards. "That was the worst shit," he continued, to the dismay of onlookers, "that I have ever heard in my life. I don't wanna see your face for at least a week." Williams, who had kept his counsel, later erupted when Columbia tried to reconvene the act in a New York studio. Pastorius' attitude provoked the normally pragmatic and mellow drummer practically to fisticuffs. Williams smashed up his drum kit and stormed out, vowing never to return. "It really tore Jaco to strips," recalled McLaughlin to Bill Milkowski. McLaughlin diplomatically ditched grudges and posthumously lauded Pastorius; "What happened afterwards was just tragic." (Pastorius, ever more deeply enslaved to his addictions, died after a beating by a Miami club bouncer in September 1987 just as his international career was edging towards the launchpad once again). McLaughlin, admittedly, was fulsome in his tribute. "We all loved Jaco," he said, "he had his faults but who doesn't? He was a lovely person. And everyone just wanted him to... be alive and just play. That's what we're here for."

At the end of the 1970s, though, to play meant to play fast. If you could play fast you could earn big money. You didn't necessarily have to play well or care very much, but you just had to play fast. The prevailing performance practise informed McLaughlin's next project, in which his virtuosity was lured down quite a different path but, on this occasion, velocity went hand in hand with vitality and not vacuity.

The question of McLaughlin and virtuosity will return. In the meantime, in the timeframe of the late 1970s, that virtuosity was still at least opening doors and filling his wallet, and had by 1979 been lured down yet another path. The reluctance of CBS to countenance much more acoustic playing in the van of Shakti hadn't stopped McLaughlin falling in with what was thought to be a commercially more acceptable acoustic line-up. This time he teamed up with two other virtuosi, the unknown Spanish flamenco guitarist Paco De Lucia and one of the lost geniuses of fusion, the then drug-addled Larry Coryell.

McLaughlin, already locking horns with Columbia over the immediate destiny of his music – acoustic or electric – was entertaining the idea of moving back to Europe, specifically France, where he felt the artistic climate wholly more sympathetic to his aspirations. One night on French radio he caught a flamenco concert, and on learning the identity of the featured guitar soloist, vowed to seek him out.

Paco De Lucia was born in the Andalucian city of Algeciras on the Mediterranean coast in 1947. He won an amateur guitar contest at 12 and flamenco dancer Jose Greco then took him on tour. Paco then toured with his brother Ramon and his own troupe of dancers. DiMeola, an inveterate guitar seeker, discovered him for America in 1976 and duetted with him (to massive public and critical acclaim) on his album *Elegant Gypsy* (1977).

Shortly after receiving McLaughlin's call, he found himself at the door of the Englishman's Parisian apartment. "I called him up," recalls McLaughlin, "invited him for some dinner, some wine, and generally discuss things... We ended up playing together for two days, and arranged a European tour with Larry Coryell as soon as was practicable."

Coryell, as we have seen, was no stranger to McLaughlin; given the prodigious nature of his talent, however, his musical bequest to history was a very sparse one. After the groundbreaking *Spaces* album in 1970, he had tried and failed to get a handle on jazz-rock with anything like the panache or singularity of McLaughlin, Corea, Hancock or any of his old New York muckers. Eleventh House, put together in 1974, was intended to finally give him the kind of global solo platform the others had achieved with the Mahavishnu Orchestra, Return To Forever and the Headhunters respectively. It failed dismally, despite a miasma of hype; it had none of the Mahavishnu Orchestra's energy or chaos, none of RTF's whimsy and none of the Headhunters' git-on-down gut instincts. It was the failure of fusion writ in six-inch headlines. Coryell had since salvaged some of his reputation in a series of impressive duets with Philip Catherine (*Splendid*, *Twin House* and *Back Together Again*, all Polydor) but was by 1979 a sorry victim of his own addictions, ill-luck, the fickleness of public opinion and misguided music-making.

This, as with many other musicians, often proved only a minor handicap on stage. A tour featuring the trio was arranged for the winter and spring of 1978-79 and played to packed, delighted houses throughout the world. The trio would later temporarily disband and reform with the Return To Forever guitarist Al DiMeola taking Coryell's place. "This," opined Charles Alexander later, "could well have had something to do with Larry's drug problem. I don't think he was clean by this time, and DiMeola taking over might well have had something to do with the fact that Larry couldn't necessarily always be relied upon."

The first incarnation of the trio was fortuitously caught on videotape by Unitel at a Royal Albert Hall gig on 14th February 1979, although it was to be the DiMeola line-up which would go down to posterity as the enduring embodiment of this perennially crowd-pulling combo. The Albert Hall concert is a revelation, once one can adjust to the surreal onstage presence of Larry Coryell, who looked utterly extraordinary in a pure-white pimp-suit (worn with the musician's trademark black thatch and professorial glasses).

The format scored for two reasons; it preserved blue-chip virtuosity but banished the perceived demon of electronics. This was virtuosity once again invested with something which could at least be sold as humanity. The reality was something more prosaic; the whole extravaganza was nothing so much as an old fashioned axe-battle, one of the tackiest rock devices in all the soiled annals of rock 'n' roll showmanship. Although certainly on the evidence of the Albert Hall concert, the standard of playing and improvisation is consistently high, and the whole is probably the equal of the CBS-recorded *Friday Night In San Francisco* concert a little less than two years later on 5th December 1980. The clowning and grandstanding in the middle of McLaughlin and DiMeola's rendition of Chick Corea's "Short Tales Of The Black Forest" on the subsequent recording by the somewhat-modified trio, lifts the lid – albeit entertainingly – on what self-indulgence such occasions could encourage. No amount of musicianly genius could entirely diminish that fact.

The American-Italian DiMeola (b.22.7.54, Jersey City) had been a pre-adolescent devotee of Tal Farlow and Charlie Burrell, and whose extrovert brilliance of technique had ensured that he autopiloted through Berklee Music College. On his emergence, he was swiftly headhunted by Chick Corea as a replacement for Bill Connors, the guitarist he was about to lose from his fast-rising jazz-rock attraction Return To Forever. DiMeola, scarcely having finished packing his theory books back into his satchel, swapped the college refectory for caviar and Carnegie Hall. He even picked up a Grammy for his involvement in the band's (frankly ordinary) 1975 album, *No Mystery*. By 1976 he had his own Columbia contract; almost by way of karmic payoff, it coincided with a mass critical backlash against guitar heroes, the majority of whose flak seemed to land in DiMeola's lap. He was regarded, not always unfairly it must be admitted, as a soulless technician, a proto-cybernetic database of syndicated licks which he applied at will to various time signatures. Certainly his playing with Return To Forever, while an exemplar of precision, raises not a hair on the neck.

With Coryell sidelined, the three plotted a profitable future. The planned world tour was set back six months after DiMeola was struck down with illness, but eventually launched in Helsinki on 14 October, 1980. The subsequent progress would be as triumphal as anything witnessed in the halcyon days of the Mahavishnu Orchestra.

As with the Coryell trio, the show was essentially a melange of showmanship and genuine musical creativity. From Stockholm to San Francisco audiences paid homage, they marvelled at the speed, they giggled at the joshing and japery (there were quotes from "The Pink Panther", "The Blue Danube", "Jumping Jack Flash", "Duelling Banjos" and "Sunshine of Your Love" randomly chucked into the Niagara of notes). In San Francisco the reaction – especially in a Hispanicized city to the fingerwork of De Lucia – is rowdily preserved for posterity on *Friday Night In San Francisco*.

Both London and San Francisco concerts are first-rate, and are testament to what was a dynamic musical entity before advancing age and commercial dictates emasculated a unique musical vision. *Friday Night In San Francisco* is a fine album, the first side of the LP in particular is dazzling. It mixes the melodically ravishing – "Rio Ancho" is probably the catchiest tune in the entire John McLaughlin catalogue – with the fun and compelling complexity of "Black Forest". Taken together, these qualities deflect any accusations of simple grandstanding. The speed and panache is there in buckets, naturally – to the hollering ecstasy of the audience – but so is some searching and wonderfully accomplished music-making. "Black Forest" is a particular gem. Arranged brilliantly by DiMeola to give a two-piano/four-hand effect, Corea's quirky melody is passed between the two men faster than a grenade with the pin out. Vivid and impressionistic, endlessly interrupted by a playful fragmentary riff, it inspires both DiMeola and McLaughlin to extraordinary levels of both velocity and sensitivity, sometimes within a matter of seconds. Side two maintains the musicianship, but defuses the tension somewhat; Egberto Gismonti's lovely "Frevo Rasgado" and McLaughlin's own deathless "Guardian Angel" are becalmed by leisurely vamping at ambling pace with little light and shade or dramatic incident. This was indicative of a slackening of intensity which would become more and more prevalent as the trio became life-expired and which by 1996 would make the three musicians' comeback recording one of the great disappointments of the whole decade.

The 1979 recording with Coryell is a different matter – there is more emphasis on straight-ahead speed and stamina. A rendition of "Meeting Of The Spirits" lasts 26 minutes and features a 12-minute solo from McLaughlin, while "Lotus Feet" from *Inner Worlds* is an exemplar of discipline and spiritual humility. "Manha de Carnaval" is again warm, tender and introspective, looking forward to McLaughlin's guitar quartet work of the 1990s.

The personalities of the musicians involved are perhaps better defined than on *Friday Night*. Firstly there is McLaughlin's ethereal eclecticism, with a high Romantic elision of individual creative brilliance and technical prowess. Then there is De Lucia's flair for flamenco drama, postponing harmonic resolutions longer and longer in his solos and with tireless rhythmic vitality. Finally, Coryell, using a semi-amplified acoustic steel-stringed guitar, sounds more evidently a neophyte hybrid of Django and Jimmy Page.

Coryell's role is missed on later recordings. DiMeola uses a six-string fully acoustic guitar, and ignores the direct European jazz guitar lineage that Coryell absorbed through his work with Philip Catherine – the discipline of Rheinhardt. His choice of harmonies are richly sentimental, almost cloyingly lyrical, not a little Gallic. Listening to Catherine and McLaughlin's own later partner, Christian Escoudé, it is clear that Coryell embodied a guitar tradition that later McLaughlin trios relegated or muted.

The main pleasure of the recordings, however, is to contextualize McLaughlin's playing with that of other guitarists, most specifically his use of harmony. The music – a hybrid of blues, jazz, flamenco and Moorish harmonies, with their mutual fluidity of language – enables us to detect how different players play with the volatile elements involved. De Lucia sounds conventionally Hispanic with inherent Moorish overtones, but McLaughlin hints at elements of further eastern provenance, and a more instinctive mélange of jazz and blues harmony. Of the guitarists involved in the trio recordings, McLaughlin provides the most vividly and emphatically flavoursome cocktail of the individual elements. It is very difficult to analyse the relationships McLaughlin constructs between these varying harmonic systems. In this respect, McLaughlin is the touchstone of the recordings. The relationship between the different musics mutually and promiscuously feed each other through his playing and his choice of notes. This is not to say he is a better or faster or more resourceful musician; it merely emphasizes once more that harmony is maybe the chief distinguishing aspect of his work and musical conception.

Critics found it difficult to locate a context in which to analyse the band's music. Despite the tireless jazzers' shibboleth that the music should only be analysed as music, the trio presented a quandary. It can be argued that jazz-rock presented just such a challenge to analysis, but that phenomenon was an immeasurably more complex musical form than this rather light-hearted piece of cross-cultural showmanship. This can really be treated as little more than adulterated flamenco music, albeit conceived and delivered with often faultless musicianship and vigorous imagination.

Flamenco critics too, though, were divided, as they had been over De Lucia's modernising tendencies in the first place. Jazz critics tended to laud the speed of execution and nothing else. So difficult was it – and it remains so – to find an idiom with which to contextualize this music it might almost be imagined that the trio had been conceived with the sole reason of giving pesky hacks the runaround. Let's see them put *this* into words, some of the music seems to say. Certainly for the most part *Friday Night In San Francisco* can only be described as a lot of cheerful, harmless fun, with virtuosity and musicality eyeing each other respectfully, like high-powered authors at a party.

"Fifty or sixty percent of the music was improvized," according to DiMeola and De Lucia – "more than that!" maintained McLaughlin bullishly. Parts were not used – De Lucia did not read music, but had "an impeccable ear" according to McLaughlin. The one exception was Chick Corea's "Tales Of The Black Forest"; which DiMeola had already recorded on his 1976 solo album *Land Of The Midnight Sun*. He therefore brought the written parts along to trio rehearsals. McLaughlin and him play it with irrepressible brio if a somewhat mechanical clownishness. As DiMeola put it, "Once we met, it was a combination of learning by ear and using... parts."

One of the more perceptive criticisms went; "the trio's self-stoking interplay heats up the momentum. Intense concentration and bursts of humour are communicated to every seat in the house with each gesture – a swivelled shoulder, a spontaneous grin, even a glance registers with the audience."

"The three of us play for each other," asserted McLaughlin robustly. "The audience is important, but secondary. Most important to me is that I want to give something to these two men. The last thing I want for them is to get bored."

So there it was; the fans didn't matter; the musicians did.

It is instructive to analyse how this mirrored the corporate thinking which backed the trio. What was needed was something to maintain the marketability of the virtuoso musician as deity and as cash-cow. The critical backlash against fusion in all its forms was gathering strength by 1978 – columns in *Down Beat, Guitar Player* and *Rolling Stone* displayed how many had lost their awed fascination with the genre and its personalities. No longer were there earnest discussions of how frontiers were being broken, gone was talk of "the classical music of the future". The musicians would still waffle on like this to their heart's content, but the unmistakable accretion of cobwebs around the fusion form, mostly thanks to an increasing infatuation with funk brought on mostly by commercial dictates, were beginning to turn off many listeners and cognoscenti. In many instances, fusion was becoming indistinguishable from the great musical AntiChrist of the 1960s generation, disco. The instrumental virtuosity so prized at the start of the decade had begun to sound more and more effete, more and more homophonic (most obviously in the music of Chick Corea, which had become so pallid by the end of the 1970s as to be almost invisible). The music was little more than high-class muzak played by Berklee graduates. By 1980 most fusion albums sounded like 40 minutes' worth of academic graduation tests in instrumental ability; functional, but emotionally arid. Attempts to get funky by using disco rhythms made the music even more lifeless.

Similarly, the pages of musicianly magazines were becoming jammed to the gunwhales with unimaginably complex equipment and hardware. This branch of the industry had, throughout the 1970s, been driven by the existence of a technically sophisticated muse operative at the heart of popular music. Progressive rock and the jazz/rock/fusion matrix and the commercial appeal thereof were largely, though not exclusively, predicated on high degrees of instrumental virtuosity and textural complexity.

The technological determinism that took root in the evolution of popular music meant that the demand for new sounds often outstripped current thinking. Before the advent of polyphonic synthesisers in 1976, for instance, the development of rock had necessitated increasing amounts of monophonic devices to meet the demand of rock musicians as more and more of them became wannabe-Mahlers. Secondly, as many critics have noted, the exponential explosion in the availability and capability of pop hardware led to an inevitable fetishization thereof. In the memorable words of the author Iain Banks in his 1987 novel *Espedair Street*, "Quantity was quality then. The bigger your sound system, the longer your double or triple concept album, the longer your tracks, the longer your solos, the longer your hair, the longer your prick (or your tongue), the wider your loon pants... the better you were." Having got into bed with rock, jazz followed suit. By 1978, for instance, *Down Beat* was featuring advertisements for drumkits featuring up to 20 tom-toms in Pearl's "astonishing new rack tom system."

From being the enabler of the Aquarian muse which jazz-rock seemed set to liberate at the start of the 1970s, technology seemed increasingly to be a dehumanizing element in rendering fusion "a pestilence in the land of jazz." In other words, there was a general concern by critics that rhythmic and melodic novelty was increasingly being subsumed by FM-radio-friendly funk grooves. These were played by overpaid progenitors who legitimized this as jazz by the simple expedient of using them as nursing homes for superannuated solos whose redundancy seemed ever more total the faster they were played.

An acoustic backlash, a rethinking of the virtuoso ideal, was inevitable. It was slow to arrive, and only with the advent of Wynton Marsalis' classic quartet in 1982 was acoustic jazz once again regarded as the future. True, intermittent retreats from the dominion of electronics had been made already. Shakti had been among the first, but McLaughlin's guitar trio was another defiant two fingers stuck up to the musical-industrial complex which seemed to be intent on colonising jazz as well as rock.

In Britain, critical opinion – and, after a while, the opinion of the record buying public – was also running against the grain of the practise and performance McLaughlin and his peers embodied. For example, as early as 1973, *Melody Maker* was reporting of the Mahavishnu Orchestra in concert that "speed had become all important". At the time, this was more endorsement than damnation, but by 1978, with the advent of punk rock, the concept of musicianship had assumed the status of a cultural pariah.

The case of punk rock in England is a highly complex one, more involved than the simple efflorescence and sudden, coincidental media worship of a disparate clique of art-school surrealists and situationists lauding anti-technique over technique. In short, by 1979 jazz-rock albums were not so much criticized in the UK music press as abused; in the offices of all popular music publications, any display of musicianship was to be frowned upon. Punk had made a cultural stand – of a kind similar to that made by Dada in interbellum Paris – against bourgeois notions of technique, power, progress and beauty. In the punk lexicon, simplicity and pop art superseded complexity and Romanticism. "Never trust a hippy" was more than simply a slogan, it was a pop-art slogan of cunning subtlety which encapsulated the entire punk project. It was a reaction to the Symbolist, Romantic 1960s, in the same way that Dada and *Neue Sachlichkeit* had been to the Romantic, Symbolist, 1900's. Technique was especially damned; it was deemed exclusive and elitist (save for artists of some assumed political or social value, usually black or female, which for instance allowed Bootsy Collins or Larry Graham to solo as long and as freakishly as they wished on electric bass).

That punk rock and post-punk rock created much fine music is indisputable; their impact on creative music-making in the UK, however, was incalculably terrible, a holocaust of musicianly attitudes only ended by the advent of a new wave of young British jazz musicians in the mid-1980s and by drum 'n' bass in the 1990s. As the musician and critic Paul Schutze points out, "The problem with punk is that it abominated anything technical. This included jazz and the avant-garde. It was a disaster in that respect." The prejudice against jazz-rock, in particular, lingers to this day, despite the avowals of affection by dance music luminaries such as Howie B and Tricky towards Return To Forever and the Mahavishnu Orchestra.

McLaughlin didn't escape, although Paul Rambali of the *New Musical Express* wrote an erudite piece – bordering on the heroic – defending the musician when reviewing *Electric Guitarist* in June 1978, cogently distinguishing McLaughlin's tasteful virtuosity from the voided note-spinning of many of his contemporaries. From *Electric Dreams* onwards, McLaughlin disappeared from British popular music magazines, a scarcely credible, if distressingly believable testimony of collective ignorance and laziness.

McLaughlin was not unaware of the hue and cry and defended himself. He compared his speed to the infinitely faster playing of Coltrane, and quoted Coltrane's "sheets of sound" approach with ingenious justification; "he's just exploring all the harmonic possibilities as soon as possible."

McLaughlin could have gone on the offensive as did many of his contemporaries, accusing his detractors of musical ignorance. This was a useless defence as musical ignorance had become a badge of journalistic excellence at most UK music papers in the 1980s. Routinely accused of self-indulgence for no very good reason, he chose not to fight back, "We need the restraints of convention and structure to help us avoid self-indulgence, since we are all self-indulgent to some extent. How do you know you're being self-indulgent? I don't know. In the end, everything's a question of taste, I suppose – up to the point when taste disappears, and you're in a state of grace where taste doesn't matter." Certainly the wonderful "Tales Of The Black Forest" from *Friday Night In San Francisco* was an example of self-indulgence, or the leeway for it, actually encouraged genuinely fine music-making given the right conditions. Horseplay here was only a shade over the line from penetrating musicality.

In spite of the eclipse brought on by press indifference, the once-rising star of jazz-rock and its virtuosi would never be entirely extinguished. But as we shall see, in the musical nightmare of the 1980s, it also brought plenty of dark hours.

* * *

CBS issued a slew of compilations in 1980 devoted to its fusion headliners. Cheaply produced in plain two-tone card sleeves, they were well-received and often – though not always – sported excellent sleevenotes. Those written by Peter Keepnews for the Mahavishnu Orchestra's LP are particularly informative and are highly complementary to the music within. Those for McLaughlin's own set, boasting a similarly broad range of tracks, are not so good.

The irony was that by now McLaughlin had fallen out of love with the electric guitar. CBS, dismayed at the free-falling profits endemic in the record industry at the end of the seventies, coldly told him that his contract would not be renewed unless his Shakti-inspired affair with acoustic music was abandoned in favour of industrial strength (and presumably fashionably funked-up) fusion. McLaughlin followed his heart and walked.

Authoritative sources insist that CBS fired McLaughlin; whatever, his exit posed a challenge. In a musical landscape where musicianship as a value in itself was being routed right left and centre, how else could he live but via his reputation. The fact that he firstly did so but then created from that reputation a wholly new guitar persona is one of McLaughlin's greatest achievements.

He began the eighties somewhat forlornly; dumped by his label, his public appearances were always either solo or in the trio format he'd developed with Larry Coryell, Paco De Lucia and others. McLaughlin once again appeared as a jobber, albeit with fatter paycheques and a bigger reputation, playing concert halls instead of speakeasies and jazz dives.

The "Meetings Of The Spirit" trio existed for as long as Coryell stayed clean, and as long as commitments spared the other two musicians. De Lucia had commitments in Spain, and McLaughlin had the odd date back in the fusion loop. There were other strange engagements which included acting as a kind of ambassador of jazz guitar at a "Crossroad Of World Guitars" in Martinique in the summer of 1981 and, at Montreux, starring in a duet cameo with Chick Corea on 15th July. The latter was document-ed on the track "Beautiful Love" released on a Corea 5-CD boxed set by GRP in the mid-1990s. More distressingly, he also surfaced at the open-ing of a Meditation Centre in Los Angeles in 1980, accompanying Carlos Santana's music and Sri Chinmoy's dodgy narratives of the beyond. Despite the split with Chinmoy, McLaughlin could obviously not make the partition definitive.

Some reports credit McLaughlin as appearing at London's Royal Albert Hall in spring 1980 playing "My Foolish Heart" (no reason is given). History records him as launching his duet project with the French gypsy guitarist Christian Escoudé around the same time (Zakir Hussain and L.Shankar opened for them, with a regular encore jam featuring all four musicians). Escoudé, a brilliant technician who had helped spear-head France's own young jazz-fusion renaissance with the violinist Didier Lockwood, was a Djangomaniac with just enough distinctive phrases to magnify his technical talent. McLaughlin played with him globally, from San Francisco to the Antibes Jazz Festival (where McLaughlin would appear regularly for many years) and Velden in Austria. In July 1980, the pair teamed up with Larry Coryell in Tokyo, Japan. McLaughlin was also there to go through the motions with the fusion track-stars of the Fuse One Orchestra, a travesty of jazz-rock made by McLaughlin and a host of other luminaries at the behest of Fusion-Lite impresario Creed Taylor. Henceforward, though, McLaughlin would throw in his lot with Paco De Lucia and Al DiMeola.

The three turned on a global public at will; by the end of December a TV documentary had already been made about them, although the origi-nal *Spirits* line-up was reconvened one last time for the recording of one track on De Lucia's 1981 *Castro Marin* album. Recorded on Christmas Day 1980, it is the sole recorded legacy of the original guitar trio (save for *The Meetings Of The Spirit* TV documentary that was syndicated throughout the world but never commercially released on video). Coryell also appeared by way of a belated encore with Escoudé and McLaughlin in December 1980 in Tokyo. But the huge tours organised by McLaughlin, De Lucia and DiMeola in the next two years made it explicitly clear where McLaughlin's preferences lay as to who he recorded acoustic guitar with. Sizeable US and European tours were undertaken in 1981 and 1983 by the trio, with the sessions for their Philips LP showcase *Passion, Grace And Fire* sandwiched in between occurring in London and New York throughout the autumn of 1982. One especially memorable concert, in Rome, on 16th June 1983, was bootlegged and is now widely available. Australian TV featured them in an obsequious profile in January 1983. The three played on until November, drunk on applause.

Aficionados of McLaughlin's fire-all-phasers kilowattage in Mahavishnu Orchestra settings were perplexed. (Most had also eschewed Shakti, having bought the debut album and taken it off the turntable for good after fifteen minutes of side one). In fact, McLaughlin would not pick up an electric guitar in anger for another five years, and even then would only toy with it, showing little conviction on two undistinguished albums.

In 1980, McLaughlin, his patience with Columbia at an end, had called the multinational from Paris to announce that his next album was to be an all-acoustic affair, recorded in Europe. Columbia, perplexed, refused. Fine, said McLaughlin, took the company to court for breach of contract and by December 1980 was free to do as he pleased. He was in the middle of a profitable guitar-trio tour and had already signed for the release of a live album. Offers, even in a musical climate turning against musical virtuosity, wouldn't be slow in coming.

They weren't. WEA stepped in, mollifyingly dismissing all talk of acoustic and/or electric. Suitably recharged, McLaughlin began planning his next album, which, he told one interviewer, would be recorded both in America and in Europe. With characteristic floridity and self-confidence, McLaughlin expanded on his ambitions. He envisaged the next album, played on acoustic guitar, as a collection with a horn section, perhaps arranged by long-time Stevie Wonder cohort Arif Mardin and with – he hoped – Steve Gadd on drums, with whom he had never before played. "I just want to concentrate purely on the guitar, on the beauty of the guitar in a number of different musical environments," he said at the time.

There was also talk of a collaboration on the album with Jack DeJohnette, Dave Holland and John Surman, pre-Mahavishnu collaborators who had been out of McLaughlin's musical orbit for more than a decade. The four shared a bandstand in Paris for a five-night residency in May 1981, further fuelling gossip. The gigs were, for McLaughlin, "a kind of reunion".

None of this ever happened, for reasons as yet unclear, but quite possibly due to the intervention of a well-turned, and very musicianly, French ankle. Settling into his new European environment, McLaughlin suddenly found a very personal and very non-musical reason to rearrange his musical horizons.

The resultant debut disc on WEA was, after all the agog anticipation, an apparently eccentric Franco-American hybrid. While little heralded, though, the band kicked out almost as many jams as any ensemble McLaughlin had yet played with. Keyboard player Francois Couturier and bassist Jean-Paul Celea had been highly-touted young virtuosi around Paris for some years and had previously played together on the quasi-legendary album *Cinq Hops* by the ground-breaking doyen of French avant-jazz, drummer Jacques Thollot. The drum stool was filled by an astounding young black American, Tommy Campbell, a Berklee graduate who combined flawless technique with a truly signature individual sound. The band played a few gigs in France in 1980, but most significantly, the line-up for McLaughlin's first LP under the terms of his new record deal, would coalesce around the guitarist's new girlfriend, Katia Labeque, the young French classical pianist. Katia, with her sister Marielle had almost single-handedly [sic] revived the piano duet/four-hand act as a concert draw in the halls of mainland Europe, thanks to an almost unprecedented empathy and technical facility, not to mention gypsyish good looks.

McLaughlin had, of course, recorded in France before, *Inner Worlds* being taped at the Chateau d'Herouville in 1975. This time he opted for the technically superior Ramses Studio in Paris, one of the finest in France and much sought-after by rock and jazz musicians. The ambience, and the work of the studio's two famed engineers, Laurent Peyron and Jean-Louis Rizet, enabled McLaughlin to record his most satisfying work since Shakti. *Belo Horizonte* was cut in a few days in June and July 1981, and released on WEA in November of the same year. Alas, distribution was patchy; the UK and the US saw only limited quantities of the album reach the shops and the supplies continued to trickle on slowly through 1982. In some areas of the UK the album did not arrive until mid-1983.

More's the pity; the album is an amazing testament to how wholly the guitarist had understood and adapted the tone of the acoustic guitar to his own style of playing. McLaughlin, of course, had never given up on the acoustic as most believed. The instrument appears regularly on Mahavishnu albums, of course, but by the early 1980s McLaughlin was at pains to stress that he had always committed just as much time to the acoustic as to the electric instrument. The acoustic, as he rightly observed, was by far the easier instrument to practise in hotel rooms or on tour buses. Also, McLaughlin's acoustic tone had changed radically. He had switched from steel strings to nylon strings at the end of the 1970s.

"It's not just a tonal thing," he said at the time. "In the upper registers the response is much better than steel. Because response is so rapid you get a percussive element that's difficult to get with steel strings." Elsewhere he testified that with acoustic playing, "articulation is pre-eminent because articulation is where you really reflect yourself and the way you feel about everything. The more transparent your articulation, the more what's beyond articulation will be seen and felt, which is what I really like to feel and hear, this vitality. It's athletic and springy, it's bouncy. On the upper strings it's less of a problem, but with the lower strings you're dealing with more weight... and you have to push that weight around... at your ease."

Electric guitar, McLaughlin now declared, was an easier option than acoustic guitar. "Acoustic requires more strength, more precision." The acoustic player, said McLaughlin, was "totally exposed." By now McLaughlin was playing Abraham Wechter's acoustic guitars exclusively. Wechter was a supremely empathetic workman, and endeavoured to make guitars ideal for McLaughlin's tall, big-fingered physiognomy.

The first solo on the opening title track sounds like nothing as much as a McLaughlin electric solo transposed for acoustic. It might have been expected that McLaughlin's vocabulary was in some way changed, but the fact that it sounds so similar and yet not at all contrived when delivered by a quite different-sounding instrument is testament to his considerable musical integrity and the courage of his convictions. "Belo Horizonte" suggests to the newcomer, that McLaughlin had been playing acoustic guitar like this for his entire career.

The album sounds wholly jazzier. The title cut is a breezily post-bop romp (it's fun to imagine the whole played note-for-note by a classic jazz quartet) boasting an absurdly elongated and complicated melody which nonetheless manages to be the most uplifting and lighthearted piece of music McLaughlin had so far committed to vinyl. Indeed the whole album, while possessing a title which suggests the fixed rictus of admass spirituality ("beautiful horizon" in translation), in fact revels in an infectiously fresh and sun-drenched friskiness which seems quite unaffected.

Couturier and Labeque's synthesisers, dominated by the Prophet 5 and Synclavier, are sensual and breathy, and Campbell's furious and sometimes over-elaborate drumming is a miracle of transparency and sparkle. He resembles here a fine hybrid of Tony Williams and Jack DeJohnette in respect of his concentration on top kit and cymbals. This quality is enhanced by the webs of sound woven by the percussion duo of Steve Shehan and Jean-Pierre Drouet.

Further top-drawer French support appears in the shape of the classical violinist Augustin Dumay (a friend and sometime accompanist of the two Labeque sisters, who kicks up a storm on the Hot Club parody "Waltz For Katia") and seasoned avant-jazz saxophonist Francois Jeanneau.

The jazz ambience is explicit if still a little tentative in execution. McLaughlin's lovely Bill Evans tribute, "Very Early" lasts a derisory one minute and fifteen seconds. Delivered as a dainty waltz or polonaise, it invites previously occluded comparisons with Evans' famous signature tune, "Waltz For Debby".

Belo Horizonte's title track begins in the fresh-scented murk of a pre-dawn Arcadia; the rustlings and feral noises in the woods promise frolicking nymphs and satyrs or pachyderms unknown. An elfin percussion band approaches, and McLaughlin's rilling acoustic guitar announces sunrise, and the hair-raising pace of the music only adds to the crazed revels of the percussionists.

McLaughlin sounds glad to be back in a congenial working situation with congenial companions. It's uncertain as to whether these sessions saw the ignition of his relationship with Labeque, but this is the work of a man inspired by freshly-detonated passion. He sounds a happier musician than for a long time. His delivery is more thoughtful, but also more unbuttoned, taking off and landing in the most unexpected places. On his early Mahavishnu albums, his notes had flown hither and thither like a silver-clad dragonfly; now he sounds like a gold-leafed moth.

"A Lotus On Irish Streams" seems to be the natural antecedent to this music, although its parentage should perhaps be jointly accredited to Shakti also. Much of *Belo Horizonte* lacks the abstruse, diffuse, highly rarefied air of the 1971 piece whose atmosphere drifted in like mist, blown intermittently as the musicianly creators saw fit and shifted their emphases. McLaughlin might have profited more from closer work with Celea, whose delightfully elastic acoustic bass notes are deployed with almost uncanny rhythmic inspiration. His urbane rumination somewhere around about the chords of "Stardust On Your Sleeve" is a superb contribution to a superb track.

McLaughlin's melodic gifts shine anew on *Horizonte*. There are the usual anaconda-length themes which entwine but never suffocate the music. "La Baleine" and "Belo Horizonte" are examples, but "One Melody", which closes side one, is a mere series of chords, stated with alacrity at the outset in the midst of a smoky musical sunset. The rest of the track is an atmospheric, locomotive improvisation on these chords, into which the crashing of warm ocean breakers and distant festivities and phantom carnival bands seem to periodically intrude. Couturier and Labeque are particularly refined here, and McLaughlin plays powerful rhythm guitar. Three *tutti* passages develop (the approaching town bands?) but fade back into the groove, undeveloped. The percussion ensemble (bongos, snare and crash cymbals) busily stoke a fierce fire under the groove, lending the whole a vaguely North African feel (albeit strictly of the Club Med variety, it must be said). Centrepiece, literally and figuratively, though, is the fabulous "Stardust On Your Sleeve", a piece which magisterially combines tender lyricism and big-band swagger.

McLaughlin's return to the acoustic guitar in a group context with *Belo Horizonte,* as well as his close friendship and professional empathy with Paco De Lucia strongly suggested a flamenco turn in McLaughlin's performing and compositional style. The closing track, "Manitas D'Oro" has the suspicious air of a brief, fill-in encore to satisfy those enthused by the *Friday Night* recordings. He would return to the studio to record a full-length album with Di Meola and De Lucia in the autumn of 1982.

The follow-up, *Music Spoken Here,* is McLaughlin's most European work. While it lacks the Ravellian/Szymanowskian surface, its language is as distant from the American black vernacular as anything McLaughlin has recorded, save for his explicitly 'classical' works; the Mediterranean guitar concerto and the accompanying duets for guitar and piano. The absence of the percussion stardust sprinkled by Shehan and Drouet on *Horizonte* denudes the soundstage of a little icing sugar, but there is a magisterial assurance about most of the pieces. The preposterously silly cover art, where McLaughlin, unaccountably afflicted with temporary male-pattern baldness, once again gets his shirt off to satisfy the whims of a particularly cliché-blown graphic designer. Record companies seemed besotted in the early eighties with having seventies figures identify themselves visually with harsh geometries. Hence scores of Progressive rock albums, storm-tossed in the post-punk commercial market, substituted airbrushed art-nouveau curlicues for cheap-shot cubism as a concession to a *zeitgeist* of alienation.

Worse, this indulgence of crass contemporary commercialism might well have alienated a substantial public from a superb album whose coherence and cogency of musical vocabulary was maintained from start to finish. McLaughlin is in control of his muse and its delivery to a degree rarely found elsewhere in his oeuvre. This album, like its predecessor, is sometimes belittled by aficionados as the distracted off-cuts of an artist in transition. Close study affirms that the musical directions which would bring him his greatest success in the 1980s and 1990s – as an acoustic guitarist in an electronic-heavy chamber environment – were thoroughly and convincingly mapped out here. The fact that the title track of *Belo Horizonte* translates so effortlessly into the vernacular of his acoustic trio with Trilok Gurtu and Dominique di Piazza (*Que Alegria*) is only incidental.

Katia Labeque is retained in the line-up, and suspicions as to her swingability, raised privately by listeners at the time of *Belo Horizonte* and still alive and well when she toured with the McLaughlin acoustic trio in the early 1990s, are quite redundant here. Francois Couturier and Jean-Paul Celea are as pine-fresh brilliant as ever. Campbell, who somewhat nervously shares the front rank of the inner sleeve group photo with McLaughlin, reins in his penchant for fussy cymbal/snare adrumbrations and turns in an even better performance than on *Belo Horizonte*. He blends a splendid contrast of physicality amid the tom-toms, combining muscularity and angel's-wing delicacy with a throwaway brilliance that would bring commissions flooding in from Dizzy Gillespie to Sonny Rollins.

On *Music Spoken Here* McLaughlin is now clearly fully in control of his instrument as the lead voice in this ensemble. There are very distinct Hispanophile tendencies also, particularly in his solos, where he cheerfully discovers and rapaciously explores the common ground between the fleet-fingering feverishness of flamenco with the passionate note-avalanches of his hero Coltrane. "Blues For L.W." in particular, with its cinematic melodrama of mighty chords crashing down through the registers, is in serious hock to several Rodrigo pieces for guitar and orchestra. It was no surprise to McLaughlin aficionados that the piece would later be cannibalised for the slow movement of McLaughlin's own first guitar concerto. McLaughlin's own soloing style on this piece reverberates with a longing for the Iberian interior, making it a slightly odd choice as a tribute to the Polish dissident leader Lech Walesa who, at the time of the piece's composition (the winter of 1981-2), had been interned by General Jaruzelski's military government.

"Aspan", the opening track, has a similar character of imaginary *noches*. Again, it is no coincidence, surely, that it was treated in more purist flamenco style by McLaughlin's guitar trio on the following year's *Passion, Grace And Fire* album with no noticeable shift of character. The comparisons with Ravel, another idealist lost in the wonder of the peninsula, become even greater. The guitar solo which sneeringly launches side two's opener, "David" (another migrant to the 1983 trio album, and another thematic source for the first guitar concerto) is positively Moorish in intent.

Both sides close with Latin-spiced miniatures. Side one with "Viene Clareando" by Segundo Aredes and Atahualpa Yutanki (originally slated for *Belo Horizonte*) and side two with "Loro", which, although authored by the Brazilian guitarist and composer Egberto Gismonti, has a folksy pan-American lilt to its harmony. McLaughlin's arrangement and delivery adds a distinctive Hispanic panache to it. "Nem Um Talvez", the classic signature piece of Brazilian composer/percussionist Hermeto Pascoal, sadly never made it onto *Music Spoken Here* which, in the context of a 39-minute album, is regrettable. Luis Eca's composition "Dolphin", although rehearsed, never made it either.

The jazz influence, while less apparent than on *Belo Horizonte* is far from dormant. The harmony to "Honky Tonk Haven" might seem a little too vivid an example, but verse-chorus structures are still predominant and the swapping of solos between Labeque and McLaughlin on "Aspan" is a wonderfully swinging moment. Nonetheless, European classicism and Spanish folk idioms are suddenly and brusquely pushed to the foreground, as though McLaughlin had turned up at the studio with a *Fodor's Guide To Spain*.

One of the album's high-points, and another decisive nod towards the Western European classical tradition, was the delightful guitar/piano duet, "Brise De Coeur". The conventional statement of a long theme at the outset, sounding not a little like a melancholy hybrid of the album's other melodies, is an effect enhanced by the measured, pragmatic delivery of the melody by both guitarist and pianist.

Beyond these, however, are some endearing oddities that seem to have neither a natural home on the album nor in the McLaughlin repertoire full stop. "The Translators" is very bizarre music indeed, a characteristically elongated McLaughlin melody played over a somnolent, reverb-heavy funk beat. It is constantly interrupted by Celea's bass prejudging the next note and, with interplay so intensive, all of the musicians seem to end up ceding space to everyone else, with the music gradually petering out. It is engaging filler material, but not nearly so outrageous as the thoroughly off-the-wall "Honky Tonk Haven", one of McLaughlin's strangest inspirations. Ostensibly heavy space-funk, it is grotesquely mutated by McLaughlin, Rizet and Peyron into a Frankenstein's monster of reverb, a cybernetic behemoth of groove that would send Bootsy scuttling for his mommy. Riffs appear and are placed on the bassline to see if they survive; they don't. Interestingly, the harshest electronic timbres are from the instruments laying down that groove, the bass and drums. It's tempting but probably unwise to regard this as a nod to late-80s rap, but there are unsettling pre-echoes of Public Enemy deep in the canyons of the mix.

If there were no plans to continue the band as a viable entity, there are few aural clues; they sound ominously together. Couturier and Labeque are much more of a duo on keyboards – their instinctive duelling on "Blues For L.W." is proof enough. Celea and Campbell, too, are self-evidently more of a pair, but probably less excitingly demonstrative than before. The absence of a further duo, Shehan and Drouet on percussion, probably adds to the band feel. Nonetheless, the Translators – as they now were billed in concert – played a few gigs during 1982; beginning in Detroit on 14th April they gigged haphazardly, including dates in Bologna and a televised session at Antibes on 21st July.

Who, or what, though, scuppered this fine band? Facts are at a premium, but logistics and inevitably money seemed to be lined up against its continuing. McLaughlin told one interviewer that he found the 1981-82 music "beautiful... I loved it very much. But live, the balance of acoustic guitar and drums was impossible."

Labeque, as we have noted, was fast approaching the peak of classical fame, and it can be assumed that McLaughlin's polyglot musicality required him to use Europe less as a base for his developing vocabulary than a building block within it. He would have been hard-pressed to maintain his exile from the US for long. Campbell, too, had seen his reputation balloon exponentially whilst within McLaughlin's circle, and was much in-demand in the US, not least from another guitarist, Kevin Eubanks, whose debut album *Opening Night* was released in the US in 1982 to ecstatic reviews. Eubanks, like McLaughlin, had backed out of fusion's blind alley and, when not using an acoustic guitar, used a finger-plucked timbre reminiscent of Wes Montgomery. The limpidity of Eubanks' tone and the puckish fleetness of his compositions suited

Campbell's style as much as the sensuous, lightly-stepping delicacy of the new McLaughlin line-up.

Couturier and Celea, for their part, would go on to release an album under their own steam on the indefatigable French modern jazz label JMS entitled *The Game* (1983). Although uneven (and, at 32 minutes, sadly attenuated) it utilises the talents of Francois Jeanneau and another French jazz giant, drummer Andre Ceccarelli. Apart from anything else, it also highlights both men's talents for tone-coloration, lyricism and quirky funk improvisation (their later albums can be found listed in the discography at the end of this book). *The Game*, now hard to find and (to the current author's knowledge not reissued yet on Compact Disc) is a must for any McLaughlin collection; from the first bar, the collector will be anticipating the guitarist's tumultuous entry. Whilst it never arrives, the music on *The Game* is nonetheless infinitely rewarding.

Talking of rewards, McLaughlin had in the meantime retreated to Monte Carlo and cohabitation with Labeque.

Chapter Six
Of Synths And Simmons Drums

From the executive eyries upon the gilded summits of the American record industry, however, all this artistry was seen as criminally spend-thrift. Here was this prodigious note-flayer, this man who made a Bren-gun of the fretboard, waffling around with antique concepts and antique instruments when the record market, crowded with guitar groupies in the wake of the global heavy metal explosion, needed a mentor as elder statesman of the hemi-demi-semiquavers. Eddie van Halen and Yngwie J Malmsteen drove a generation back to the practise rooms in the planet's guitar stores; now was the time for a living mentor of high speed and higher volume to throw his cap into the marketplace and reassert his sovereignty.

Naturally, it didn't happen like that. The Mahavishnu Orchestra mark IV was a marketing man's dream and a pragmatist's nightmare. The move was almost certainly inspired by the remarkable rehabilitation of Miles Davis – the exceptional albums *We Want Miles* (1982), *Star People* (1983) and *Decoy* (1984) had defied Jeremiad predictions by elevating the former demigod's reputation to deific levels rarely seen before in jazz. The reason, of course, lay in Miles' own uncanny instinct for extrapolating the musicianly elements that lay within the contemporane-ous ghetto, which at the dawn of the 1980s were funk and rap. Even crit-ics venomously antithetical to both conceded Miles could wring blood from both of these apparently featureless musical stones. But the radiant return of the king reflected badly on his courtiers. Those who had forged careers on reputations made with Miles had, for various reasons been found cowering in the shadows. Corea, addled by Scientology, was chasing his tail around ever more tired licks of less and less chirpiness, whether rendered acoustically or electronically. Hancock had sold his soul to disco but, unlike Miles, had bargained away all his musicianship when performing his newer music.

There were exceptions; Dave Holland, Keith Jarrett and Jack DeJohnette, excluded from the big-buck mainstream, forged rewarding careers with the European label ECM. Only Zawinul and Shorter were immune from the judgement of passing time. This was mostly because their Weather Report ensemble were insulated by years of repeated Grammy nominations; and, to be fair, a dogged dedication to render solos the slave to music and not vice versa, a policy only briefly undone by the tenure on bass of Jaco Pastorius.

McLaughlin, as a guitarist, was potentially the most errant sheep of the flock Miles had so profitably assembled and nurtured. His stewardship of the most iconographic instrument in popular music, and his genius at playing thereon made him, in a decade when the record industry was dominated by soft-metal guitar-led bands (from REO Speedwagon and Styx to Bon Jovi), the fusion talent most likely to clean up with white America.

Mahavishnu, the album which resulted, was a jarring together of McLaughlin's muso-musing desire to renew partnerships, with cold-blooded record company policy. It is a shambles with a smile, a well-intentioned wreck. It contains passages of fine music, but can never quite become anything but a guest at a record company marriage of convenience. Even the workaday, carefully non-elitist titles give it away – "Nostalgia", "Nightriders", "Radio Activity", "Pacific Express". It is as though the music is being fastidiously designed by PR committee, hand-tooled to appeal to an affluent twenty-something US market composed of *Down Beat* readers or their girlfriends/boyfriends. Whereas the original Mahavishnu Orchestra had been a buccaneering journey into musical darkness, a collective sortie into uncharted territory, Mahavishnu IV rarely rises above the opportunistic. These are musicians who know what works commercially in a musical field their leader did much to invent. Saddest of all, little effort is made to disguise the fact.

From track one on *Mahavishnu*, the texture is almost slavishly adherent to that of Miles' *Star People* and *Decoy* albums. Miles, over the course of four albums, had consecrated poppin'-and-fonkin' bass, funky torrents of saxophone, zappy electronic snare-shots and horribly cheesy synthe-siser chords as the new Word of 1980s jazz – an old man's summary of a new young black take on music technology. Praised by critics on both sides of the Atlantic, it had been a startling revivification of funk among white musicians. What this apparent revolution didn't disclose was the sheer emptiness of the raw material Davis was working with; rhythmical-ly enticing but often harmonically and texturally limited, only someone of Davis' native common-sense and artistic sensitivity could have made something of it. Alas, his pioneering spirit served only to prove to would-be emulators that the new material was so thin that only the most musi-cally sensitive could hope to wring anything from it. No matter; the furore that the "new Miles" created was enough to pose a fait accompli to his ex-cohorts and would-be heirs, to match or exceed the master's new achievements. In some cases, the attempts were risible, as with Chick Corea's often jarringly predictable New Elektric Band, an even greater subordinator of good taste to showboating than Return To Forever. McLaughlin, an even more slavish acolyte of Davis than Corca, hardly distinguished himself.

Miles' second coming had an almost incalculable effect on young jazz musicians in America. Here was a generation which had been introduced to music via both the actuality and the hype of the original fusion experi-ment and its commensurate musical virtuosity. The years of *Bitches Brew* and *Inner Mounting Flame* had epitomised the idealism of elder brothers and sisters; now Miles' resurgence, hybridising black popular and white art forms with apparently as much panache as ever, was captivating thou-sands. Similarly, the recent eruption into popular music of the emasculat-ed American version of 'punk' (about as venomous as low-grade acne) and the growing cash-cow of ghetto chic in the forms of breakdance and rap, had made blue-collar sweatiness a noble attribute in popular music forms in the US of the early 1980s. Ghettos were hip, and this counted even in Berklee; every college boy or girl on any kind of music course donned a backwards baseball cap. The result was a tsunami of some of the most vapid hybrids ever to call themselves music. It's little more than well-intentioned slumming, whites contributing talents as charitably to black music as they might contribute hours at a soup kitchen in the Chicago projects. The act of participation in black cultural discourse feels liberating and refreshing – "hey! impeach Reagan!", "Run, Jesse, Run!" – but is of a dilettante nature that does little but retard the musi-cianly integrity of the charitably-minded protagonist. It persists today in the micro-particles of thousands of leaden jazz-rock CDs and across most of American TV – the famed solo bassline which introduces every episode of *Seinfeld* is a throwback to the wannabe-Miles fever of the mid-80s.

Ironically, with hindsight, the most complete integration of black and white music in the 1980s came not from Miles but from the guitar of Prince, the genius of Minneapolis, a musical avatar whose talents McLaughlin has rightly recognised and apostrophised. Prince's lowly status as pop, rather than jazz, musician, prevented the (mostly white) movers and shakers of jazz and fusion from cocking anything but a cursory ear. When black jazz did produce a new hybrid of its own – that of New York's M-Base collective in the late 1980s – it was regarded as being simply too esoteric, too far removed from the coffee-coloured funk mainstream to be taken seriously. Here were white youngsters who wanted as much to engage with black music as kids who wore Air Jordans and back-to-front Mets caps wanted to adopt black lifestyle iconography as bricolage of imagined rebellion. The bricolage here is a succession of mutated heavy funk basslines with the odd, obligatory twist, upon which tunes seem gratuitously grafted at odd angles. Instead of sounding urban and threatening, it just sounds tiresomely noisy. McLaughlin's generation of musicians didn't set out to create fusion – they discovered it by accident, which, frankly, is why so much early fusion sounds so much more organic and convincing than later, funk-based, 80s fusion.

Miles Davis achieved in the 1980s what he set out and failed to do in the 1970s; engaging directly with the street music of urban black America. Making something musicianly of this rested on using simple forms in a musicianly way, not trying to make them something they weren't. It also required a feel for basic funk and, crucially, pop music which many fusion musicians simply didn't possess.

McLaughlin's involvement in this sorry episode of epigonism and misguided, commercially-driven musical rainbow-nationism reflects not at all well on his career. He was, and remains, considerably less culpable than most who, having grown up to the beat of Miles' drum, unthinkingly changed step when it changed pulse. None of the tracks recorded under the Mahavishnu mark IV rubric remotely ranks with McLaughlin's best work. The fact that it is bracketed by two of the most musically rewarding collaborations of his career (i.e. in France in 1980-2 and with Trilok Gurtu at the beginning of the 1990s) poses even more questions as to the motivation and musical impulse behind this ill-timed and ill-favoured reincarnation.

Others had their own problems with the whole Mahavishnu IV schtick; Billy Cobham, for one. In 1987, he told *Down Beat* of a bad experience at its hands. "The Hahavishnu [sic] became a real bad joke. I extended myself to a point with John McLaughlin and his ideas, and I chose to really push it. It became more of an obsession for me, in a way, than for anybody else, and I ended up being the one hurt most. It cost me almost a year's setback in work. I had nothing. It was the closest I've ever come to being destitute, because I lost all the work I could have had that summer. I made the full commitment, and I lost out because their plans apparently changed and they decided not to tell me."

Danny Gottlieb, ex of Pat Metheny's band, got the gig instead. "About two or three weeks after the tour started," groused Cobham, "I found out from a guy who works at Paiste cymbals... I was still getting ready to go. The last time I spoke with McLaughlin he was supposed to get back to me with information on how I was supposed to transport my equipment." And then, silence, which an incandescently angry and personally hurt Cobham stoutly maintained.

The new band featured two recent and/or contemporary Miles players, saxman Bill Evans and keyboards player Mitchel Forman. The bass player was a relatively unknown Swede, Jonas Hellborg – who had wowed the 1981 Montreux Festival with a solo bass show and was now given to such gimmicks as shaving his head and tossing his axe in the air during solos – and who has since toured, amicably and profitably, with Billy Cobham.

Hellborg had been contacted by McLaughlin, one of those impressed at Montreux in June 1983. The results, however, were uniformly depressing. The opener on *Mahavishnu*, "Radio Activity" is one of the most enervatingly derivative pieces McLaughlin has ever recorded. The fact that it could so seamlessly fit into *Star People* or *Decoy* (given that Miles had been out of the room and thus unable to contribute trumpet) reveals McLaughlin as at least a man capable of understanding contemporary musical trends if not being able, in this instance, to contribute much towards their enhancement. Forman's keyboards chant tinnily, Evans' soprano saxophone skirls showily but unthreateningly around the root chord, and bassist Hellborg blacks up his sound, but unfortunately does it with all the conviction of a Black 'n' White Minstrel. The texture is wholly different from the original Mahavishnu line-ups. The keyboards-bass-drums triumvirate is utterly sovereign in the establishment of texture and rhythm, often asserting top lines and riffs, with McLaughlin merely a decoration.

It had all begun, perhaps predictably, with a massive fanfare. WEA, who'd shepherded McLaughlin's solo career since 1981, believed they had a major coup on their hands. With Miles reborn, fusion seemed reborn, and one of the biggest stars of the rebirth was on their roster. They slated the sessions for the new Mahavishnu Orchestra for April and May of 1984. In May, Jonas Hellborg and Billy Cobham accompanied McLaughlin in various sessions shown briefly on French TV, and by the summer, minus Cobham, the band were on the road. They checked in at London's Hammersmith Odeon on 12th July 1984 to reviews of warm enthusiasm, but not unanimous conviction, and spent the summer dazzling the festival circuit (notably North Sea on 14th July 1984 and Antibes on 27th July 1984 – again recorded for French TV), with Chick Corea in tow on some dates.

This episode effectively nullified and, under cover of darkness, interred McLaughlin's relationship with the Synclavier guitar, almost as embarrassing a commercial failure as Mahavishnu IV. For two years, he had apostrophised the new technology with unflagging volubility in the muso press, outdoing any company hype with his pronouncements that the Synclavier technology was the future of music as western man knew it. In the May-June 1985 issue of *Jazziz* magazine, McLaughlin waxed lyrical about the instrument with Pat Metheny, whose pioneering use of it on his albums *Offramp* (1982) and *First Circle* (1985) had had critics reaching for the thesauri in praise.

The Synclavier, in layman's terms, allowed a guitar player access to the library of textures and voices available to a keyboard player, but with infinitely greater speed than any previous guitar synthesiser. Given McLaughlin's long-term fascination with technology, and the failures of his previous attempts at easy guitar synthesis, it was inevitable that the Synclavier would attract him. Given the extraordinary beauty of Metheny's work with it – McLaughlin was an admirer of the younger man's music – it seemed that the Synclavier was the next logical step in McLaughlin's development. Unfortunately, it helped make him all but mute; any fan of the man listening to *Mahavishnu*, for example, would find it hard to locate McLaughlin's instrumental voice at any given point.

McLaughlin threw himself into the concept, talking it up endlessly to any journalist that would listen, even going into exhaustive detail on the mounting of a little onboard control panel on the Roland G303 he used to control the Synclavier. He worked, he told reporters, for "15 hours a day" just creating his "own timbres", to avoid working with the preset factory timbres. "Thirty different timbres" were used on *Mahavishnu* alone, it was triumphantly asserted, with 25 being used in concert. The problem was, McLaughlin didn't sound like a guitarist. He sounded like a synthesiser player, and one just learning the instrument at that. In interviews, he enthused that the Synclavier allowed him to play in a different way. "Conventional electric and acoustic guitars don't lend themselves to the horn-like flow of improvisation that's very dear to me", he told one magazine, evidently having left off listening to his own back catalogue for some time. Elsewhere he is reported as saying that the instrument affected his timbre and phrasing. "When you get involved in the creation of timbres with the synthesiser, you're creating a whole new world of sound... once you've got a particular timbre, its characteristics will directly influence you as soon as you start to play. It's as if you're suddenly playing another instrument". In short – thoughts had to be rethought. "The good thing about a guitar synthesiser," said McLaughlin, "is that it helps you to know what to leave out... some of the sounds... are not like guitar at all... and that timbre would oblige you to think in a different way... I think this is very healthy, because it would oblige me to stop thinking with habits that I'm accustomed to."

McLaughlin's logic is expectably sound. But the problem with these arguments was that for better or worse people paid to hear McLaughlin play guitar, not bassoon or glockenspiel. The Synclavier robbed him of the grain of his playing, his attack, his ability to use the voice of the *guitar* as the voice of his inspiration. It even diminished his characteristic electric guitar voice. As he said in 1987, synthesiser technology abominated "overtones and vibration, which computer technology reads as additional but garbled information." Overtones and vibration had been two qualities that McLaughlin had masterfully manipulated for twenty-odd years to universal acclaim. With the synthesiser technology of the mid-1980s, he inexplicably muted this mastery. By 1986, he at least had recognised the malaise and commissioned luthier Mike Pedulla to build him a guitar to eliminate the overtones in the body of the synth-control guitar. But it did little to incite the flow of human blood through his playing once again. Comparisons with Metheny's work are almost too painful. Even on *Offramp*, Metheny's first interface with the Synclavier, he has developed a language of voicing and phrasing which sounds sufficiently *unlike* a keyboard player, sufficiently *distinctive*, to make the technology viable. McLaughlin, over the space of two albums, never achieved this; perhaps his most outstanding musical failure.

For all their crudity, the band was in demand. A lengthy US tour in autumn 1984 was followed by a brisk circuit of Europe the following spring. Intermissions for McLaughlin to record with Davis' saxist Bill Evans and Davis himself (the masterpiece *Aura* in Denmark, in March 1985), were succeeded with a series of concerts doubling McLaughlin with bassist Hellborg. Twice in one ignominious evening at London's Royal Festival Hall the pair were billed to support the king of fuzak guitar, Lee Ritenour. After that, the now-flagging Mahavishnu bandwagon, on autopilot and shedding wheels at every turn, tooled mechanically round the festival circuit one more time. Most notably was their participation on the bill of Carlos Santana and Zakir Hussain at Keystone San Francisco and Palo Alto in California on 8th and 9th August 1985 respectively.

McLaughlin was once again being reduced to hawking himself, albeit with panache; whether for money or for music is uncertain. What is certain is the contrast between the opportunistic showboating of Mahavishnu mark IV and the stylishly unassuming mastery of jazz guitar he anonymously displayed in Francois Truffaut's film masterpiece *Round Midnight*. Recorded between 1st and 12th July 1985 and slap-bang in the middle of his most freakishly tasteless spectacles with Mahavishnu mark IV, the contrast couldn't have been greater.

Things may have looked good on the surface. On 19th November 1985 McLaughlin played briefly with the Mahavishnu Orchestra IV on Johnny Carson's *Tonight* show on CBS TV in the US, also giving the venerable talkshow god a five-minute interview. But slogging away with Hellborg in places like Saalfelden in Austria and Bratislava in Czechoslovakia, a thread of gigs leading through to the spring of 1986 and one short appearance on German TV betrayed to perceptive fans an uncomfortable truth. Mahavishnu mark IV was simply costing too much, and McLaughlin's workload in covering its outlay was becoming intolerable and degrading. Mahavishnu mark IV had lost WEA's backing, and its frantically criss-crossed web of routes between the European festival venues throughout the summer of 1986 (Hollabrunn (Austria), Neuwied, Schondorf (Germany), Ravenna, Milan (Italy, 20th July, with an appearance by David Sanborn on alto sax), North Sea (Holland), Antibes (France), Lugano (Switzerland) and London's Royal Festival Hall merely set the scene for one last desultory club tour of the States towards the end of the fall and the band died a natural death.

The music on the band's next eloquent testimony to the ill-conception of the entire Mahavishnu mark IV idea, *Adventures In Radioland* (1986) is, if anything, an even worse affair. McLaughlin himself, however, admitted his still-considerable affection for the album to the author in an interview ten years after the event. But even the staunchest apostle of McLaughlin's art must interpret this as the floundering, drowning-not-waving piece of bombast that it is. Just as one might scramble for terms on which to praise *The Inner Mounting Flame*, one has to rummage at the bottom of the barrel for terms with which to approach *Radioland*. Had *National Lampoon* decided to spoof post-Miles jazz-rock, they could surely have come up with no more toe-curling a parody than this. It is without question McLaughlin's weakest album, in terms of composition, performance and cultural relevance.

This would only work with real soul, or really good compositions, or quirky, effectively non-funk ways of dealing with ordinary ones. The album was maybe the most catastrophic failure of McLaughlin's career; issued intermittently in various territories through the offices of the US independent Relativity, it seemed to signal a sad ebb tide for a hero in eclipse.

The endless tumble of Gottlieb's horrid Simmons drums is almost single-handedly an indicator of the musical bankruptcy of the decade; only the spikiness of "The Wall Will Fall" and the rather sweet Joe Zawinul tribute "Jozy" come close to inviting the needle back onto the vinyl a second time. The arrival of Jim Beard, who contributes the quirky opener "The Wait" but does not play on the record, at least necessitated McLaughlin's return to straight electric guitar. Hitherto, Mitchel Forman's doubling on piano had allowed McLaughlin unobstructed freedom to indulge in the Synclavier axe. Beard, first and foremost a synthesiser player, presented textural conflicts, and McLaughlin obligingly picked up unmediated electric Gibson guitars again. At first, it sounds like a mistake – McLaughlin sounds uncharacteristically ubiquitous and syndicated – this could, surely, be any chart-friendly axe hero? He finds his feet, though, and his playing on the admittedly excellent "The Wall Will Fall" is as blisteringly agile and mean-sounding as anything since *Visions Of The Emerald Beyond*.

Beyond that, though, a parlous mess ensues. While he is a formidable tenor horn player, Evans' soprano playing is often just an annoying interference, so boilerplate is its sound (it *could* be Kenny G). As ever, the problem was the same; the unpalatable ugliness of the electronics and the contrivance of much of the music. "Gotta Dance" and Evans' "Half Man Half Cookie" are particularly culpable, random splatters of supposedly 'happening' basslines and 'quirky' tunes and riffs which, while promising as individual musical properties are hopeless together. They seem to call for both street and intellectual appeal and fail to garner either.

The usual sheaf of rent-paying but mechanical guest slots came down like confetti. An attempt to reconvene the De Lucia/DiMeola trio in 1986 came to naught, but other opportunities weren't thin on the ground; McLaughlin playing with the Japanese Philharmonic Orchestra in Tokyo in 1987; McLaughlin and Hellborg in a trio with ageless Japanese jazz-funk trumpet warhorse Sadao Watanabe (27th January 1987). McLaughlin grinding on with Hellborg (a televised concert at Bourges, France in 1987, a British date at Croydon Fairfield Halls – he couldn't even make the biggest London halls this time – in March the same year, a TV concert in Frankfurt). Violinist Gidon Kremer and cellist Yo Yo Ma were reported to be interested in collaborations, but nothing came of them. McLaughlin made a guest appearance playing electric guitar with Gil Evans' orchestra at an outdoor date during the Ravenna Festival in July 1986 and also contributed polite curtain-call acoustic guitar solos to tracks on solo albums by Mahavishnu mark IV sideman Bill Evans (*The Alternative Man*, 1986) and Danny Gottlieb (*Aquamarine*, 1987). He also began producing albums of classical two-piano four-handed works by his girlfriend Katia Labeque and her sister Marielle. As already mentioned, he made a rather enjoyable appearance – alongside many other modern jazz and fusion luminaries playing incognito – as an anonymous club guitarist in Bertrand Tavernier's sensational 1987 movie *Round Midnight*, in which Dexter Gordon plays a broken-down American tenor saxophonist on his last legs in 1950s Paris, in effect a fictional biography of Lester Young.

The partnership with De Lucia was resumed for a money-spinning summer (Royal Festival Hall, Berlin, Frankfurt, Montreux), but many spectators and commentators felt this was less spinning money than spinning out a past whose inspirations had deserted McLaughlin in his hour of need.

It wasn't so, of course. But the fact that McLaughlin's most luminous statement of his art at the time was on an obscure release by tabla player Zakir Hussain, who the guitarist had once employed in Shakti, seemed to sum the whole sad situation up. The world, it seems, had had enough of the guitarist, who many assumed would be forced to ply his trade on further and further shores from the mainstream to express himself to his full potential.

The Hussain recording, *Making Music*, was taped in Oslo by the maverick German producer Manfred Eicher for his award-winning ECM label which had for years specialized in pushing the envelope of jazz, art and world musics. While McLaughlin found Eicher's intensity a little overpowering, he nonetheless produced, along with his bandmates, some great playing and contributed to a splendid session which, had it appeared a decade or so earlier, would have been hailed worldwide as a masterpiece even exceeding the achievements of Shakti.

Hussain used Hariprasad Chaurasia, a master of the Indian flute who was a student of Annapurna Devi, the ex-wife of Ravi Shankar, and also the Norwegian jazz saxophonist Jan Garbarek, whose keening sound approximated to the Indian reed-instrument the nagaswaram but retained a luxuriant classical warmth as well as a bluesily playful jazz inflection. Although skeletal in texture, the music was more westernised and more luxurious in harmony than much of Shakti's, although melody and rhythm are still paramount.

The album was of an intimacy and compression of statement that wowed critics; sometimes the unit wanted for cohesion and the players seemed unfamilar with the settings, but this merely added a nice edge of innocence and discovery to the music. Shakti had been pure possession, total commitment, high octane; this was low-key, thoughtful, an epigram not a manifesto, a Himalayan valley rather than a Calcutta stew. Hussain didn't shirk his responsibilities as frontman and star, unleashing some stellar solos but also, most importantly, providing a constantly shifting pattern of rhythmic impulses which served as much as melody and texture as they did rhythms. By way of an example, "Water Girl" is a particular delight.

McLaughlin even contributes a number of his own, the first appearance of his lovely ballad "Zakir". His guitar solos now trace the contours of tabla soloing technique even more closely, evident from a few minutes into the first title track of the album. In Garbarek and Chaurasia he encounters two musicians whose idiosyncratic voicings and considerable range matched if not outdid his own. McLaughlin has for the most part to contribute a 'drone' effect with his strings, and achieves it ably without the use of anything more than a simple nylon-stringed Abraham Wechter six-string guitar and judicious use of reverb.

The album is fifty minutes of largely uninterrupted joy, whose relative obscurity in the McLaughlin pantheon is entirely undeserved. It is one of the most rewarding collaborations of his career, one of the few albums upon which he plays *throughout* as titularly-subordinate sideman and one whose value mounts when the listener remembers that it's a unique arte-fact, the only recording made by this quartet. Its distance from the phoney bombast of Mahavishnu IV is even more startling and cleansing than the gaiety that elevated Shakti's first recordings above

Mahavishnu's last. It reveals McLaughlin as a musician at peace with the world and his art, and in its serenely disciplined guitar language it also points forward – although he, like his public, could not know it at the time – towards musical, cultural and commercial redemption as the eighties drew to a close. The integrity he found in the Hussain quartet came to his own music again, only this time, he was the boss. In parting with one percussion virtuoso, he found another. Only this time, with a talent so unique that nobody could resist him or the man who employed him. His name was Trilok Gurtu, a dark magus with the cheekiest grin in jazz.

Chapter Seven
Half Century Limited

It would be unwise to call the 1980s a decade of decline for McLaughlin. But compared to the 1970s, they were like a Job-like medley of *anni hor-ribili* for the player. Bankrupted by the almost total systems failure of the ill-advised Mahavishnu mark IV project, label-less and with the potentially exciting new acoustic trio format with Jeff Berlin and Trilok Gurtu only engaging intermittently with critical and public sensibilities, he seemed in career downturn of a potentially terminal nature. He appeared like a venerable laureate of the festival circuit whose only income came from the glories of the past endlessly reheated for the demanding present.

In 1989, McLaughlin was lucky to still have a career of any kind after a horrific and potentially catastrophic domestic incident. Rearranging some furniture at home, he overbalanced a TV set which promptly fell on his left hand. "Well," he rather sheepishly told *Down Beat*, "I've got a big bump... [pointing to left index finger], and I don't think it's ever going to go away. But, I can play. Fortunately, it missed the bone by a sixteenth of an inch. I was very lucky." Just as luckily, it forced only the cancellation of one short spring tour, but it was two months before McLaughlin could even touch, let alone play, a guitar. But this unfortunate incident was merely the prelude to one of the most successful periods of McLaughlin's life, a portent to a career actually salvaged and wholly reoriented, in which he firmly re-established himself not only as a superstar of jazz but as master of an entirely new domain. He wasn't hailed as a pioneer as he had been with Mahavishnu mark I, but for the first time since Shakti, McLaughlin could once again do no wrong, and was regarded, at forty-eight, as a renewed creative voice in the genre.

In the autumn of 1989 audiences greeted a new incarnation of his acoustic trio with unprecedented acclaim. Berlin had been dropped and a young, relatively unknown German-born electric bassist, Kai Eckhardt-Karpeh, stepped in. The German, who had already featured in the *Auditions* page of *Down Beat* promoting new jazz talent in January 1986, had previously played with pianist Tiger Okoshi and drummer Alphonse Mouzon while studying at Berklee.

Given Berlin's unimpeachable pedigree, it's hard to understand how the new boy Eckhardt's introduction suddenly had such an effect on the trio's public profile. Perhaps it was no more than the purest coincidence, but the new constitution of the trio seemed to transform its fortunes, and notices went from enthusiastically interested to unanimously enraptured. McLaughlin's own playing even holds its own in the face of phenomenal global interest in the breathtaking skills of percussionist Gurtu.

The following spring, CBS released McLaughlin's concerto and JMT unleashed the compellingly brilliant, if infuriatingly abbreviated, recording of the trio's barnstorming London concert the previous November. McLaughlin, it seemed, had never been away. His face smiled out again from publicity and magazine features and interviews that once again ravenously discussed the promise of the future and not the wonders of the past or the stasis of the present. He seemed revitalised, and the smile shone ever brighter having emerged from the long dark of the '80s, a decade in which he had seen the music and the values he believed in dismissed, in his own life and career as well as in the wider world beyond.

It's hard to understate the importance of Gurtu in all this. The dynamic, hardworking little drummer from Bombay was just enough of a sideshow in the act to attract publicity of the how-the-hell-does-he-do-it variety. Even so, this was not freakish enough to overshadow McLaughlin, and the ingenious good taste and brio imparted by new arrangements which now somehow made his tunes distinct and fresh and desirable. Compare, for example, the unassuming swing that is the mercurially fleet hide-and-seek composition "Florianapolis" on *Adventures In Radioland* with the technicoloured cartoon of movement and magic it becomes in the hands of the trio.

The group made Gurtu the major star he deserved to be, to the extent that by the late 1990s many critics were lauding him as one of the greatest drummers ever, almost as colossal a figure in his discipline as

McLaughlin was in the field of the guitar. His fame and laurels even eclipsed those of Billy Cobham in his prime as Mahavishnu Orchestra drummer. Top Percussionist category in the *Down Beat* polls became a no-contest. All in all, for anyone who cared about jazz, or the power of music to cross barriers and to heal, the massive success of McLaughlin's trio was a singularly feelgood story; the only sadness being that Eckhardt wasn't around longer. While the young German did well out of the association, it's a shame he was ousted by Dominique di Piazza for live dates in the autumn of 1990 and for the group's only studio recording, *Que Alegria* (1992). Di Piazza acquits himself very well indeed, but the grooves developing on the live album suggest a future of pure gold for the Eckhardt incarnation of the band. Labeque would also join the trio for sundry dates throughout the latter half of 1991 and beyond. TV appearances were forthcoming in Germany (1990, 1991) and Australia.

The *Mediterranean Concerto* was (according to McLaughlin's self-penned sleeve-notes to the premiere recording), inspired by the generosity of Ernest Fleischmann, executive director of the Los Angeles Philharmonic Orchestra. Having played a concert at the Hollywood Bowl in which his girlfriend Katia and her sister Marielle were also performing a piano duet, McLaughlin was having dinner with Fleischmann when the enterprising orchestra boss offered him the opportunity to play Rodrigo's evergreen *Aranjuez* concerto with the orchestra. McLaughlin accepted, joking that he would do it on the condition that Fleischmann allow him to perform a piece of his own for guitar and orchestra. To his amazement, Fleischmann immediately consented, and McLaughlin set to work. The premiere of the finished work was eventually given in Los Angeles under the baton of the young Englishman Jan Latham-Koenig on Thanksgiving Day 1984. Notices were polite, if hardly adulatory.

The intervention of the Mahavishnu debacle in the mid-1980s kept McLaughlin out of the recording studio, and certainly starved him of funds to convince a major label to take a chance on such an ambitious project. It finally made it to the recording studio in 1988, in CTS Studios, Middlesex, with McLaughlin's old friends Tilson Thomas and the LSO. Even then, CBS held back the recording for two years, and in the meantime McLaughlin teamed up with Katia for a few leisurely, affectionate duets in Ramses Studio, Paris, meditating on some of McLaughlin's sunnier and more intimate themes.

The piece makes no pretence at being a lighthearted, un-serious if ludicrously virtuosic attempt at making straightforward, colourful symphonic music for a mass audience. McLaughlin admits the inspiration of the

Mediterranean, and freely admits the weight of his debt to 20th century French and Hispanic cultures (rather than owning up to directly pastiching Rodrigo, Ravel and Turina). Nonetheless, his admission that, "should (anyone) listening to this piece... accuse me of creating a vast potpourri, I shall be delighted, for it is nothing if not that, and if it gives pleasure to only one person, then all the work would not have been in vain" is disarmingly unassuming. Interestingly, one critic did suggest that the slow movement might have had 'too many tunes' for its own good.

This modesty was a far cry from the admittedly naive rather than megalomaniacal pronouncements of his Chinmoy days, when McLaughlin declared his aim to be a "cosmic instrument of God". McLaughlin made fewer claims to prowess as a classical composer than he did as a classical soloist – after all, Michael Gibbs is credited conspicuously as the orchestrator. The concerto is a suitably unassuming piece which is perhaps diminished for the McLaughlin fan by the familiarity of many of the themes.

There was also the issue of performance method; McLaughlin was, of course, a picker rather than a conventional classical finger-player, which he freely admitted would cause other soloists to maybe think twice about tackling the work. "If a finger-style player does eventually attempt it, he'll have to be very flexible and open to adaptation." Clearly McLaughlin had few rewritten compromises in mind. Wechter made him a special guitar for the piece, nylon stringed and with conventional fingerboard and a large body to bring out a rich bass mid-range. The scalloped models had died the death when McLaughlin switched to nylon strings, which required more pulling behind the string than he thought was conducive to good playing on a scalloped fingerboard.

There is no report of McLaughlin making cuts to the work, but reviews of the premiere gave its length as 42 minutes (the recording takes a little under 37) with the slow movement clocking in at a gargantuan 18 minutes alone (it occupies 12 on the CD). The action gets underway immediately, as a snappy triplet-based flamenco-style figure introduces the soloist, who appears in the soundstage almost incidentally. The first theme develops from here, a chatty, capricious little thing. Transitions are somewhat pedestrian, as the emergence of the second subject reveals, although transitions back are accomplished with panache – a rising figure from 1981's "One Melody" brings us back into the thick of idealised Hispanic picture-painting (all a bit school-of-Woolworth's sometimes it has to be said). McLaughlin's lines rarely deviate too much from polite variations on the figures involved. His solo voice seems oddly subdued in the mix, however, and during his cadenza, he seems fastidious and inhibited, although playing some delightfully inventive figurations.

The slow movement, based on "Aspan" (from *Music Spoken Here*) is unashamedly derivative; McLaughlin's serene chords, the lamenting solo trumpet theme and the dimly attendant divided strings are pure *Aranjuez*. There is even a hint of Gil Evans' own arrangement of Rodrigo on Miles Davis' *Sketches of Spain* (a key album in McLaughlin's musical development). No matter; McLaughlin's solo lines, while still recessed, are passionately lyrical yet constrained from rhetoric, and his use of space, pausing, emphasis and phrase-shaping quite exquisite. One has the impression that this was the first and easiest movement he wrote. The finale is a celebratory romp, inspired "by Indian beats" in the composer's words, but also overflows with not-always-well-concealed homages to Bernstein and Copland.

Mike Gibbs' orchestration is spotlessly connoisseur, if lacking in individuality. Solo lines for instruments abound, but never overshadow the concertino soloist, apart from one seductive flute solo in the finale. There are nice ideas – the celesta in the slow movement, for example. But Gibbs does tend to indulge McLaughlin rather than act as an authoritative counterweight to him. At times his arrangements over-egg the pudding, and make comparisons with McLaughlin's influences too painfully obvious. If a figure sounds Ravelian, then the orchestration undergoes a Pavlovian switch to sound that bit more Ravelian. If it sounds like Gershwin, as in the finale, then the soundstage switches magically to that of Gershwin's *Piano Concerto in F*. Even when evoking other composers, he can evoke the composers those composers evoke. For example, the trio section of the slow movement is a percussion-heavy rhythmic fantasia, which not only suggests Leonard Bernstein and the maverick Mexican Silvestre Revueltas, but also, uncannily, their respective debts to the works of Stravinsky.

Performances since the premiere and the recording have been few and far between, and mostly in Europe, notably with the Orchestre de Paris, the Frankfurt Radio Symphony Orchestra and the Tonhalle Orchestra in Zurich. A commission for a second guitar concerto was soon forthcoming from Tilson-Thomas and his newly-minted youth orchestra, the New World Symphony Orchestra, based in Miami, Florida, a work premiered in February 1991.

At fifty, McLaughlin looked and sounded in rude health; tanned and lean, with the silvering hair neatly coiffed, he looked every inch the Euro-sophisticate. Additionally, the similarly-revitilised Verve Records, now a Polygram subsidiary, offered him a new contract in 1991 which happily bore fat fruit both for the musician and for his new – and old – publics. He was greeted like a conquering hero at the Guitar Legends festival in Seville in October of the same year.

But it was the acoustic trio that really restored McLaughlin to the pantheon. Aside of the sheer joy and resourcefulness of the playing, critics vied as to the essence of what made the line-up so emotionally stimulating and musically fascinating. Comparisons with Shakti were seen as odious, but were probably the best thing to hang onto in the meantime. It would be a while before there was some formulation of McLaughlin's new direction in a critical fraternity still mesmerised by the novelty of 'world music'.

"When I asked Trilok to join me in a musical venture," said McLaughlin to one interviewer, "it was without any thought of Shakti. I love the way he plays. He has a very interesting concept and approach to time. In a way, he's a mirror image of myself, though coming from the Orient – because, he's a jazz drummer, he's a classical, tabla-trained, North Indian classical musician. But he's a jazz musician more than an Indian musician... I had classical training, but I'm not a classical musician."

John Ephland, in *Down Beat* magazine suggested to McLaughlin that the trio "seemed to revolve around a strong harmonic foundation, much like early Shakti". Harmony and melody, he offered, accounted for a great deal, but Gurtu's presence seemed the pivotal one. McLaughlin disagreed; "the harmonic movement that goes on in this show is quite complex in some pieces. It may not be evident because there's no keyboard playing behind me. You don't hear it, but the construction is there nevertheless; and some of it is quite complex, which never existed in Shakti.

"This became a problem in Shakti, because I really wanted to contribute more Western music. [It] was a wonderful group but as long as I kept going in the Indian tradition, Northern or Southern, you revolve around a tonality and you can change a raga or change a scale, but harmonic movement is definitely a no-no. I would do it in a kind of spiral movement around the central tonality, and I would expand on it that way. And I would tell Shankar, 'you can put this scale over this, even though it sounds funny.' Or, I [would try to] put this chord over that tonality, because we have this drone all the time.

"I wanted to work with Shankar to develop more incorporation of western movement, which is really, more or less, harmonic. Indians know a lot about melody but harmony, this is really the Western contribution to music... the trio is very much harmonic movement, but you don't hear it, you hear it in a linear way because there's no keyboard pad."

This is perhaps a little disingenuous; with some smart new toys to play with, McLaughlin didn't need a keyboard to acquire that western chordal harmonic movement. Together with Abraham Wechter and one Larry Fishman, he could now play sustained, synthesised legato chords from his guitar, as well as transposing rhythmic and solo lines with the use of a transducer.

This was a triumphant conclusion to and culmination of McLaughlin's decade-long search for the ideal guitar synthesiser and a wholly more artistically satisfying use of MIDI technology than the ill-fated Synclavier experiment of 1984-87. The transducer was capable of providing a separate output signal for each of the guitar's six strings. Those signals were sent to his Photon Guitar synthesiser (made by Phitech). MIDI connections, taken from the bridge via microchips, were forwarded to two book-sized Yamaha synthesisers which enabled him to combine complex voicings and textures (as, for example, with the voice-like sounds heard at the start of the track "Baba" from *Que Alegria)*. Arpeggio-like sequences could be played and held indefinitely, likewise chords and layered voicings. The signal from the Fishman Piezo transducer was used to pick up the guitar's acoustic sound and transmitted through a TC digital 31-band equaliser and dynamic equaliser.

Convenience was the first advantage – there were no questions of schlepping huge amounts of equipment as of yore. Musically, it was a treasure trove. It gave McLaughlin his own tonal centre to improvise over, as well as offering the possibility of simultaneous *unisono* voices playing at any chosen speed. McLaughlin cited "Hijacked" on *Que Alegria* as an example; there was no overdub, he stated to one interviewer, despite the apparent presence of one or more. This, McLaughlin added, "can provoke Trilok or Dominique into different directions."

One thing that the transducer technology guaranteed was the extinction of McLaughlin's scalloped fingerboard, which confused the transducer. It also cemented McLaughlin's relationship with nylon strings, once again altogether more sympathetic to the technology than steel strings.

It's worthwhile comparing the two albums, *Live At The Royal Festival Hall* and *Que Alegria* to examine the development of the music, the composition of which is contributed by three out of the four musicians directly implicated in its execution. Gurtu contributes "Pasha's Love" to *Live* and "Baba (for Ramana Maharshi)", while bassist di Piazza has a short chance to shine on the six-string bass solo "Marie".

The live album boasts fewer but more memorable originals – tunes by Miles Davis and Mitchel Forman fill out the session in London. That said, the band originals are handled with greater vitality – *Que Alegria* sometimes outstays its welcome, the music unable to sustain its spans. The Eckhardt band swings with infectious gusto on the askew flamenco pastiche "Pasha's Love". Eckhardt's muscular and agile bass lines in the first section of the long McLaughlin-composed jam "Mother Tongues" lead into a stunning solo which underpins some of the most intoxicatingly virtuosic ensemble playing in McLaughlin's entire catalogue. The later band is more restrained, dignified almost; only on "One Nite Stand" and "Reincarnation" do they stretch out. The retread of 1981's "Belo Horizonte", a longstanding favourite of the trio's stage act, for example, remains indecisive about a pulse compared to the original's headlong gallop.

One writer cited di Piazza as the "new Jaco" and, while this may have erred on the side of hyperbole, the comparison is by no means odious. The Italian has the same singing, rounded tone and can switch at will between bass and melody lines without a batted eyelid or missed beat or at any cost to the drive of the music. The problem is, the music di Piazza was asked to play on *Que Alegria* emphasised his melodic as opposed to his rhythmic prowess. Live, this was not the case, but *Que Alegria* occasionally ruminates a little too long, and di Piazza either lacks or is constrained from a necessarily articulated, funky, kick-ass style. This is not to suggest indiscriminate Bootsying. It would merely have provided a more focused sense of forward movement. More than once, the pace lags a little; the music seems slack, tensionless. The finale, seeking nostalgic contemplation, manages only narcotically-enhanced navel-gazing. Gurtu and McLaughlin's sensational interplay of tabla and guitar in the central section, however, wholly redeems the piece. Eckhardt manages to imbue even slow, meditative music with an implicit muscle and sinew, as on "Blues for L.W." and the opening pages of "Mother Tongues", with its alternately slinky and thoughtful moods.

Que Alegria is more of a complete musical statement; its unashamed homage to the blues ("Baba" and "Reincarnation") and wider-ranging scope place it ahead of *Live At The Royal Festival Hall*. The harmonies are more adventurous too; McLaughlin makes less use of western harmony with more sparing and sensitive use of the chords played on his guitar synthesiser; *Que Alegria*'s harmony is altogether more linear. But for sheer excitement and avalanching musical inspiration, the live album is unassailable, and remains one of McLaughlin's finest statements.

Regrettably, aside of a few rare bootlegs and a quasi-official tape supposedly endorsed by McLaughlin for private release among fans in Estonia in 1991, no other recordings of the Eckhardt group survive. The di Piazza line-up, a wholly different proposition in concert settings (helped by Gurtu's evolving understanding of the music) is uncatalogued in concert on any disc.

One common denominator between all the trios was the employment of extended vocal improvisations around a set pattern, led from behind the drums by Gurtu. First heard occasionally on the Shakti albums, these took the form, in the simplest terms, of onomatopoeic substitution of percussion tones by voices. In short, collective impressions of tablas. At first, slightly unsettled western audiences saw this, performed in concert, as a piece of light relief, maybe shading a little too deeply into gimmickry. But McLaughlin included passages of such improvisation not only on the *Live* album but also, and at much greater length, on his *Que Alegria* studio effort.

In attempting to explain, he observed that, for Indian classical music, instruments – the tamber [sic], flute or sitar – didn't "go to the core of the music, which is the human voice. My understanding is that the voice is central and I discovered that if I wanted to learn Indian music, I must first learn to sing. In the West if you tell someone I'm a musician, they ask, 'What instrument do you play?' And they may ask, 'Do you also sing?' In India, if you say, 'I'm a musician', people ask, 'In what style do you sing?"

Gurtu and McLaughlin's improvisation was based on the Hindustani *Khayal*, meaning literally imagination, improvised nonsense syllables. "In *Khayal*", explains Warren Senders, "There are words that have semantic meaning but are not treated in a meaning-intensive way... six words may be sung over two minutes of tonal space. The vowels are open and the words are varied. Indians may also improvise on syllables and there are also nonsense songs with meaningless vocal components." Echoing McLaughlin's observation about the role of vocal music in Indian music as perceived by Westerners, Senders says it is a cultural fluke that Americans prejudge Indian music as predominantly instrumental (that may, as he acknowledges, be because of the prominence of the instrumental Indian musican Ravi Shankar, with whom many Americans are familiar). But *Khayal*'s improvisatory kernel suggested further parallels between the subcontinent's classical repertoire and jazz, for *Khayal* and other Indian vocal improvisations are little other than a form of scat-singing.

The trio played its last gigs together in 1992 to support the release of *Que Alegria*. By this time, Gurtu had his own solo record deal with the German specialist fusion label CMP, for whom he continues to record and, in the case of 1997's *Bad Habits Die Hard* has been recording some of the most dynamic jazz-rock of the last decade. Gurtu has, however, maintained a personal and professional adherence to McLaughlin, not least on the soundtrack for the 1996 movie *Molom*; he must now be rated as one of McLaughlin's most durable and valuable musical partners.

The demise of the trio was seen by some as a tragedy, and by others as a commercial and artistic mistake. McLaughlin, however, would prove both diagnoses wrong; as usual, he was staying one step ahead of the game, or, in the case of 1993, two steps ahead. What he would do that year would prove indisputably that he was once again one of the major creative forces in jazz.

Firstly, the trio merely bore another, one which, if anything, won McLaughlin even more respect. This was the potentially-risky Free Spirits trio, debuting in Paris in May 1993. Then, towards the end of the year, came another album, which didn't so much drop out of left field as flutter gently down; *Time Remembered: John McLaughlin Plays The Music Of Bill Evans*, hailed as one of the guitarist's greatest triumphs.

The mêlée of critical opinion that greeted the announcement of the Free Spirits centred mostly, and inevitably, on McLaughlin's return to electric guitar after over a decade in which he had become associated – Mahavishnu IV aberrations aside – with the acoustic instrument. Foreboding settled in; was this to be an atavistic throwback to the excesses of the late 70s? McLaughlin's ill-judged, if probably ironic, comment on the new configuration as a "power trio" and the hefty presence of drummer Dennis Chambers, whose double bass-pedal attack and hyperactive grandstanding had been an occasionally tiresome highlight of the early-90s fusion revival, boded ill. But before anyone could pre-judge, the organist Joey de Francesco announced his presence in the music with a performance of singular note. The sheer novelty of Francesco's sound, and the way in which he and McLaughlin had combined their playing into a beautifully rounded and distinctive unit, enchanted reviewers everywhere. Chambers, too – who McLaughlin had met by chance backstage at a George Duke gig in which the drummer was participating in Seville – was hailed as a giant.

McLaughlin was relieved and pleased by the exceptional critical acclaim that greeted the Free Spirits; "I really wanted to play with Dennis Chambers, and the idea of a Hammond organ trio was very attractive to me. I grew up with the Hammond organ – Georgie Fame, Graham Bond, Larry Young, Mike Carr. And the idea of playing acoustic guitar in a Hammond organ trio was just ridiculous. But it had been so long since I played electric guitar that I needed to have a big guitar, I mean an acoustic-electric guitar, so of course you've got to go and find all those jazz guitars".

The English journalist Mark Gilbert, in an excellent 1996 interview with the guitarist in *Jazz Journal,* observed a more chromatic, straightforward jazz voice creeping back into McLaughlin's music; something not just apparent with the straight-ahead throwback experiments like the Free Spirits trio, but throughout the 1990s.

McLaughlin responded; "I think in the last few years I've been working systematically on trying to find new harmonic approaches to the guitar. Like when you start to play a blues, like 'No Blues' or an 'I Got Rhythm' structure, or a piece like 'Vukovar', there's some very, very interesting harmonic movement. How you move from A to B can be done in a great number of ways, and so I work on that. I can never get to the end of a 12-bar blues... I mean, you can never get to the end of where you can take it, and still stay in the blues.

"A lot of work has gone into just examining my own compositions, and looking at the harmonic structure, and how can you get from A to B and not bore yourself to death. You systematically have to wipe your old ideas out. You have to have habits – you can't go on stage and think. You've got to go on stage and play."

This was little more than a riff on themes he'd explored before; the very great depth to which the blues was inculcated into his music. He'd patiently explained the blues colourings in the provenance of the harmonic language of *The Inner Mounting Flame*, although that music displayed explicit textural and timbral alienation from traditional blues voicings to a far greater extent than the music of the Free Spirits. As McLaughlin blithely admitted, this 1990s line-up was fuelled not inconsiderably by the resonance of his own musical nostalgia for the organ-led blues sounds of his youth.

For a kick-off, the guitar does not lead – another throwback to days of yore in Lifetime and with Graham Bond. All three voices are democratically deployed. DeFrancesco solos at greater length and with greater volubility than McLaughlin. The guitarist's solo voice seems altogether changed; restrained, polite, dignified even, although the attack still has bite. His playing is slower, if no less fluid, the phrases clipped and curt. Again as with Lifetime, McLaughlin shoulders the majority of bass duties, an active rhythmic spur, and an emotionally sensitive one. He adds oomph, moving in urgently to fatten up climaxes as at the end of deFrancesco's long solo on "Hijacked". Chambers, for all his dexterity, keeps both feet firmly within a basic foursquare pulse. "Hijacked", for example, contrasts his elaborated rock beat with the zigzagging, schizophrenic rhythmic lines which Trilok Gurtu scattered all over the tune on *Que Alegria*. With Gurtu, for most listeners, all that remains is the memory of a pulse.

McLaughlin's originals on *Live In Tokyo* certainly seem rootsier; ditto their execution. Sometimes almost raucously bluesy, in a vein that make them sound not a little like the jokey variations on older material McLaughlin might have once included as contrast in a live show, notably the almost perky "Little Miss Valley".

"Vukovar", as McLaughlin pointed out, was more complex; ostensibly a lament for the lost of the Croatian town recently shelled by Serbs during the war in the former Yugoslavia, it's nonetheless taken at a lively clip, and hints at "Electric Dreams, Electric Sighs" from some fifteen years previously. McLaughlin is at his most assertive here, and he also impresses on the very long "Mattinale", where he's once again very much restored as the *leader* of the band and quotes at length the theme from the 1982 track "Aspan".

The problem with the record, however, is de Francesco. A splendidly gifted musician, his tone is nonetheless too effete by far for the setting. Glassy, transparent almost, it sits ill here, like a church organist auditioning for the Red Hot Chilli Peppers. His own work is often exciting, but here he sounds out of place. The climax of the twelve-minute "Vukovar" for example, is an upward-spiralling riff that has been building for minutes, and de Francesco, while playing fast enough, simply can't provide the visceral edge the music needs. He swings ably, but doesn't rock. One writer once described McLaughlin's old mucker Larry Young as the Coltrane of the Hammond organ with Jimmy Smith as its Charlie Parker. De Francesco is notably Parkerish in his solos, and can be beautifully sensitive as support for quiet music, although the laurels in *Tokyo* for sensitivity go to his trumpet playing alongside McLaughlin in a heartrending rendition of the guitarists' "When Love Is Far Away", derived from 1978's "Do You Hear The Voices That You Left Behind?"

McLaughlin's next album *After The Rain*, in spite of multifarious awards and critical panegyrics, falls flat. Ostensibly a tribute to Coltrane, through performances of the saxophonist's own music and that which inspired, or was inspired by him, it smacks of verisimilitude. It sounds

145

like something McLaughlin felt obliged to follow his heart and do, ditto the inclusion of veteran jazz drum genius Elvin Jones on the session. The ensemble playing is of course excellent. Jones is so efficient he's practically undetectable but alert to every requirement, like a Michelin-starred waiter. Whereas on *Tokyo* the emphasis was on blues, here a more explicit post-bop feeling is evident. The music passes uneventfully, although McLaughlin's soloing on "My Favourite Things" is appealing. "Naima", Coltrane's own composition is a much better stab at trio playing, striking real sparks between the three musicians despite the restrained, almost preoccupied intimacy of the reading. Similarly, McLaughlin's passionate playing of the lovely chords which introduce "Crescent" recall memories of so much of his own musical language in a little shiver of *deja vu*.

The Bill Evans tribute *Time Remembered* seemed, initially, a wilful piece of obscurantism; it was, of course, nothing of the sort, in fact one of the most logical moves McLaughlin's discography has made. His renditions of Evans' mood-pictures had been a feature of his live performances since the late 1960s; "Peace Piece" on *Extrapolation* was the first evidence of it on record. "Very Early" followed in 1981, and occasionally an Evans piece would crop up in guitar trio performances. What distinguished *Time Remembered* was the novelty of its arrangements, made by McLaughlin himself for a quartet of acoustic guitars.

This arose from his association with a young French guitarist, Yann Maresz, whom McLaughlin had taken on as a student in the late 1980s. He helped the young man with theory, specifically the chord structures and theory of jazz harmony. Maresz in turn introduced McLaughlin to his own friends, who helped form the Aighetta Guitar Quartet.

McLaughlin spoke little in public of the gestation of the Evans project, which made its arrival all the more serendipitous for reviewers. As tributes go, it's a heroic one, done with the maximum of good taste and the minimum of personally subjective or self-aggrandising rhetoric. *Time Remembered* does not say "this is what Bill Evans meant to John McLaughlin" so much as "this is what Bill Evans *meant*".

Nothing here cloys. At times, if anything, the music becomes a little too chromatically introspective and formless; it is more fugitive even than Evans' performances at their most ruminative. A precise rhythmic path is followed through each, but so colourful and lyrical are the *divertissements* improvised by the soloists that rhythm quickly seems to become secondary. Only "Waltz For Debby" is delivered with any directness.

"Very Early" makes an instructive comparison with McLaughlin's 1981 recording. Here, his choice of notes emphasises the abstract, the chromatic, rather than the prettily picturesque inflections of the lovely melody. But it is nostalgic, affectionate, and even optimistic in places. It's not music for mourning, but for celebrating, appreciative friends gathered swapping reminiscences. *Hey... do you guys remember when Bill...?* Only McLaughlin, ironically, could have remembered him as a person, but all five musicians involved on the recording seem to have assimilated his musical personality pretty well into their own.

Paradoxically, however, while the mystical, contemplative aspects of Evans' music are pointed up by this ensemble, if anything the acoustic guitars, singly or in tandem, add charm to and better distinguish the shape of Evans' writing. He was, after all, lauded more as a performer and improviser than a gifted composer. Only his "Waltz for Debby" established itself as a deathless standard. For example, far more pianists – even including the great Michel Petrucciani, perhaps the most sovereign of jazz pianists to follow the American – reproduce Evans' keyboard stylisms than his actual compositions. The ensemble here allow Evans' phrases and lines, and most of all his dreamy harmonic language to emerge in greater relief. We are reminded just what a wonderfully quirky little take on the musical love-letter "Waltz for Debby" really is.

Predictably, fast playing is at a premium; the music is handled gently, phrases passed around like a newborn baby. A top line leads for the most part, and the lower register and bass figures are varied amongst other players, often assuming different forms within single songs.

The acoustic guitar was now vying once again for favour with McLaughlin against the electric instrument. With the extensive use of electric guitar in the Free Spirits and again on the forthcoming 1996 album *The Promise* it looked like McLaughlin had opted once again for electric. But even so, one more acoustic album before the millennium was forthcoming. McLaughlin called up Al DiMeola and Paco De Lucia turning one unassuming and somewhat somnolent get-together into a fully-fledged comeback bandwagon. Unfortunately, nobody screwed the wheels on.

The guitar trio of the 1996 album *Trio*, or more particularly the trio tour, was an ill-conceived move made expedient by the cutting of the album. One assumes that permission for the one was dependent on the other; certainly shortly into the tour it was evident that very serious personal differences were emerging. By the time the triumvirate reached London, rumours were flying that they had stopped speaking to each other. *The Guardian* published a now-famous photograph of the three men spaced out across the stage of the Royal Festival Hall with enough space between them to drive two low-loaders through. This was a far cry from the fiendish fun of the Coryell/De Lucia nights when the three players had been sat so close together that they risked entangling the machine heads of their instruments.

"Do these look like three men who want to be on the same stage together?" asked the reviewer rhetorically. At one stage DiMeola, when his turn came to introduce a piece, stated to the London spectators that it was "nice to be back someplace where they speak English". De Lucia's thunderous glower, held stonily throughout the evening until then, turned even blacker. That evening De Lucia left the stage after the last encore like a scalded cat, clearly angry. Reports abounded that he gave the American a fat lip after the London gig.

Some blamed DiMeola for the bad feeling. Some said that De Lucia had accused McLaughlin of being unable to keep time; some maintained DiMeola had told anyone who'd listen that McLaughlin couldn't tune a guitar. Others blamed McLaughlin for vacillation, ignoring the conflicts in the interests of corporate profit, of letting the tour go on for mercenary purposes when it was quite plain from the body language of the participants, and the often mechanical quality of the performances, that this was something nobody wanted to happen. Certainly the whole exercise lacked the good-natured duelling and sense of revelry in musicianship which infused previous trio outings.

It might have been a less sorry affair had the music of the new trio been anything to write home about. For the most part it wasn't; the album in particular was at best mannered, at worst truly enervating, perhaps one of the worst albums in McLaughlin's discography. Many of the pieces seem to provoke little but a doze, and bad dreams to boot, or perhaps fond recall of the triumvirate's illustrious past. The 1983 effort, *Passion Grace And Fire* had little passion and the mere ember of a fire, but on *Trio* there's not much grace either. Frankly, it seems as if nobody really cared. There's a lack of relish about the disc that is singularly unique in McLaughlin's repertoire. Once again the production, despite responsibilities being shared out between the three guitarists, who produced their own three tunes on the CD, is unexciting and unresponsive. Playing is never less than excellent – expectably, one might think – but while the album cannot be called bad, it is wooden to a disappointing degree. All energy has gone – it's hard to credit these are the same three musicians as made *Friday Night In San Francisco*. All pieces are amiably mid-tempo, and licks and solos are politely exchanged rather than traded as the gentle thrum of the bassline continues below. It sounds at times like a listless swarm of bees, so uniform are the textures. Not even the compositions stand up for themselves – a telling point, because all three men are proven composers. The aridity of inspiration apparent here is probably more down to a lack of commitment than to any sudden loss of creative powers. Even Luis Bonfa's provocatively sensuous "Manha de Carnaval (Morning of the Carnival)", a trio staple in live shows since the days of Coryell, is a mirage in the desert. It sounds less like the happy preparation of celebrations than a civic committee planning a low-key arts festival. Arguably maturity, even advancing years, had mellowed the three; but even the dynamics between the musicians are negligible. The music of *Time Remembered* is low-key in character, but infinitely more appealing thanks to the intensely concentrated interplay of the musicians involved.

The contribution made by the trio to McLaughlin's massive career retrospective, *The Promise*, that same year, might have set alarm bells ringing. "El Ciego" was lacklustre, but at least had the benefit of a pleasant melody and at least the memory of an ensemble brio from the three.

The Promise was a media event of some size; McLaughlin toured the promotional circuit tirelessly. His record label, Verve, hammered the chief selling-point; McLaughlin covering all the bases of his talent, including the ceaselessly hyped return to full-steam jazz-rock fusion and the many reunions with former compadres in new line-ups. Reviewers, daunted by the sheer scale of the enterprise (nearly 74 minutes, the equivalent of a double vinyl LP) muttered darkly about spreading things too thinly, and it takes time for the album to assert its qualities. On the whole notices were tolerant, shading towards guardedly endorsing. It remains an overblown effort, but has considerable merit, given the immense ambition of it all; jazz-rock fusion, the organ trio, a reconstituted 'new Shakti' line-up, contributions from the guitar trio and quartet, as well as party pieces with starry guests such as Sting, Jeff Beck and Vinnie Colaiuta.

The Promise, said McLaughlin, "just grew out of a desire to play with some people". It also seemed to stem from a desire to inflict maximum pain upon himself and collect Air Miles. For the two numbers recorded with saxophonist Michael Brecker, for example, he flew from Japan to New York City for three days, with sessions on two afternoons, then on the third day flew back to play live in South Korea. Recordings were made in a total of nine different locations.

On the whole, the album is problematic; after five or six years of great success and intense diversification, *The Promise* is less promise than problem. What is it? What is it trying to say? It is neither calling card (John McLaughlin – look how much he can do! – available for birthdays and barmitzvahs) or inventory for the future (now which direction can he take next from all of *these*?)

What is McLaughlin *saying* here? We never really find out, not even from the cutesy 3D computerised cover art. The hidden message therein might imply certainty, but the music doesn't.

Curate's eggs are best approached from the bad side first. There's no stink here, but "The Return" is clearly a piece that should have been removed from the shelf for health reasons. It begins promisingly, with a snatch of sampled found sound, a voice which might be an impression or an actual recording of Miles Davis' grating a "let's go" and a snippet of drum'n'bass. Unfortunately this resolves with horrid incongruity into a tune of unusual triteness over a feelgood reggae beat, the sort of tricksy guff that all too many jazz-rockers had fallen into by the 1990s. The chorus' lovely, yearningly romantic chord sequence almost redeems things, as does Joey De Francesco's very capable impersonation of a Harmon-muted Miles Davis.

"Django", a composition by MJQ pianist John Lewis, is treated with genial disrespect by McLaughlin in a line-up featuring Jeff Beck, veterans Tony Hymas (keyboards) and Pino Palladino (bass) as well as the brilliant young British drummer Mark Mondesir. Comparisons maybe odious but can be informative, and we learn much about Beck's and McLaughlin's respective approaches to soloing, and it provides yet another example of McLaughlin's comparative harmonic audacity in his solos, and the wealth of material he finds within the blues tonalities. McLaughlin's modified tone is also apparent; while Beck remains faithful to distortion, reverb, feedback and the whole grab-bag of rock guitar devices, McLaughlin is altogether more transparent, more subdued; it's almost as if he is retracing backwards the steps he made from jazz to rock styles in the late 1960s. Explaining this is difficult, but it seems that, given his comments on his experience in the Free Spirits, his teaming with Joey de Francesco forced him to adapt an altogether more mellifluous, mellow timbre.

"Django" is hobbled by the somewhat tiresome and gratuitous switch to twelve bar blues in the middle. For McLaughlin though, the song was "played just as it was written out, harmonically and rhythmically." The Free Spirits number is very much a simple post-bop continuation of their previous work. The nod to McLaughlin's subcontinental influences came with "The Wish", featuring Nishat Khan on sitar, Trilok Gurtu on percussion and Zakir Hussain on tablas. This line-up was "consciously looking for more equilibrium between east and west" than the previous group. This almost shades into world-musical vulgarity with the western elements deeply underscored by the four-square accenting of Gurtu's percussion and cymbal work. It may be an aural illusion, but it's hard to say whether this enhances the apparent effect that Khan's sitar solo seems to follow distinctly rocky phrasing. Also, the recurrence of a small fragmentary theme also seems to act by way of a surrogate chorus here and there and is hardly based on classical Indian tradition. It's a pleasant enough piece, however, and McLaughlin solos with great power and discipline, playing fast and intently and with great restraint, possessed by a desire to rock out but apparently always holding his impulses in check.

The two jazz-rock numbers, "Jazz Jungle" and "Shin Jin Rui" are, of course, central to the album, because of their size and volume if nothing else; but both are viable pieces of music. Much was made of the 'new freedom' and 'energy' of the former. McLaughlin indeed enthused to this author about the simultaneous soloing on "Jazz Jungle". While it does present McLaughlin at his most uninhibited and least obsessed with form since Shakti, it has a tight underlying structure. While Chambers subdivides the rhythm almost to infinity, until McLaughlin's solo entrance at around the six-minute mark, the basic pulse remains foursquare fatback. Brecker's saxophone-playing, while full of athleticism, vim and invention is simply too syndicated a sound in the 1990s. There seems to be a conscious attempt to recreate the Miles Davis era of *Jack Johnson*; random interjections by bass and keyboard fall like rain onto molten metal, sizzling and steaming. Guitar and saxophone, meanwhile, duel furiously, and significantly speed is less of the essence here. There is an apparently genuine desire to experiment again with timbre and texture and the rhythmic possibilities of solo playing rather than simply time-trialling velocity of execution. At two points around ten minutes and fourteen minutes in, "Jazz Jungle" is a minefield of uncued explosions from McLaughlin and Brecker.

McLaughlin certainly gives his all here; he almost tries too hard to prove he can still 'rip it out' and very consciously muddies his otherwise somewhat domesticated electric guitar tone. To one reviewer he explained that he was once again using a ring modulator as he had years previously with the Mahavishnu Orchestra. "...it's like the saxophone players – just by changing their embouchure, they get this rough sound;

it's just harmonic. And that's basically what a ring modulator does it just messes with your harmonics." Using an ATM vibrato arm ("an old Bigsby"), McLaughlin admitted that harmonic randomness, or at least the freest flexibility possible, was a "technique I'm working on, it's tricky, but I'm learning how to control it more. I really like it because it reminds me of Indian music, and sometimes, they'll just drop a quarter tone... then there's Miles. Miles would bend his note. Trane would do a slurred run down but Miles would bend the note. You can go up on the guitar. You can bend it up but to bend it down is impossible, unless you begin with the note bent up and release it. I tried to do that with the Shakti guitar and that's one of the reasons I had the scalloped fingerboard. It's hard that way, a very tricky technique."

"Shin Jin Rui" is an altogether looser exercise, redolent of late Weather Report in its conversational interplay of bluesy, funktified bass guitar and chirpy keyboards with warm-hearted and off-centred reed work. The broken, hiccupy, hesitant melody, delivered unisono on sax and guitar, recalls the days of David Sanborn's guest appearances on *Electric Guitarist* and *Electric Dreams*. Brecker is entirely at home here; in the best tradition of McLaughlin and his best soloists, he uses the complexity of McLaughlin's melodies to build up to songlike, melodic passages in his own improvisations.

Jimmie Rowles' "The Peacocks" is another original given the guitar sextet treatment with Maresz and Co; as with the Evans pieces, forward movement seems almost entirely diffused here, and once again the mood is ardent but never saccharine.

Curiosities and novelties, and not just the disembodied voices reciting poetry between the tracks occupy the remainder of the album. "English Jam", a bizarre collision of plodding Britrock (Sting and drummer Vinnie Colaiuta both wasted) with a startlingly good passage of drum'n'bass, which shows that while McLaughlin might seem more delighted with the novelty of this musical device, he hadn't quite yet figured how best to deploy it. "Tokyo Decadence", thirty-nine seconds of birdsong, is a shot at ambient soundscaping and "Amy and Joseph" sounds like an outtake from an abandoned concerto, with synthesisers and samplers providing the orchestral arrangement. These three, it's tempting to imagine, might all have been included as teasers, loose-talk hints dropped into the texture of the record as a whole, like subliminal advertisements to signpost further developments.

Perhaps inevitably, the direction that swiftly became apparent as the most financially rewarding was for McLaughlin to play to the gallery and continue the nostalgic stint in the land of jazz-rock fusion which had delighted so many of his fans on *The Promise*. Within a year he was rehearsing a new electric quintet, to much fanfare.

The concept underlying the configuration of the band was, presumably, to whet the appetite of those who had enjoyed the adrenalised fusion of "Shin Jin Rui" and "Jazz Jungle" on *The Promise*. At the time it seemed that, rather like the album's other tracks, these were simply an extended cameo of one among McLaughlin's many musical interests. The response to these tracks was to garner an inevitably large acreage of review space. There was delighted surprise at their evasion of the most obvious and heinous jazz-rock clichés and the evident commitment that went into their execution. It seems that McLaughlin could scarcely resist the temptation to venture back into amplified music. In the fashion of the *Promise* quintet, he used a saxophonist (the highly-rated young cohort of Brooklyn's M-Base collective, Gary Thomas), a keyboard player (Jim Beard, a veteran of the ill-fated Mahavishnu Orchestra IV), a bassist (Matthew Garrison – son of Coltrane pianist Jimmy) and redoubtable drummer Dennis Chambers, fast becoming one of McLaughlin's most rewarding collaborators.

The Heart Of Things was released in the fall of 1997 to reviews that mingled caution with relieved approbation and only some brickbats. What could have been omitted was the hokey cover art with its absurd sub-Tarantino theme – Johnny Mac and the boys (sorry, *boyz*) patrolling their patch in the projects, five enforcers spilling off-kerb into the street (they don't care – this is their territory, man). That said, the formidably-pumped Chambers, with a chest broad enough to play a game of gridiron on, looks like he sounds – as though he could take on an army or as if he owns the neighbourhood, or could if he really wanted to. The other four look like they've never walked such streets in their lives. The whiteboy slummers-in-the-hood imagery, so tiresomely and infinitely trawled by record companies after Miles restored what corporate America imagined to be a semblance of ghetto timbre to fusion in the 1980s, suggests a fuzak disaster waiting to happen.

That it doesn't, and indeed comes off against expectations as a rather good, thoughtful album, owes little to Chambers' seemingly incorrigible grandstanding. Even Cobham at his most garrulous knew when to stop, but not Chambers. Having toured leisurely through the Free Spirits recordings, he puts the pedal to the metal here; both feet, and both hands, too, at every available opportunity. The album's main problem, however, is that everyone puts their foot down apart from McLaughlin himself.

The whole is a coherent, searching fusion album, whose leader, it appears, just happens to have taken time out for a coffee break and omitted to tell the band to stop playing.

No other McLaughlin album sidelines him so wholly as *The Heart Of Things*. His compositions have merit and trigger good grooves and solos; so where, pray, is McLaughlin himself? Save for the odd polytonal string of notes, meekly receded within the mix, he may just as well be a guest.

The recurring referent for the album's overall soundprint is Weather Report; the exemplary Gary Thomas' soprano and tenor lines act as melodic leads while the rest of the band falls in as textural improvisers on whatever fragments they choose to pick up. The group collectivises its voices, with McLaughlin's acting more of a prompting role as does Zawinul's keyboard work on classic Weather Report tracks. That said, Zawinul's was an altogether deeper upholstering, harmonically spurring role, than that of McLaughlin on this strange album.

Textures are somewhat *pointilliste*, with no strict hierarchy in the music; lines randomly overlap each other, save for the omnipresent blanket-bombing of Chambers' drums. There is, in other words, no room for McLaughlin's melodic gift to be borne above the clamour. This would be perfectly acceptable if his other gift, that of grimily mixing it with the most reprobate of blues scales (and winning) was given a chance to assert itself. But McLaughlin, here, seems to be merely the director, not the leader. "Seven Sisters" and, especially, the languorous "Fallen Angels" are eloquent cases in point. There is lots of interesting rhythmic interplay – the bass and drums undemonstratively play with the tempo – but come the entrance of the sax and the guitar, McLaughlin seems to cop out after one chorus. Once, a track like "Fallen Angels" would have been a cue for McLaughlin to raid the deepest recesses of his musical imagination in crushing the heart and drawing the tears. Not here. "Ladies and Gentlemen," the track seems to declare, "John McLaughlin presents Gary Thomas." It's tempting to gloss McLaughlin as playing the Gil Evans/Mingus card, of forsaking his own gift for those of younger men, but this doesn't quite work – McLaughlin's always musical solos are buried deep within the velvety, somewhat anonymous mix. Clearly, McLaughlin himself, despite moments of inspiration is not entirely convinced of the value of his own contribution to this band. It seems that he thinks they could probably do as well without him, as long as they were nourished by his compositional input.

The problem with *The Heart Of Things* is that, while it never ceases to be interesting and pleasing and coyly funky (it's devilishly hard to turn off) it rarely surprises. McLaughlin knows the genre, but seems content to conceive exercises on the rhythmic and harmonic flexibilities rather than impose his own melodic and harmonic stamp upon it *as well*. It *knows* it's cleverer than 75% of fusion, but for some reason shirks candidacy for greatness due to the leader's reluctance to brand his own melodic and harmonic soul upon it. The economy of McLaughlin's contribution as a player to *The Heart Of Things* outdoes even *The Promise*. At least on that album one sensed a polite withdrawal for the benefit of the guests, but on *The Heart Of Things* McLaughlin seems afflicted by chronic musical generosity – *here, take my solo, it's yours...*

What became apparent, however, was that even after pledging to take the new quintet on the road in 1997, McLaughlin had finally learned to live and let live with his guitar favours. By 1997, to mark the fiftieth anniversary of the independence of the republic of India, he was touring as an acoustic guitarist with an all-Indian line-up of musicians who would eventually form the Remember Shakti band; also, he was selling out halls worldwide with *The Heart Of Things* band. Unwieldy of title but hot of reputation, McLaughlin found himself back on the stardom trail again.

This was far from the days of Mahavishnu, when critics and public strewed palms in his path – the music was, as we have seen, structured quite differently in terms of responsibilities for soloing and spotlight-hogging. Even in live concert situations, outright display was minimised when compared with days of yore; McLaughlin's interplay with Dennis Chambers proved that. An inveterate addict of flashy soloing, Chambers was by and large reined in, as were McLaughlin's own tendencies towards the florid. McLaughlin's tribute to the drummer, "Mr DC" when played live, featured neither a drum solo nor a guitar solo. As with the record, the less demonstrative passages, rather than the frantic self-indulgent breaking of musical speed limits, was the order of the day. No matter; he might not have been a speed king any more but he was a king of guitars again. The sudden reappearance in interviews of very long extemporisations on technical and musicological themes relating to guitar practise and performance testified to a man once again, in the words of one writer, "hopelessly in love with the guitar".

By 1996, McLaughlin was using three different Johnny Smith guitars – 1962, 1968 and 1977 models. There was no conventional amplification and the sound went straight through the PA and McLaughlin used a monitor. An electronic box of tricks – a Sony M7 – placed between himself and the PA transformed a mono signal into a stereo output making for a broader sound. For acoustic concerts, Abraham Wechter's instruments were still reigning supreme. And onstage, McLaughlin was yet again a leader of people.

In 1997, McLaughlin allowed Verve to issue on CD the soundtrack music he had recorded in 1994 with Trilok Gurtu for the independent movie feature *Molom*. He also toured with, among others, the prototype for the new Shakti line-up, who were immediately booked into the studios to record an album due for release in March 1999. A tribute album to McLaughlin, featuring other guitarists' renditions of his tunes, was also on the drawing board. In the wings, other events were unfolding; his relationship with Katia Labeque, the longest of his life, ended in 1995, which explained her absence from his LP *The Promise*; he remained resident in Monaco, quickly married, and once more became a father, thirty years on.

He approached sixty in fine fettle; neither as cutting-edge innovator or elder statesman, but respected, even lauded, nonetheless.

* * *

During the course of his interview with *Jazz Journal International* in 1996, McLaughlin responded to a question about his appetite for work with slightly amused surprise. "I never stop working," he attested.

This is not an idle boast. McLaughlin's career has been one of relentless workaholism and of almost ascetic dedication to music, or more precisely, his own musical imagination. It's an indication of how barren the mid- to late-1980s were for the musician that so little new territory was explored and so few contacts made with the people who might guide him therein. In the 1990s, he has been almost constantly travelling, as though to make up time lost somewhere; there's always another jam or another collaboration, always something to explore, always a rainbow to chase. Sometimes there's no crock of gold at the end – witness the horribly ill-fated guitar trio reunion of 1996 – but McLaughlin at least sees fit to make the journey the destination.

This might seem tediously obsequious; but McLaughlin's work rate is not necessarily a virtue in itself. It's a career choice, for better or worse, and it makes the job of the chronicler very difficult, as constant change renders the demarcation of a manageable biographical period very hard to call.

There is no easy way to end a biography of a musician like McLaughlin, in the same way as it might be when writing the stories of

Miles Davis, Duke Ellington, Art Tatum, Jimi Hendrix, John Coltrane, Ornette Coleman, Keith Jarrett, Bix Beiderbecke, Charlie Parker, Billie Holiday or Dizzy Gillespie within their lifetimes. With each, it is hard to say whether destiny, or their own willpower and creative genius, is unfurling life-events faster. Only death can provide a full stop with any authority. The story must be forever unwritten until then, so evolutionary are these players. I begin the conclusion of this book thus, because there is no other way to end it except by saying that the action rolls on, and we're leaving the picture early. McLaughlin has hit many heights and plumbed many depths, and the journey will go up hill and down dale many times more.

But before the book ends, there are a few more things to say; most significantly, why John McLaughlin is, and was, so important. Why, in the end, this book had to be written.

Epilogue
Musical Virtuosity And Virtue
In The Late 20th Century

Why bother writing this chapter? Why bother justifying what I have spent over a hundred and fifty pages explaining? Because McLaughlin, and a lot of his generation, deserve explanation and cultural justification. While among technically the greatest exponents of their musical style, they are somehow excluded, beyond the pale, beyond common cultural currency, marginalized by a music industry which once looked up to them and their synthesizing ideals. Mention them in polite conversation, and your new friend will say that he or she has *heard* of them, no more. Why, though? Why are such technically gifted musicians so excluded from the popular culture they graduated from and still remain a part of?

To expose McLaughlin's gifts means first tackling how they were belittled and marginalized. McLaughlin – by most accounts, one of the most gifted musicians in popular music – is a marginal figure in his native land, not to mention in a world transfixed by the American-derived music he usually performs with innovation and invention. There seems to be, in the English-speaking world at the end of the century, not just a commercial attitude but a popular attitude that asks 'why?' to anything that does not rake it in at the box office. Furthermore, a hostility to the imposing, the self-consciously ambitious, is afoot. To that end, having listened to McLaughlin's music inside out, I will boldly ask the question that his detractors might ask at the end of the century. What is John McLaughlin for? What purpose does he serve?

To many readers, this question will seem ludicrous. But in writing this book, even with the limited musicological knowledge at my disposal – or perhaps because of it – it seems to me to be very important indeed. I have been confronted with a musician of genuinely exceptional means. Yet at the same time we live in an age when certain people have seen fit to question the use of his gifts. *Why* play that fast? *Why* play for that long? Music isn't about athletic performances. On the other hand, many readers will contend that because McLaughlin is that fast, he's *good.* Equally fatuous, really.

Much of the argument is politico-cultural. To those revolted by the phrase, let me touch a rawer nerve. Why, for example, does nobody slate Prince when Sheila Escovedo detonates one of her thrilling drum solos in his show? Why, though, is white, male instrumental rock damned for any attempt at similar display? To western ears, the tabla solo unleashed by Zakir Hussain on the title track of his 1987 album *Making Music* is as dazzling a display of physical dexterity as anything played by McLaughlin? Why is an hour-long Coltrane solo 'the real thing' and an Eddie Van Halen extemporization not so?

Here we confront a critical faultline.

Much musical criticism in the late 1970s and 1980s was informed – often for good reason and with good results – as much by sociology as musicology. White men flourishing technical gifts were irretrievably bourgeois. Here was music as a badge of quantitative and acquisitive success implicated in the entire Dead White European Male project. This explained the rise of disco as a cultural force, divorced as it was from 'stuffy' and 'outdated' and 'Eurocentric' concepts of expressivity or subjectivity. After all, how could the drumbeat, the heart of disco, be described in subjective terms – it couldn't be described in terms of something else, of representation, only as a quality in itself. Disco, like punk, was nothing to do with music as beautiful art object, music as vessel of the gods, music as art discourse. Music could no longer 'express' an 'other', a fundamental 'truth'; it could only be a plastic entity to be moulded and interpreted as much by listeners as authors. Thus, what did the fannying around by McLaughlin and his virtuoso chums really mean when push came to shove? Nothing.

This critique made fair points but was riddled with misconceptions. As with all pseudo-revolutionary music criticism, it ignores historical elements, even facts. It ignores the often crucial, but supposedly neutral,

element of musical discourse – rhythm – in determining the subjective
and representative qualities immanent in melodic or textural input in
white European twentieth-century music. It ignored the possibility of
doing anything progressive or forward-thinking with rhythm.
McLaughlin, on the other hand, has been innovative and rhythmically
inventive. He had derived much of his inspiration from rhythm, from his
use of the subtle blurring of the boundary between rhythm and melody in
the work of tabla players – and in his own interaction with drummers.
With Williams, Cobham, Walden, and had many critics bothered to
notice, with Shakti's tabla star Hussain, rhythm and melody were often
interchangeable. Ultimately, though, anyone with eyes and a brain could
comprehend, you couldn't dance to it, i.e., tumbril time for the white
guys with the fast fingers. But again, why?

A point always worth restating is the English terror of the exceptional.
The late-1970s anti-virtuosic agenda was dictated, particularly in Britain,
by quite extra-musical critical criteria; by a native fear and distrust not
only of the academic – which musical dexterity is associated – but also
by a far more deep-rooted antipathy to the grand, to the self-consciously
imposing. Britain, as the cultural critic Jonathan Meades has pointed out,
is a nation terrified of the grandiloquent, the technologically explicit. In
the case of antipathy to modernist architecture – as Meades' discourse
refers to – this is an antipathy based on intrusion into primary cultural
spheres, into the social environment at a very basic level of existence.
Understandable of course, but extending this fear into secondary cultural
spheres is inexcusable. The Mahavishnu Orchestra and many Progressive
artists nonetheless found themselves branded as inimical to a rockist
mythology of immediacy and youth, in which the form took shape not in
the recital room but upstairs above a pub and divorced all rock discourse
from representational, classically-derived discourse. That most
Progressive artists had bridged these two environments was overlooked
in the cultural rush to overwhelm a perceived distraction from rock fundamentalism.

In Britain, this, as Paul Schutze observes, threw the baby out with the
bathwater. While it dispensed with the more ludicrous whimsies and
affectations of Progressive rock, it also extinguished any attempt to render rock expression as spiritual or intellectual exercise. Anything disdain-
ing the 'won't/want' linguistic spur (to paraphrase Simon Frith) was of
no importance. It was never imagined that there was anything good about
Progressive rock or jazz-rock, but even Emerson Lake and Palmer, for
example, made some stunning music – but who could tell the good in

their repertoire from the appalling? The whole Progressive project was, in effect, musically cleansed from the landscape.

Rock fundamentalism, truth-to-feeling, reigned supreme. The wussy elements of 1960s progressives were swiftly silenced or driven underground. Lost with them was their belief that the European musical traditions of Romanticism and the avant-garde were as 'authentic' as the American traditions of blues, jazz and bluegrass. Anglophonic, largely American pop vernacular was what mattered now, and anyone who didn't echo the 'feelings' of this curious community of rock-weaned 'kids' was ultimately disposable.

By 1974, McLaughlin and his whole jazz-rock ilk were said to have exorcized 'feeling' from their performance. But how does one measure the 'heart' or the 'commitment' in a performance? Many classical conductors – notoriously, Herbert von Karajan – have been accused of removing any 'life' or 'spontaneity' from music-making. In the classical world, even peerless critics such as Norman Lebrecht tend to want it both ways – performances without a wrong note, yet without lapsing into 'cold' or 'mechanical' playing. But what was, and is, feeling? It's usually termed as 'commitment' or 'caring' for the music. But how can one prove, for instance, that punk rock, even in its early, unformed days in the garage culture of mid-60s America, embodied 'heart and soul'; likewise soul and r'n'b. How many musicians in these genres ever played *every note* as though their lives *really* depended on it? Almost none. The "heart" and the "soul" are cultural constructs, comparable to applying a spurious 'national characteristic' to a music. We can hear, in Roland Barthes' terms, a "grain" to a singing voice, which sets it apart as a vessel of emotion – for instance, compare Otis Redding to Jack Jones – but again, isn't this "grain" at least partly a cultural construct, similar to that which equates "virtuoso" playing with quality in European middle-class thought processes. How can one attribute immane qualities to music? How, for example, is Grieg's music Norwegian? "Grieg's music does not remind me of Norway," George Bernard Shaw once noted, "because I have never been there."

That must lead us elsewhere; we have revealed the cultural constructs we bring to music. Let us now investigate the cultural constructs the musicians bring to it.

The punk assumption in Britain – and the blues assumption in America – presupposed that excessive musical ability was somehow superfluous, that it didn't matter, that anyone who bothered with all that extraneous fluff had somehow lost the plot, that the heart had gone out of the playing. This is hardly surprising – listen to many live rock albums from the 1970s, particularly those of fundamentalist virtuosos like Emerson, Lake and Palmer. But listen, too, to many free jazz albums from 1960 onwards – to Archie Shepp, for example. To the initiated, are Shepp's interminable honks and squeals any less dull – or, for the culturally committed, any less 'real' – than Emerson tearing his Hammond organ to bits or Carl Palmer playing a bell with his teeth? Who cares more about what they are playing? Can we guess? Do we have the possible or potential motivations to guide our judgement?

The simple answer is no: Shepp's defenders would marshal ethnomusicological defence of the endless improvisation, with good reason. Similarly, Emerson and Palmer's cronies might – albeit with a little more strain – cite the European Romantic virtuoso tradition of Paganini and Lizst.

But neither are pure extensions of fact; neither are pure cultural expressions. Shepp is not a Yoruba priest; Emerson and Palmer are not classical whizz-kids in starched collars with a grounding in conservatories (Bernstein, on hearing Emerson run through his First Piano Concerto as a prelude to having the New York maestro conduct it, swept out of the studio after two minutes crying 'how can you be so crude?'). The musical expressions of both had been shaped in the 1960s through a fundamentally confessional cultural bent, in which subjectivity and expressivity was all. Shepp's music was probably the purer; he expended everything in trying to subvert the 'precision' of European classical execution, whilst Emerson and Palmer never skimped on emphasising how their music came from the 'heart', as all good pop music (and Romantic classical music, incidentally) aspires to. Both Shepp and Emerson might have emphasised the heart, but both played from the mind and memory first and from the heart second.

Musical virtuosity and extemporization thereby became difficult to call; it was hard to tell who was trying to say what and for what reason. But instead of simply buckling to postmodern relativism and saying *this is all equally valid whatever it is,* perhaps a better approach to musical virtuosity and harmonic exploration is to examine what role it fulfils in the performance of the music in which it takes place.

I am not entirely a cultural relativist. I believe the music made by the likes of McLaughlin and DiMeola infinitely more worthy of preservation and more in touch with the loftiest human aspirations than, say, the music of Sash! or B*Witched. Conversely, I believe the music of McLaughlin and DiMeola similarly subsidiary in the same hierarchical scheme to that of Beethoven or Wagner. In the overall Western scheme of things, relativism does not apply. But I believe that *within a given musical constituency,* terms of discrimination can be established. For instance, the conditions facing Beethoven and Wagner were similar, but were very *dissimilar* to the comparable conditions facing McLaughlin and B*Witched.

All forms have their paradigms. What distinguishes the Spice Girls from their innumerable contemporaries, for example, is the skill with which their songwriters choose their emotional syntax, in which harmonic devices as old as mass music itself are deployed resourcefully. The music may be pure cheese, but it can still be blended well and with imagination. Even the most minimal of minimalism, working in the right harmonic context, is able to apply almost unlimited permutations of unlimited compositional devices. All Pop music, and all its creatures, is a bourgeois commodity. End of story. Its ability to reshape itself within those terms and how that music is critically judged is important.

But what then, of McLaughlin? By what critical criteria can we judge him? Within what parameters? McLaughlin asks more questions than he gives answers. There are questions of rock, jazz, classic European and Northern and Southern Indian musics to be accounted for. And there are other levels of enquiry. For instance, the conflict between the schematic memory of notated music and folkloric memory of improvised music. Where does that stand us with McLaughlin's music?

On a more elevated plane, McLaughlin's music pits the irrational against the rational with almost sadistic glee. But at the same time, his musical thought processes occur simultaneously with two bourgeois notions of music-making, the irrational (the 'gift', handed down from the universal will or ether) and the rational (the work ethic). So how to explain, how to justify McLaughlin in a world culturally and politically unfriendly to his music? How to explain McLaughlin in a world whose critical faculties have lost the wherewithal to deal with him?

I'll repeat; McLaughlin (and his ilk) ask more questions than give answers, and he was one of the first to ask the questions. With McLaughlin, ditto Hendrix, writ larger; what was he trying to say? Could he know what he was trying to say? And did he care? How can we write about him?

For a start, let us scotch romantic myths about playing from the heart or in the cause of some greater power – even though McLaughlin himself might deem it as a deified 'Music'. Playing music requires intellectual decision-making which cannot be divorced from social and cultural realities. Neither, however, can it be divorced from intellectual decisions based on discrete and subjective interpretations of those realities. In McLaughlin's case, those realities are often socio-musical, and the results evident in his playing suggest that he is re-interpreting an extraordinarily varied musical experience through it.

McLaughlin, for this writer, is a musician who understands with uncanny ease the emotional syntax of every music he attempts to play across a wide cultural frame – like Hendrix. Moreover, he understands the way in which certain emotional syntaxes not only engage with native listeners but also how they cross cultures. Listening to his recordings of *The Inner Mounting Flame* or *Shakti,* for example, reveal to western ears a bewildering harmonic babel where the family of blues, jazz and rock not only meets European classical music but also Moorish and Indian classical music. The language is, however, primarily familiar to western ears – the work of an interpreter of flawless sensitivity. Note also that McLaughlin has never been tempted beyond the harmonic esperanto he perceives to exist within these apparently disparate elements. There has been no venture into East Asian, Eastern European, or Australasian musics, for example. Even the Hispanic echoes are strictly those of Moorish Spain, and by implication the near East. But for the time being McLaughlin has clearly established a harmonic empire and isn't afraid to use a phenomenal technique to get around that vast empire as fast as possible. Little wonder, for example, that Ravel, lover of European lushness, subcontinental pentatonics and jazz's rhythmic spurs, is one of McLaughlin's heroes.

In that respect, McLaughlin's formidable insistence on playing fast loses much of its reputation as playing fast for its own sake. His citation of Coltrane's penchant for billowing flurries of notes as justification, sounds just a tad disingenuous when McLaughlin was so well aware of the rewards awaiting the fastest axe hero of the 1970s. There's no doubt that McLaughlin simply loves to show what he can do – his stage career attests to that. But when listening to him play opposite, say, Carlos Santana, one realises just how careful he is to make as many notes as possible count in the musical context in which they are being played. On *Welcome,* in particular, Santana plays much the faster but provokes the mind and the heart far less.

That, I feel, is the heart of why McLaughlin is one of the greatest popular musicians. He can use one of the hoariest twentieth-century cultural cliches – the rock guitar solo – and bend it out of shape and then gloriously reform it. Only major guitar virtuosos – Derek Bailey, Sonny Sharrock – have done this, but only rarely in a tonal, accessible context, never in a context which remains rooted in the musical discourse from which it first arose. Also, no rock guitarist is able to stray quite so far from those rock/blues roots and sound convincing. McLaughlin is able to use it as a lightning rod for many different musical ideas from various cultures and is able to cannily lead fixed musical preconceptions into new avenues. Nobody – Beck, Clapton, not even Page, was able to emerge from Britain with such tirelessly exploratory credentials to go with their rabble-rousing speed of execution. As a polyglot of pop guitar, only Hendrix can match McLaughlin.

McLaughlin's tricks, at least those he employed once he was fully established as a solo artist, are well-known. They emphasise, primarily, the *sounds* of emotional tensions and releases upon consonant harmonies within the European tradition. However, the harmonic freedom of jazz, the rhythmic impulse of the blues and the melodic extemporization of Carnatic music are jostling for equal position immediately thereafter in the hierarchy. Yet his mixture of musical syntax is so accomplished, it is hard to decide who is best served by one particular climax – or perhaps, by extension, one note – of his solos. Everyone will be well-served who knows well the musical traditions in which he is working. To this end, listening to his work with Shakti is intensely instructive, for it places his choice of notes for electric guitar in quite another context. Often that choice is echoed in his subsequent acoustic guitar-based work, but once again sounds quite natural within its setting both as a contribution to a group endeavour and as a solo endeavour. He can thrill as a virtuoso, seemingly, in all these musical contexts. No matter in what genre he chooses, his soloing sounds natural, yet closer inspection, and biographical knowledge, reveals much more.

Significantly, much of his least rewarding music has come in situations whose cliches tend to overpower even the best efforts to deploy that polyglot approach – the European aspirations of Prog rock on *Apocalypse,* the pandering to ho-hum funk textures and rhythms on *Love Devotion Surrender* and *Inner Worlds* (and to a lesser extent on *Electric Dreams),* the enervating dash to renew fusion to Miles Davis' hesitant and crowd-friendly blueprint *(Adventures in Radioland)* and a too-affectionate *hommage* to the organ trio on *Live In Tokyo* and *After The Rain.*

To this end, he can be seen as globally manipulative by the weasel-worded and short-sighted. But his unerring ability to tap into the emotional well-springs not only of different musical genres but also of musical cultures makes his speed of execution less of a foreground attraction and more of a musical adjunct, something else he happens to do.

For this reason I believe he is a great musician. His virtuosity is dependent entirely on the thorough knowledge of that music's own syntax and emotional effect. Calculated? Any musician not clinically insane makes rational calculations about which notes to play. Commercially, in the 1970s, yes maybe. This was when McLaughlin was maybe naive enough to believe that the meliorism of the 1960s, mediated by Chinmoy's verses, would conquer. He calculated that the music on *Apocalypse* and *Visions Of The Emerald Beyond* – a similar synthesis of eastern and western idealism – would become the new world's soundtrack. But once that panacea fell apart in the 1970s and began to die horribly, McLaughlin just played on and got deeper into his musical quest, and it became evident that the man was for real.

No accident, surely, that some of his greatest music comes in his fallowest years, the early 1980s. If this was calculated music, it was paradoxically the calculation of a madman. Who, given the industry climate of the time, would have brought out *Belo Horizonte* or *Music Spoken Here?* The UK was in the grip of electronic pop and postpunk; the US had its own anodyne 'New Wave' explosion. It is musical performance calculated only on the premise that others share a similarly global musical outlook to his own obstinate cross-culturality. Had McLaughlin calculated, he would have become a doppelganger of Carlos Santana.

What distinguishes McLaughlin from his peers? He is better than some, the equal of others. But what, say, makes him different, or better, say, than Al DiMeola? If I proceed via the criterion of technical ability, any notion of hierarchy becomes difficult to establish. How is a guitarist of fabulous technical ability 'better' than another of equal technical ability? Does this reduce music once again to time-trialling? How does one 'grade' the quality of one composition or performance against another except via wholly irrational individual preference, or wholly rational technical criteria?

I would prefer to cite a musician who can imbue the mainstream of a culture's music with riches of which it was ignorant, and do so in style. The inestimable Chris Cutler quotes Schoenberg, Varese, Beefheart, Sun Ra, Mingus, Eisler and Coltrane as conduits to the world outside the mainstream. McLaughlin, as a prisoner of time and his society, used what he could from outside and what he could from inside that loop, but remained a mainstream musician in the terms of musical linguistics while transcending its bourgeois myopia to do so. That he did with such panache distinguishes him alongside other unhailed toilers in the crevices between musical genres (in pop, Beefheart, Zappa, Todd Rundgren,

Steely Dan, Prince; in jazz, Ellington, Coltrane, and Miles; in classical music, Ravel and Ives). This is not an attempt to compare like artist with like, save on the grounds of virtuoso genre-bending. But all of them belong together as maverick musical miscegenators who hit a critical *zeitgeist* at the right time and helped – sometimes posthumously – to immeasurably enrich the musical mainstream of the western culture in which they operated. Ravel and Ellington, sure enough, were cultural icons, but not for the random pollination of musics they encouraged, and this is my point here, and the point that justifies McLaughlin's endeavours.

McLaughlin's dignified residency within the mainstream, whilst continuing to pursue his own musical vision drawn from any number of elements from without that mainstream, is something surely that elevates him to the nobility of jazz, and maybe of twentieth century music. Jazz, after all, is perhaps the ultimate musical expression of the twentieth century. It explores musical cultures finding each other by serendipitous accident through the economic expediency of greater things.

McLaughlin may sometimes have used the vernacular of a workaday rock guitar soloist (yet few, save the ideologically-blinkered or supernally gifted, could support his critical status *as just another axe hero)* and as such a leading propagandist for one of the most pervasive of American cultural-imperialisms. But surely nobody has better traced the vocabulary of the rock guitar through its entire family tree – India, Spain, the delta, Chicago, Central Europe (by dint of Prog-rock bastardization). He has done so with such innate understanding of the emotional effects, not only of each music, but also of the potential effects each music could have on another culture.

McLaughlin is not coffee-table musical tourism. It doesn't demand mere window-shopping on other cultural musical devices – as, say, Martin Denny's mood music might use devices from Malaysia or Mexico as an adjunct. It presents an international hybrid which is all too often interpreted as a musical travelogue or the equivalent of a Miss Universe contestant complacently invoking world peace. True, it is more immediately accessible to a musical mind versed in western pop practises than one versed in Latin pop or African hi-life. Critics would call it an exotic soup which only the seasoned western musical tourist could understand – the equivalent of westernized food.

But McLaughlin *is* a product of western society, and can hardly be expected to produce authentically ethnic fare. The fact that he produces fare as wonderfully cross-ethnic as he does and with such panache ought to be enough to excuse him from all but the most excoriatingly liberal critic. How can anyone interested in esperanto start but from building on his own musical language? The fact that McLaughlin seems to have built a syntax for that esperanto before a recognisable vocabulary, is perhaps his greatest achievement.

Bibliography

Books etc.

Banks, Iain, *Espedair Street*, Abacus, London, 1992
Berendt, Joachim-Ernst, *The Jazz Book*, Paladin, London 1984
Carr, Ian, *Music Outside*, Latimer, London 1973
                Miles Davis: A Biography, Quartet, London 1982
                Keith Jarrett: The Man And His Music, Paladin, London 1992
Coryell, Julie and Friedman, Laura, *Jazz-Rock Fusion*, Marion Boyars, London, 1978
Davis, Miles with Troup, Quincy: *Miles: The Autobiography*, Simon and Schuster, New York, 1989
Feather, Leonard,   *The Encyclopaedia of Jazz in the Sixties*, Quartet, London 1982
                The Encyclopaedia of Jazz in the Seventies, Quartet, London 1982
Heckstall-Smith, Dick, *The Safest Place in the World*, Quartet, London 1989
Milkowski, Bill, *Jaco: The Extraordinary and Tragic Life of Jaco Pastorius*, Miller Freeman Books, San Francisco, 1995
Nicholson, Stuart: *Jazz-Rock: A History*, Canongate Press, Edinburgh, 1998
Redd, Adrienne, *EastJazz: Intricate Connections, Cultural Contradictions and Coming Home, The Influence of Indian Music in World Music Genres*, WorldWideWeb essay, 1997

Articles, Monographs

Aledort, Andy, 'Translating The Language Of The Spirit', *Guitar*, December 1987
Berg, Chuck, 'John McLaughlin, Evolution Of A Master', *Down Beat*, June 1978
Berendt, Joachim E.,   'John McLaughlin', *Jazz Forum* #71
                       'John McLaughlin's Jazz Odyssey', *Jazz Times*, May 1982
Blumenthal, Bob, 'McLaughlin's New Quintet Is Full Of Heat And Heart', *Boston Globe*, 25 November 1997
Bourne, Michael, 'The Magic of Mahavishnu', *Down Beat*, November 1972
Cariaga, Daniel, 'McLaughlin Concerto In Premiere', *Los Angeles Times*, 29 November 1985
Chappell, Jon, 'John McLaughlin: A Promise Delivered', *Guitar*, May 1996
Charlesworth, Chris, 'McLaughlin's Dream Comes True', *Melody Maker*, 15 June 1974
Ephland, John, 'A Lifetime Of Devotion', *Down Beat*, July 1994
Ferguson, Jim, 'John McLaughlin: From The Symphonic Stage To The Frontiers Of Technology', *Guitar Player*, November 1985
Fripp, Robert, 'John McLaughlin with Robert Fripp: Coffee And Chocolate For Two Guitars', *Musician* #41 (1982)
Gilbert, Mark, 'John McLaughlin', *Jazz Journal*, November 1996
Isaacs, James, liner notes, Tony Williams Lifetime, *Emergency*, Polydor Records 1991
Jerome, Jim, 'For A Song: McLaughlin Pulls the Plug on his Guitar, But He's As Electrifying As Ever', *People*, 21 June 1976
Jeske, Lee, 'Johnny McLaughlin, Acoustic Guitarist', *Down Beat*, April 1982
Kalbacher, Gene, 'Satori With Strings', *Hot House*, April 1992
Keepnews, Peter, 'John McLaughlin's Discipline: Ultimate Devotion To His Instrument', *Guitar World*, July 1981
Korall, Burt, 'Extending Beyond Mahavishnu', *Down Beat*, March 1973
Little, Charles, 'John McLaughlin and Pat Metheny, Guitar Synthesists, More or Less In The Jazz Tradition', *Jazziz*, May/June 1985
Mandel, Howard, 'John McLaughlin: Spirit Of The Sine Wave, *Down Beat*, March 1985
McLaughlin, John: liner notes, The Mediterranean Concerto (CD), CBS Records, 1990
                   'My Life and Guitar' (w. Rosen, Steve), *Guitar Player*, February 1975
Menn, Don and Stern, Chip, 'After Mahavishnu And Shakti, A Return To The Electric Guitar', *Guitar Player*, August 1978

Milkowski, Bill,   'Split Second Abilities and Disabilities', *Jazziz*, June/July 1990
'Past Present and Future', *Jazz Times*, August 1992
'Woodshedding With The Heavenly Timbres: Mahavishnu's Hot New Band Allows The Master To Rock Out On His Synclavier', *Guitar World*, March 1985
'After Mahavishnu And Shakti, A Return To The Electric Guitar', *Guitar Player*, August 1978
Nash, Jesse, 'Hopelessly In Love With The Guitar', *Jazz Times*, May 1990
Primack, Bret, 'A Conversation With Herbie Hancock And John McLaughlin', *Jazz Times* May 1996
Ross, Penelope, 'Love Devotion And Surrender, McLaughlin Tosses Santana To The Lord', *Circus*, August 1973
Rotondi, James, 'John McLaughlin: A Continuous Process of Discovery', *Guitar Player*, July 1992
Schaffer, Jim, 'Mahavishnu's Apocalypse', *Down Beat*, June 1974
Shulgold, Marc, 'McLaughlin Steps Into A New Arena', *Los Angeles Times*, 27 November 1985
Stephen, Bill, 'The Cultural Improvisation of John McLaughlin', *International Musician and Recording World*, March 1979
Stump, Paul, 'Muso In The Promised Land', *The Wire*, March 1996
Trigger, Vic, 'Mahavishnu John McLaughlin', *Guitar Player*, December 1972
Varga, George, 'Mahavishnu's McLaughlin: Obsessed With Musical Exploration', *San Diego Union-Tribune*, 27 September 1986
Wheeler, Tom, 'A Victory of The Acoustic Guitar', *Guitar Player*, March 1981
Woodward, Josef, 'John McLaughlin's Life In the Emerald Beyond: Guitar Great Seeks Clarity In Conception', *Musician*, March 1987
Zwerin, Mike, 'Monaco's Resident Prince of Fusion', *International Herald Tribune*, 30 May 1992
also, with no bye-line: 'What's In The Changer'? *Dallas Morning News*, 5 November, 1998, George Martin talks about his work on *Apocalypse*.

Radio broadcasts

Impressions, BBC Radio 3, November 1996. John McLaughlin interviewed by Brian Priestley. The Language Of The Spirit'

Discography

Author's note: the compilation of this discography has been extremely problematic. One of the joys of jazz is the spirit of flexibility, eclecticism and adventure of its practitioners. While making for some great music, it soon proves a headache for historians, cataloguers, anyone interested in charting the history of its musicians.

I am indebted almost wholly to the invaluable work of Johann Heidenbauer, author of the definitive McLaughlin discography [now posted on the Internet]. I have made the tiniest corrections and additions here and there, but these have been of an *extremely* minor nature. The main problem has been to revise Herr Heidenbauer's work into a form which best reflects the narrative of this book and its emphasis on divorcing McLaughlin's solo work from his collaborative work. Even here, of course, the discographer encounters difficulties, and rarely as much as in the case of a musician like McLaughlin, one of whose greatest assets is to work intuitively with others, and to create by the presence of others' creativity. Therefore, in the case of his work with Shakti and the DeLucia/ DiMeola/ McLaughlin trio, the borders between solo and collaboration are blurred almost to the point of invisibility. But to break the discography down into too many categories is to obscure the development of McLaughlin's recorded output. Therefore I have decided to render this discography in four sections; solo work in which McLaughlin is either the solo artist or is nominally the leader or co-leader of a collective act, including bootlegged recordings. Secondly, work in which he is billed solely as a sideman, including bootlegs; thirdly, recordings in which he features as solo artist, nominally featured artist or sideman which do not fall into the previous two categories; and finally, his production work.

John McLaughlin Solo

Including recordings by: John McLaughlin, Mahavishnu Orchestra, Shakti, McLaughlin/ DeLucia/ DiMeola

JOHN McLAUGHLIN - *EXTRAPOLATION*
Recorded Advision Studios, London, January 16, 1969
Marmalade Records 608007
John McLaughlin (electric guitars/ acoustic on "Peace Piece") Brian Odgers (bass) Tony Oxley (drums), John Surman (soprano and tenor sax).
Extrapolation/ It's Funny/Arjen's Bag/ Pete The Poet/ This Is For Us To Share/ Spectrum/ Binky's Beam/ Really You Know/ Two For Two/ Peace Piece

JOHN McLAUGHLIN - *DEVOTION*
Recorded Record Plant Studios, New York City, February 1970
John McLaughlin (guitar), Larry Young (organ, electric piano), Billy Rich (bass), Buddy Miles (drums, percussion), Ralph McDonald (conga on "Devotion").
Douglas 0004
Devotion/ Dragon Song/ Marbles/ Siren*/ Don't Let The Dragon Eat Your Mother/ Purpose Of When
Note: Douglas issued an edited version of "Siren" with "Marbles" on a French 7" single (Douglas 100011)

JOHN McLAUGHLIN - *MY GOAL'S BEYOND*
Recorded New York City, March 1971
Douglas Records 9
John McLaughlin (guitars), Dave Liebman (tenor, soprano saxes, flute), Jerry Goodman (violin), Charlie Haden (bass), Eve McLaughlin [alias Mahalakshmi] (tamboura), Billy Cobham (drums), Airto Moreira (percussion), Badal Roy (tabla).
Peace One/ Peace Two/ Goodbye Pork-Pie Hat/ Something Spiritual/ Hearts and Flowers/ Philip Lane/ Waltz For Bill Evans(*)/ Follow Your Heart/ Song for My Mother/ Blue In Green
Note On some re-issues (*) is titled "Song Of The Wind"

MAHAVISHNU ORCHESTRA - *THE INNER MOUNTING FLAME*
Recorded New York City, early August 1971
Columbia KC 31067
John McLaughlin (electric guitar), Jerry Goodman (violin, electric violin), Jan Hammer (electric piano), Rick Laird (bass guitar), Billy Cobham (drums)
Meeting Of The Spirits/ Dawn/ The Noonward Race/ A Lotus On Irish Streams/ Vital Transformations/ The Dance Of Maya/ You Know You Know/ Evolution

MAHAVISHNU ORCHESTRA - *BIRDS OF FIRE*
Recorded London & New York City, September & October 1972
Columbia KC 31996
John McLaughlin (electric guitar), Jerry Goodman (violin, electric violin), Jan Hammer (piano, electric piano, synthesiser), Rick Laird (electric bass), Billy Cobham (drums)
Birds of Fire/ Miles Beyond/ Celestial Terrestrial Commuters/ Sapphire Bullets of Pure Love/ Thousand Island Park/ Hope/ One Word/ Open Country Joy/ Sanctuary/ Resolution
Additional track: "Open Country Joy" (b) CBS 1664
(b) is an edited version of (a) issued on a 7" single together with "Celestial Terrestrial Commuters".

MAHAVISHNU ORCHESTRA - *LIVE BETWEEN NOTHINGNESS AND ETERNITY*
Recorded Central Park, New York City, August 17/18, 1973
Columbia KC 32766
John McLaughlin (electric guitar), Jerry Goodman (violin), Jan Hammer (electric piano, synthesiser), Rick Laird (electric bass), Billy Cobham (drums)
Trilogy (The Sunlit Path/La Mere de La Mer/Tomorrow's Story Not The Same)/ Sister Andrea/ Dream

MAHAVISHNU ORCHESTRA – *APOCALYPSE*
Recorded AIR Studios, London, March 1974
Columbia KC 32957
John McLaughlin (guitars), Jean-Luc Ponty (electric violin), Gayle Moran (keyboards, lead vocals), Ralphe Armstrong (electric and acoustic bass, vocals), Michael Walden (drums, percussion, vocals), Carol Shive (violin, vocals), Marsha Westbrook (viola), Philip Hirschi (cello, vocals), Michael Gibbs (arrangements)/The London Symphony Orchestra; Michael Tilson Thomas (conductor, piano-1)
Power Of Love/ Vision Is A Naked Sword (-1)/ Smile Of The Beyond/ Wings Of Karma/ Hymn To Him

MAHAVISHNU ORCHESTRA - *VISIONS OF THE EMERALD BEYOND*
Recorded New York City, December 4 to 14, 1974
Columbia PC 33411
John McLaughlin (12-string guitar, guitar, vocal), Bob Knapp (trumpet, flugelhorn, flute, vocals), Russel Tubbs (soprano, alto saxes), Jean-Luc Ponty (electric violin, Barytone-Violectra), Gayle Moran (keyboards, lead vocals), Ralphe Armstrong (electric and acoustic basses, vocal), Michael Walden (drums, percussion, vocals), Steven Kindler (violin), Carol Shive (violin, vocals), Carol Shive (violin, vocals), Philip Hirschi (cello)
Eternity's Breath (Parts 1 And 2)/ Lila's Dance/ Can't Stand Your Funk (a)/ Pastoral/ Faith/ Cosmic Strut/ If I Could See/ Be Happy/ Earth Ship/ Pegasus/ Opus One/ On The Way Home To Earth
Additional track; "Can't Stand Your Funk" (b) CBS 3007
Note (b) is an edited version of (a) issued on a 7" single together with "Eternity's Breath (part 1)".

SHAKTI - *SHAKTI WITH JOHN McLAUGHLIN*
Recorded South Hampton College, Long Island, NY, July 5, 1975
Columbia PC34162
Lakshminarayana Shankar (violin), John McLaughlin (acoustic guitar), Ramnad V Raghavan (mridangam), T H Vinayakaram (ghatam, mridangam), Zakir Hussain (tabla).
Joy/ Lotus Feet/ What Need Have I For This – What Need Have I For That – I Am Dancing At The Feet Of My Lord – All Is Bliss – All Is Bliss

MAHAVISHNU ORCHESTRA - *INNER WORLDS*
Recorded Chateau d'Herouville July and August 1975
Columbia PC33908
John McLaughlin (guitar, guitar synthesisers), Stu Goldberg (keyboards, vocals), Ralphe Armstrong (bass, vocals), Michael Walden (drums, piano, organ, percussion, vocals)
All In The Family/ Miles Out/ In My Life/ Gita/ River Of My Heart/ Morning Calls/ The Way Of The Pilgrim/ Lotus Feet/ Planetary Citizen/ Inner Worlds (Parts 1 And 2)

SHAKTI WITH JOHN McLAUGHLIN - *A HANDFUL OF BEAUTY*
Recorded London, August 1976
Columbia PC 34372
Lakshminarayana Shankar (violin), John McLaughlin (acoustic guitar), T. H. Vinayakaram (ghatam, mridangam), Zakir Hussain (tabla)
La Danse Du Bonheur/ Lady L/ India/ Kriti/ Isis/ Two Sisters

SHAKTI WITH JOHN McLAUGHLIN - *NATURAL ELEMENTS*
Recorded Geneva, Switzerland, July 1977
Columbia JC 34980
Lakshminarayana Shankar (violin, viola, vocals), John McLaughlin (acoustic guitar, vocal), T.H. Vinayakaram (percussion, vocals), Zakir Hussain (percussion, vocals)
Mind Ecology/ Face To Face/ Come On Baby Dance With Me/ The Daffodil And The Eagle/ Happiness Is Being Together/ Bridge Of Sighs/ Get Down And Sruti/ Peace Of Mind

JOHN McLAUGHLIN - *ELECTRIC GUITARIST*
Recorded North Hollywood, California, January 16 (6), January 18 (2), January 20 (1) 1978 and New York City, January 26 (5), January 28 (7), January 30 (3), February 2 (4) 1978
Columbia JC 35326

John McLaughlin (electric guitar), Stanley Clarke (acoustic bass), Chick Corea (electric piano, mini Moog (-1), Jack de Johnette (drums -1), Jack Bruce (bass, -2), Tony Williams (drums -2), Billy Cobham (drums -3, -5), Stu Goldberg (keyboards -5), Fernando Saunders (electric bass -5), Jerry Goodman (violin -5), Tom Coster (organ -6), Carlos Santana (electric guitar -6), Neil Jason (electric bass -6), Michael Walden (drums -6), Alyrio Lima (percussion -6), Armando Peraza (conga -6), David Sanborn (alto sax -7), Alphonso Johnson (electric bass -7), Anthony Allen Smith (drums -7), Patrice Rushen (keyboards -7)

Do You Hear The Voices That You Left Behind/ Are You The One? Are You The One?/ Phenomenon- Compulsion/ My Foolish Heart/ New York On My Mind/ Friendship/ Every Tear From Every Eye

JOHN McLAUGHLIN WITH THE ONE TRUTH BAND - *ELECTRIC DREAMS*

Recorded Soundmixers Studio, New York City, November & December 1978 Columbia JC35785

John McLaughlin (6, 12 and 13-string acoustic guitars, 6 and 12-string electric guitars, banjo, vocals -5), Lakshminarayana Shankar (violin), Stu Goldberg (keyboards), Fernando Saunders (bass guitar, vocals -4,-5), Anthony Allen Smith (drums, vocals -4), Alyrio Lima (percussion)

Guardian Angels/ Miles Davis/ Electric Dreams, Electric Sighs/ Desire And The Comforter (-4)/ Love And Understanding/ Singing Earth/ The Dark Prince/ The Unknown Dissident

AL DiMEOLA / JOHN McLAUGHLIN / PACO DE LUCIA - *FRIDAY NIGHT IN SAN FRANCISCO*

Recorded Warfield Theatre, San Francisco, December 5 1980
Columbia FC 37152

Al DiMeola (1, 2, 4, 5), John McLaughlin (2-5), Paco De Lucia (1,3-5) (acoustic guitars)
Mediterranean Sundance - Rio Ancho/ Short Tales Of The Black Forest/ Frevo Rasgado/ Fantasia Suite/ Guardian Angel
Additional Tracks; Tres Hermanos/ Morning Of The Carnival/ Spain/ Meeting Of The Spirits/ Splendido Sundance/ My Foolish Heart (not released)

JOHN McLAUGHLIN - *BELO HORIZONTE*

Recorded Ramses Studio, Paris, June-July 1981
Warner Brothers B5K3619

John McLaughlin (acoustic guitar), Francois Jeanneau (tenor sax -4, soprano sax -5), Augustin Dumay (violin-6), Katia Labeque (piano, Prophet 5 synthesiser, Synclavier), Francois Couturier (electric piano, Prophet 5 synthesiser), Jean-Paul Celea (bass), Tommy Campbell (drums), Jean-Pierre Drouet, Steve Shohan (percussion), Paco de Lucia (acoustic guitar-8)

Belo Horizonte/ La Baleine/ Very Early (Homage To Bill Evans)/ One Melody/ Stardust On Your Sleeve/ Waltz For Katia/ Zamfir/ Manitas D'Oro (for Paco de Lucia)

JOHN McLAUGHLIN - *MUSIC SPOKEN HERE*

Recorded Ramses Studio, Paris, June-July 1982
WEA 23723-1

John McLaughlin (electric guitar, acoustic guitar)/ Katia Labeque (piano, synthesisers)/ Francois Couturier (electric piano, synthesisers) Jean-Paul Celea (basses) Tommy Campbell (drums)

Aspan/ Blues for LW/ The Translators/ Honky Tonk Haven/ Viene Clareando/ David/ Negative Ions/ Brise de Coeur/ Loro

JOHN McLAUGHLIN / AL DiMEOLA / PACO DE LUCIA - *PASSION, GRACE AND FIRE*

Recorded London September and October 1982, New York City November and December 1983
Columbia FC 38645

Al DiMeola, John McLaughlin, Paco De Lucia (acoustic guitars)
Aspan/ Orient Blue Suite*/ Chiquito/ Sichia/ David/ Passion Grace and Fire
* titled "Orient Blue" on some European issues

JOHN McLAUGHLIN & MAHAVISHNU - *MAHAVISHNU*

Recorded Paris, April, May 1984

Warner Bros 25190-1
John McLaughlin (guitar, Synclavier II digital guitar)/ Bill Evans (tenor and soprano sax, flute)
Mitchell Forman (Fender Rhodes, synthesiser, acoustic piano)/ Jonas Hellborg (fretless bass,
bass guitar)/ Billy Cobham (drums, percussion)/ Danny Gottlieb (percussion)/ Katia Labeque
(Synclavier II synthesiser, acoustic piano -1)/ Hariprasad Chaurasia (flute on -1), Zakir
Hussain (tablas, -1)
Radio Activity/ Nostalgia/ Nightriders/ East Side West Side/ Clarendon Hills/ Jazz/ The
Unbeliever/ Pacific Express/ When Blue Turns Gold

JOHN McLAUGHLIN & MAHAVISHNU - *ADVENTURES IN RADIOLAND*
Recorded Milan, Italy, January and February 1986 [Relativity Records 88561-8081-1]
John McLaughlin (Gibson Les Paul Special, Mike Pedulla guitar/ interface with Synclavier
digital guitar), Abraham Wechter acoustic guitar/ Bill Evans (tenor and soprano saxes, flute,
keyboards ("Half Man Half Cookie"))/ Mitchell Forman (keyboards)/ Jonas Hellborg (Wal double neck electric bass guitar)/ Danny Gottlieb (Premier drums and Paiste cymbals, Ludwig
drums, Simmons 5D57 drums, Sycologic PSP Drum Interface)/ Max Costa (computer pro-
gramming and drum sequences)
The Wait/ Just Ideas/ Jozy/ Half Man Half Cookie/ Florianapolis/ Gotta Dance/ The Wall Will
Fall/ Reincarnation/ Mitch Match/ 20th Century Limited

JOHN McLAUGHLIN -*THE MEDITERRANEAN CONCERTO*
Recorded CTS Studios, Middlesex, England, September 1988 (concerto); Ramses Studio
Paris,
November 1988 (duets)
John McLaughlin (acoustic guitar)/ London Symphony Orchestra; Michael Tilson Thomas
(conductor)/ Katia Labeque (piano ("Duets" only)
Concerto for guitar and Orchestra "The Mediterranean" (arranged. Michael Gibbs); i)
Rhythmic; ii) Slow and Sad; iii) Animato)/ Brise de Coeur/ Montana/ Two Sisters/ Until Such
Time/ Zakir

JOHN McLAUGHLIN TRIO - *LIVE AT THE ROYAL FESTIVAL HALL*
Recorded Royal Festival Hall London, November 27 1989 [JMT 834 436-2]
John McLaughlin (acoustic guitar, Photon guitar synthesiser)/ Kai Eckhardt-Karpeh (electric
bass)/ Trilok Gurtu (percussion)
Blue In Green/ Just Ideas/ Jozy/ Florianapolis/ Blues for LW*/ Pasha's Love/ Mother Tongues
*Omitted from LP and cassette release

JOHN McLAUGHLIN TRIO - *QUE ALEGRIA*
Recorded Ludwigsburg, Germany, November 29-December 3,1991
Verve 837280-2
John McLaughlin (acoustic guitar, Photon guitar-synthesiser)/ Dominique Di Piazza (electric
bass)/ Trilok Gurtu (percussion)
Belo Horizonte/ Baba (for Ramana Maharshi)/ Marie/ Hijacked/ Milarepa/ Que Alegria/ Three
Willows/ One Nite Stand/ Reincarnation

JOHN McLAUGHLIN - *TIME REMEMBERED*
Recorded Milan, Italy, March 25-30,1993
Verve 519861-2
John McLaughlin (acoustic guitar)/Yan Maresz (acoustic bass guitar)/ The Aighetta Quartet:
Francois Szony, Pascal Rabatti, Alexandre Del Fa, Philippe Loli (acoustic guitars)
Prologue/ Very Early/ Waltz For Debby/ Hommage/ My Bells/ Time Remembered/ Song For
Helen/ Turn Out The Stars/ We Will Meet Again/ Epilogue

THE FREE SPIRITS FEATURING JOHN McLAUGHLIN - *TOKYO LIVE*
Recorded Blue Note Club, Tokyo, Japan, December 16-18 1993
Verve 521870-2
John McLaughlin (electric guitar)/ Joey de Francesco (organ, trumpet)/ Dennis Chambers
(drums)
One Nite Stand/ Hijacked/ When Love Is Far Away/ Little Miss Valley/ Juju At The
Crossroads/ Vukovar/ No Blues/ Mattinale

JOHN McLAUGHLIN - *AFTER THE RAIN*
Recorded Clinton Studios, New York City, October 4, 5,1994
Verve 527 467-2
John McLaughlin (electric guitar)/ Joey de Francesco (organ)/ Elvin Jones (drums)
Take The Coltrane/ My Favourite Things/ Sing Me Softly Of The Blues/ Encuentros/ Naima/
Tones For Elvin Jones/ Crescent/ Afro Blue/ After The Rain

JOHN McLAUGHLIN - *THE PROMISE*
Recorded at Wessex Recording Studio, London (1), Blue Note Club, Tokyo (2), Studio
Ygmas, Monaco (3,11), Tribe Studio, Milan and Sumit Bernet Studio, Dallas, Texas (4),
Studio Ferber, Paris (5), Clinton Studios, New York City (6,10), Mill House Studios, Wiltshire,
England (8), Tribe Studio, Milan, Italy (9), all 1995
Verve
John McLaughlin (electric and acoustic guitars, keyboards (3,4), Midi guitar (9), Birdsong (9))/
Tony Hymas (keyboards, 1), Jeff Beck (electric guitar, 1), Pino Palladino (bass guitar 1),
Marc Mondesir (drums, 1), Joey de Francesco (Hammond B3 organ 2, trumpet 4), Dennis
Chambers (drums 2,6,10), Paco De Lucia (acoustic guitar 5), Al DiMeola (acoustic guitar 5),
Michael Brecker (tenor saxophone 6), James Genus (bass guitar 6), Jim Beard (keyboards
6), Don Alias (percussion 6), Zakir Hussain (tabla 7), Nishat Khan (sitar 7), Trilok Gurtu (per-
cussion 7), Sting (bass guitar 8), Vinnie Colaiuta (drums 8), Toto (birdsong 9), Susana
Beatrix (voice, birdsong 9), David Sanborn (alto saxophone 10), Philippe Loli (acoustic guitar
11), Yann Maresz (acoustic bass guitar 11)
Django/ Thelonius Melodius/ Amy And Joseph/ No Return/ El Ciego/ Jazz Jungle/ The Wish/
English Jam/ Tokyo Decadence/ Sin Jin Rui/ The Peacocks
Note: The voices of Stephania Bimbi, Nishat Khan, Susana Beatrix and Mariko Takahasi can
also be heard between tracks on this album

JOHN McLAUGHLIN AND TRILOK GURTU - *MOLOM (OST)*
Recorded Ramses Studio, Paris, February 1994
Verve 529 034-2
John McLaughlin (guitar synthesiser, acoustic guitar) Trilok Gurtu (percussion)
Um Mani Padme Hum*/ Molom Theme Song 1/ The Boy's Theme 1/ Breakfast - The Cave/
The Four Seasons (*)/Horses/ Boudamchou (*)/ Little Girl's Theme 1/ Cows In The Water/
The Man Hunts/ The Camel Walk*/ Hunting- The Witch/ The Boy Walks/ Melody */ The
Dream Of The Boy/ The Boy Cries/ Traditional Song */ Introduction Of The Boy To The Monk/
The Little Girl Says Goodbye To The Boy/ The Boy Leaves/ National Song*/ Molom Theme
Song End
Notes: Soundtrack to the film "Molom, A Legend Of Mongolia" directed by Marie Jaoul de
Poncheville. The tracks marked with an asterisk (*) are traditional Mongolian songs not per-
formed by John McLaughlin and Trilok Gurtu

PACO DE LUCIA / AL DiMEOLA / JOHN McLAUGHLIN - *THE GUITAR TRIO*
Recorded Real World Studios, Bath, England, May-July 1996
Verve 533215-2
Paco De Lucia, Al DiMeola, John McLaughlin (acoustic guitars)
La Estiba/ Beyond The Mirage/ Midsummer Night/ Manha de Carnival/ Letter From India/
Espiritu/ La Monastere Dans les Montagnes/ Azzura/

BOOTLEGS, OTHER RECORDINGS

MAHAVISHNU ORCHESTRA - *ONE WORLD*
Recorded Hunter College, New York City, May 15,1972
Cuttlefish CFR 006 (bootleg)
line-up: as *The Inner Mounting Flame*
[Symphony Hall, Boston, January 26, 1972]
Celestial Terrestrial Commuters/ The Noonward Race/ Meeting Of The Spirits/ You Know
You Know/ The Dance of Maya/ Sanctuary/ The Noonward Race
Additional tracks "One Word - Resolution" (unissued)

MAHAVISHNU ORCHESTRA - *THE INNER FLAMMING AXE*
Recorded Syracuse University, Syracuse, NY, April 29 1972 [All of Us 27 (bootleg)]
line-up as *The Inner Mounting Flame*
Meeting Of The Spirits/ You Know You Know/ The Dance of Maya/ One Word- Resolution*/
Dawn/ The Noonward Race/ A Lotus On Irish Streams * cover says "Awakening"

MAHAVISHNU ORCHESTRA - *DANCE OF THE MAYA*
Recorded unknown venue, USA, early May 1972
Phonygraf TPGRL 1112 (bootleg)
line-up as *The Inner Mounting Flame*
The Dance Of Maya/ Meeting Of The Spirits/ You Know You Know
Note: Also issued as *In Hommage Of The Bird God* (HHCER 112) and as *Live* (CD; OH BOY
1-9014).

MAHAVISHNU ORCHESTRA - *LIVE, KING OF GUITARS*
Recorded Kongress Saal, Munich, August 17,1972
Atmosphere S03478 (bootleg)
line-up: as *The Inner Mounting Flame*
Meeting Of The Spirits/ You Know You Know/ The Dance Of Maya/ A Lotus On Irish
Streams/ Binky's Dream
Additional tracks; One Word / Resolution (unissued)
Note: Identical to the bootlegs *Birds Of Pray* (Aftermath 15) and *Bundled Sunspray Demise*
CTAKRL 1923).

SHAKTI WITH JOHN McLAUGHLIN - *IN CONCERT 153*
Recorded - Golders Green Hippodrome, London, May 12, 1977
BBC Transcription Services
Lakshminarayana Shankar (violin), John McLaughlin (acoustic guitars), T H Vinayakaram
(ghatam, mridangam), Zakir Hussain (tabla), Eileen, Monique (sruthibox)
La Danse Du Bonheuri/ India/ What Need Have I For This - What Need Have I For That - I
Am Dancing At The Feet Of My Lord - All Is Bliss - All Is Bliss
Note: First broadcast on BBC Radio 1, May 28,1977.

JOHN McLAUGHLIN/ AL DIMEOLA/ PACO DE LUCIA
Recorded Rome, Italy, June 16 1983
All Of Us AS 18/2 (bootleg)
line-up. as *Friday Night In San Francisco*
Spain/ David/ Passion Grace and Fire/ Mediterranean Sundance/ Scenario/ Chiquito/ Sichia/
Guardian Angel/ Orlent Blue Suite
Note; this is a 2-CD set.

JOHN McLAUGHLIN TRIO - *LIVE AT THE FIESTA INTERNATIONAL '90*
Recorded Paernu, Estonia, June 18 1990
Line-up: as *Live at the Royal Festival*
No track details
Note: This is a cassette allegedly authorised by John McLaughlin for distribution in Estonia
only.

JOHN McLAUGHLIN TRIO - *LIVE IN EUROPE 1991*
Recorded unknown venue, Europe, 1991
All of Us ASOS (bootleg)
Line-up: as *Que Alegria*
One Nite Stand/ Baba (for Ramana Maharshi)/ Florianopolis/ Three Willows/ Belo Horizonte/
Jozy/ Are You The One?

* MILES DAVIS - *HILL AUDITORIUM 2/21/'70*
Hill Auditorium, Ann Arbor, USA, February 21,1970-
Miles Davis (trumpet), Wayne Shorter (soprano), Chick Corea (electric piano), John
McLaughlin (guitar), Dave Holland (electric bass), Jack DeJohnette (drums), Airto Moreira
(percussion)
It's About That Time/I fall In Love Too Easily/ Sanctuary/ Bitches Brew

JM-008 Masqualero
Note: This is a Japanese bootleg CD
*MILES DAVIS - LENNIES ON THE TURNPIKE BOSTON '71
Jazz Masters
Miles Davis (trumpet), Gary Bartz (soprano, alto saxes), Keith Jarrett (piano, electric piano),
John McLaughlin (guitar)?, Michael Henderson (electric bass), Jack DeJohnette (drums),
Airto Moreira (percussion)
Inamorata/ Funky Tonk/ What I Say/ Inamorata (reprise)
*Note: Though McLaughlin's participation in this session is claimed on the cover of this boot-
leg CD, no guitar is audible on the recordings. McLaughlin is also not implicated in the other
CD of this 2-CD set.*

COLLABORATIONS/SESSIONS
DUFFY POWER WITH THE GRAHAM BOND QUARTET
Recorded London, March 1963
Parlophone R5024 (45rpm single)
Featured musicians: Duffy Power (vocals), Graham Bond (organ), Big Jim Sullivan (guitar-1),
John McLaughlin (guitar-2), Jack Bruce (bass), Peter 'Ginger' Baker (drums)
I Saw Her Standing There/ Farewell Baby

GRAHAM BOND - *SOLID BOND*
Graham Bond (alto sax), John McLaughlin (guitar), Jack Bruce (bass), Ginger Baker (drums)
Recorded: Klook's Kleek Club, London, June 26, 1963
Warner Brothers WS 3001 (2LP)
The Grass Is Greener/Doxy/Ho Ho Country Kicking Blues
Note: McLaughlin is not implicated in the other tracks on this 2-LP set.

GRAHAM BOND - *RARITIES*
Duffy Power (vocals-1), Graham Bond (organ), John McLaughlin (guitar), Jack Bruce (bass),
Ginger Baker (drums)
Radio show: *Pop Goes The Beatles*
Recorded: London July 1963
GB 1 -19-94
I Got A Woman (-1)/ Cabbage Greens/ I Saw Her Standing There (-1)/ Spanish Blues
Note: McLaughlin is not implicated in the other tracks on this CD. This is a private pressing
from Norway, 1994.

TONY MEEHAN
Tony Meehan (drums, vocals, guitar), Glenn Hughes (alto, baritone, soprano saxes), Chris
Hughes (soprano, tenor saxes, clarinet, percussion), Joe Moretti (lead guitar), John
McLaughlin (rhythm guitar), John Baldwin (aka John Paul Jones) (bass guitar); unidentified
strings
Recorded: London, December 1963
Decca F. 11801 (45rpm single)
Song Of Mexico/ King Of All

ROLLING STONES - *METAMORPHOSIS*
Mick Jagger (vocals), Arthur Greenslade (percussion), Keith Richard, Brian Jones (vocals,
guitar), Joe Moretti, John McLaughlin (guitar), Jimmy Page (guitar, bass guitar), Bill Wyman,
John Paul Jones (bass guitar), Charlie Watts (drums), Glyn Jones (percussion), Mssrs.
Leander and Whittaker (backing vocals).
Recorded: London, July 1964 Decca SKL 5212
Heart Of Stone/ Some Things Just Stick In Your Mind/ (Walkin' Thru The) Sleepy City
Notes: Details about this session are lacking. Thus the given personnel are not complete and
not all listed musicians are presumably featured on these recordings. McLaughlin is not impli-
cated in the other tracks on this LP. These demo tracks differ from commonly known versions
of some of the songs.

LONDON ALL STARS - *BRITISH PERCUSSION*
Stan Roderick, Ray Davis, Bert Ezard, Albert Hall (trumpet) Keith Christie, Gib Wallace,

Johnnie Edwards (trombone), Jack Thurwell (bass trombone), Roy Willox (alto sax), Don Honeywell (baritone sax), Keith Bird, Rex Morris, Bill Skeat (sax), Jim Buck Sr., Jim Buck Jr.(frn), Kenny Salmon (organ), Arthur Greenslade (piano), Jimmy Page (lead guitar), John McLaughlin (rhythm guitar), Alan Weighall (bass guitar), Arthur Watts (bass), Ronnie Verrall, Andy White (drums), Eric Allan, Barry Morgan (percussion).
Recorded: Pye Studios, London, February 23,1965
Barclay BB86
Stop The Drums/ Mexican Shuffle/ Coming Home Babe/ Drum Stomp/ Watermelon Man/ More/ Beefeater/ Image/ Night Train/ Spanish Armada/ Lord Byron Blues/ Salvation

THE NIGHT-TIMERS FEATURING HERBIE GOINS
Hubert 'Herbie' Goins (vocals), Mike Eve (tenor sax), Harry Beckett (trumpet, flugelhorn), Steve Morse (organ), John McLaughlin (guitar), Dave Price (bass), Bill Stevens (drums).
Recorded: London, October1965
Parlophone R5355 (45rpm single)
The Music Played On/ Yield Not To Temptation

DUFFY POWER - *INNOVATIONS*
Duffy Power (vocals), John McLaughlin (guitar), Jack Bruce (bass-1), Phil Seaman (drums-1), Nick Blythe (congas-1)
Recorded: London, Autumn 1965
Transatlantic TRA229
God Bless The Child/ Rosie (-1) (see also below)

DUFFY POWER - *JUST STAY BLUE*
Duffy Power (vocals), John McLaughlin (guitar), Jack Bruce (bass), Phil Seaman (drums).
Recorded: London, Autumn 1965-RMB Retro 802
Dollar Mamie
See also below

HOWARD BLAKE - *THAT HAMMOND SOUND*
Howard Blake (organ, percussion, vibraphone, xylophone, marimba, celeste), John McLaughlin (guitar), Russ Stapleford (bass), Dick Harward (drums), Ron Seabrook (bass*).
Recorded: London, 1966
Columbia TWO 192
Meditation/ Bluesette/ Moon River/ More/ Till There Was You/ Alfie (HB only)/ Perdido/ Recada/ Oasis*/ Gypsy In My Soul*/ Scorpio* (last three tracks Stapleford out)

DUFFY POWER - *INNOVATIONS*
Duffy Power (vocals, harmonica), John McLaughlin (guitar), Danny Thompson (bass), Red Reece (drums), Terry Cox (drums)
Recorded: London, February 1966, November 1966
Transatlantic TRA229
Mary Open The Door/ It's A Boy Blue*/There You Go/ Red White and Blue (last two tracks Reece out)
* also available on Decca 457.142 M, a French EP. RMB Retro 802
Little Boy Blue (-1)/ Little Girl/ Mary Open The Door*/Hound Dog (-1)*/ Hound Dog (alternate take) (-1)/ Rags and Old Iron**/ Just Stay Blue
Note: - available also on Decca F.22547 a 45 mm single, Decca 457.142M, the latter a French EP. These are available on "THE BRITISH R'n'B EXPLOSION Volume 1 '62-'68" (See For Miles - See CD 224).
McLaughlin is not implicated on the other tracks on this LP

HERBIE GOINS & THE NIGHT-TIMERS
Herbie Goins (vocals), Mike Eve (tenor sax), Harry Beckett (trumpet, flugelhorn), Mike Carr (organ), John McLaughlin (guitar), Dave Price (bass), Bill Stevens (drums)
Recorded London, July 1966
Parlophone R 5478 (45 mm single)
No.1 In Your Heart/ Cruisin'

TWICE AS MUCH - *OWN UP*
David Skinner (vocals, piano), Andrew Rose (vocals), Arthur Greenslade, Nicky Hopkins (piano) John McLaughlin, Joe Moretti, Jimmy Page, Jim Sullivan (guitars), Alan Weighall (bass), Andy White, Eric Ford (drums), Red Weller, Alan Hakin, Eric Allen (percussion); unidentified strings and wind.
Recorded: London, July 1966
Immediate IMSP 007
I Have A Love/ Help/Is This What I Get For Loving You Baby?/ Night Time Girl/ Life Is But Nothing/ The Spinning Wheel/ Happy Times/ Sha La La La Lee/ We Can Work It Out/ As Tears Go By/The Time Is Right' The Summer's Ending/Play With Fire/ Why Can't They All Go And Leave Me Alone?

TWICE AS MUCH - *THAT'S ALL*
David Skinner (vocals, piano) Stephen Rose (vocals) Arthur Greenslade (md), Nicky Hopkins (piano), John McLaughlin, Joe Moretti, Jimmy Page, Jim Sullivan, Eric Ford (guitars), Alan Weighall (bass), Andy White (drums), Vashti Bunyan (vocals-1).
Recorded; London, 1966-1967
Immediate 1M033, Immediate IMCPO13
Sittin' On A Fence/ Hey Girl/ Listen/ You're So Good For Me/ Green Circles/ Life Is But Nothing/ Do You Wanna Dance/ True Story/ Simplified*/ Step Out Of Line*/ You'll Never Get To Heaven/ Crystal Ball**/ Coldest Night of the Year (-1)
Released as A and B side of 45rpm single, Immediate IM 036
**Released as A side of 45 rpm single, Immediate IM 042-

DUFFY'S NUCLEUS – "JUST STAY BLUE"
Duffy Power (vocals; harmonica-1), John McLaughlin (guitar), Jack Bruce (bass), Ginger Baker (drums, not **), Terry Cox (drums, only)/ Mike Carr (organ only), Binky Mackenzie (bass*** only)/ unidentified drummer/ unidentified horn section
Recorded: London, mid 1966, mid-November 1966, early 1967 at Abbey Road Studios, London, October 13,1967?
Parlophone R5631 (45 rpm single)
Davy O'Brien (Leave That Baby Alone)/ July Tree

HERBIE GOINS & THE NIGHTIMERS - *NO.1 IN YOUR HEART*
Herbie Goins (vocals), Mike Eve (tenor sax), Harry Beckett (trumpet, flugelhorn), Mike Carr (organ), John McLaughlin (guitar), Dave Price (bass), Bill Stevens (drums)
Recorded London, 1966/67; July 1967?
Parlophone PMC 7026
Outside Of heaven/ Looking At Granny Run Run/ I Don't Mind/ Pucker Up Buttercup/ No.1 In Your Heart/ Cruisin'/ I (I Can't Get No) Satisfaction /Good Good Lovin'/ Knock On Wood/ Thirty Six - Twenty Two - Thirty Six/ Turn On Your Love Light/Coming Home To You/ The Incredible Miss Brown Additional: Coming Home To You (live edit)
Note: McLaughlin left The Nightimers in mid-1966. Though this LP was issued about one year later he is possibly featured on some of these tracks. 'Coming Home To You' was released on Parlophone R 5533 as a 7" single issued in November 1966. 'Coming Home To You (live edit)' was released on a compilation LP titled "SIGHTS & SOUNDS OF LONDON" (Columbia 5AX9001) released in 1966. All tracks are also available on the CD release HERBIE GOINS & THE NIGHT-TIMERS "SOULTIME!" on See For Miles Records SEECD 362.

GEORGIE FAME
Georgie Fame (vocals, organ), Eddie Thornton (trumpet), Johnny Marshall (baritone), Lyn Dobson (tenor sax), Derek Wandsworth (trombone), John McLaughlin (guitar), Ricky Brown (bass), Hughie Flint (drums), Jimmy Scott (congas)
Recorded London March 1967
CBS 202587 (45rpm single)
Because I Love You/ Bidin' My Time

GEORGIE FAME - *KNOCK ON WOOD*
Georgie Fame (vocals organ), Eddie Thornton (trumpet), Johnny Marshall (baritone sax), Lyn Dobson (tenor sax), Derek Wandsworth (trombone), John McLaughlin (guitar), Ricky Brown

(bass), Hughie Flint (drums), Jimmy Scott (congas)
Recorded: London March 1967
CBS 2781, CBS EP 6363
Knock On Wood/ All I'm Asking/ Didn't Want To Have To Do It/ Close the Door/Road Runner
Note: CBS 2781 is a 7" single which was issued only in the Netherlands
McLaughlin is not implicated on the other tracks on this LP

THE EMCEE FIVE - *BEBOP 61*
Gary Cox (tenor sax), Mike Carr (organ), John McLaughlin (guitar), Jackie Denton (drums)
Recorded: New Orleans Club, Newcastle, Spring 1967
Birdland MC587
Bells Blues
Note: McLaughlin is not implicated on other tracks on this LP

DAVID BOWIE - *THE WORLD OF DAVID BOWIE*
David Bowie (vocals, guitar), John McLaughlin (guitar), Herbie Flowers (bass), Tony Visconti (bass, backing vocals), Andy White (drums); unidentified strings
Recorded: Advision Studios, London, September 1,1967
Decca 5PA58
Let Me Sleep Beside You/ Karma
Note: McLaughlin is not implicated in the other tracks on this LP

BIDDU
Biddu (vocals), Nicky Hopkins (piano), John McLaughlin, Jimmy Page (guitar), John Paul Jones (bass); other musicians unknown
Recorded: Advision Studios, London, September 1967?
Regal Zonophone RZ3002 (45 rpm single)
Daughter Of Love/ Look Out Here I Come

THE GORDON BECK QUARTET "EXPERIMENTS WITH POPS"
Gordon Beck (piano), John McLaughlin (guitar), Jeff Clyne (bass), Tony Oxley (drums)
Recorded; London, December 7,1967
Major Minor MMLP2I
These Boots Are Made For Walking/ Norwegian Wood/ Sunny/ Up, Up and Away/ Michell/ I Can See For Miles/ Good Vibrations/ Monday, Monday

GEORGIE FAME "THE THIRD FACE OF FAME"
Georgie Fame (vocals, piano), Ian Hamer, Derek Healey, Derek Watkins, Les Condon, Albert Hall (trumpet), John Marshall, Gib Wallace (trombone), Tony Coe, Tommy Whittle, Art Ellefson, Harry Klein, Ronnie Scott, Cyril Reubens (sax), Gordon Beck (piano), John McLaughlin, Terry Smith (guitar), Phil Bates (bass), Bill Eyden (drums), Harry South (conductor)
Recorded: London, February/March 1968
CBS 63293
When I'm Sixty Four/ Ask Me Nice/ Exactly Like You/ Someone To Watch Over Me/ Blue Prelude/ Bullets Laverne/ This Is Always/ Side By Side/ St James Infirmary/ Mellow Yellow
Additional; Kentucky Child
Notes: The last track is obviously an out-take from the sessions for "THE THIRD FACE OF FAME" and has been released on a 7" single in some countries (Epic 10347). McLaughlin is not implicated in the A-side of this 7". (Johann Heidenbauer)

KEN WHEELER - *WINDMILL TILTER*
Ken Wheeler (flugelhorn), Tony Coe (clarinet, tenor sax), John McLaughlin (guitar), Dave Holland (bass), John Spooner (drums).
Recorded: London, March 1968
Fontana STL.5494
Preamble/ Sweet Dulcinea Blue/ Sancho*/ Propheticape/ Altisidora*
Notes: On (*) the whole quintet plays some parts of these titles only.
Note: McLaughlin is not implicated in the other tracks on this LP.

JACK BRUCE - *THINGS WE LIKE*
Dick Heckstall-Smith (soprano, alto saxes), John McLaughlin (electric guitar), Jack Bruce (bass guitar), Jon Hiseman (drums).
Recorded; London, August 24 & 25,1968
Polydor 2343 033
Sam Enchanted Dick/ (Medley: Sam's Sack/ Rill's Thrills)/ Born To Be Blue/ Hckhh Blues/ Ballad For Arthur/ Things We Like
Note: McLaughlin is not implicated in the other 2 tracks on this LP.

SANDY BROWN AND HIS GENTLEMEN! FRIENDS *HAIR AT ITS HAIRIEST*
Kenny Wheeler (trumpet, flugelhorn), George Chisholm (trombone), Sandy Brown (clarinet), John McLaughlin (guitar), Lennie Bush (bass), Bobby Orr (drums).
Recorded: London, December 23-27,1968
Fontana SFJL 921
Ain't got no/ Aquarius/ Black Boys/ Easy to Be Hard/ Hair/ Underture: Where Do I Go?/ Manchester England/ Air/ Electric Blues/ Overture: Where Do I Go?
Note: McLaughlin is not implicated on the other tracks on this LP

MILES DAVIS - *IN A SILENT WAY*
Miles Davis (trumpet), Wayne Shorter (soprano), Herbie Hancock, Chick Corea (electric piano), Joe Zawinul (electric piano, organ), John McLaughlin (electric guitar), Dave Holland (bass), Tony Williams (drums)
Recorded New York City, February 18,1969
Columbia C59875
Shhh - Peaceful/In A Silent Way- It's About That Time
Notes: Track 2's end uses the first four minutes of track 1. Track 3 is an excerpt of the LP version (Columbia AE13)

JIMI HENDRIX - "HELL'S SESSIONS"
Jimi Hendrix, John McLaughlin (electric-guitar), Dave Holland (bass), Buddy Miles (drums).
Recorded: Record Plant Studios, New York City, March 25, 1969
Bootleg (no label)
Instrumental jam
Notes: McLaughlin is not implicated in the other tracks on this bootleg LP. The song titles given on this LP are made up. This track is also available on the other Jimi Hendrix bootlegs "ELECTRIC LADY JAMS" (Sure Nice Shoes Records H-3600; US), "LET'S DROP SOME LUDES AND VOMIT WITH JIMI" (Sure Nice Shoes Records H-3600; US) and "RECORD PLANT JAMS" Cram Studio; UK). Contrary to the claims on the cover McLaughlin is, however, not implicated in the Jimi Hendrix bootlegs "MUSIC FOR FANS" (MOD 1003) and "ELECTRIC BIRTHDAY JIMI" (no label details).

TONY WILLIAMS LIFETIME - *EMERGENCY!*
Larry Young (alias Khalid Yasin) (organ), John McLaughlin (electric guitar), Anthony 'Tony' Williams (drums; vocals-1)
Recorded: Olmsted Sound Studios, New York City, May 26 & 28,1969
Polydor 25-3001
Emergency/ Where (-1)/ Beyond Games (-1) Nashkar/ Sangria for Three/ Via the Spectrum Road (-1)/ Spectrum/ Something Spiritual

TONY WILLIAMS LIFETIME - *NEW YORK 1969*
Larry Young (alias Khalid Yasin) (organ), John McLaughlin (electric guitar), Tony Williams (drums ;vocals-1)
Recorded; New York City, 1969
JR-004
To Whom It May Concern- Us/ Emergency/ Unknown Title/ A Famous Blues (-1)/ Something Spiritual
Note: This is a 'live' CD released in Japan. The track titles given on the cover are all made up.

MILES DAVIS - *BITCHES BREW*
Miles Davis (trumpet), Wayne Shorter (soprano), Bennie Maupin (bcl), Chick Corea, Joe

Zawinul (electric piano), John McLaughlin (electric guitar), Harvey Brooks (electric bass),
Dave Holland (bass), Jack DeJohnette, Lenny White (drums), Charles Don Alias, Jumma
Santos (percussion)
Recorded: New York City, August 19,1969
Columbia C5999516 (2LP)
Bitches Brew
same as above plus Larry Young(electric piano)
Recorded New York City, August 20,1969-Spanish Key/Spanish Key*
*Columbia 4-45171 (excerpt of LP version)
Miles Davis (trumpet), Wayne Shorter (soprano sax), Bennie Maupin (bass clarinet), Chick
Corea, Larry Young (electric piano), John McLaughlin (electric guitar), Harvey Brooks (elec-
tric bass), Dave Holland (bass), Jack DeJohnette, Lenny White (drums), Charles Don Alias,
Jumma Santos (percussion)
New York City, August 20,1969-Miles Runs The Voodoo Down/ Miles Runs The Voodoo
Down*
*Columbia 4-45171 (excerpt of LP version)
same as above plus Joe Zawinul (electric piano)
New York City, August21, 1969
Pharaoh's Dance
John McLaughlin (Miles Davis, Wayne Shorter out)

WAYNE SHORTER - *SUPER NOVA*
Wayne Shorter (soprano), Chick Corea (vib, d), John McLaughlin, Sonny Sharrock (guitar),
Miroslav Vitous (bass), Jack DeJohnette (drums).
Recorded: A & R Studios, New York City, August 29,1969
Blue Note BST 84332
Capricorn/Super Nova/ Water Babies/ Swee-pea
Note: McLaughlin is not implicated in the other tracks on this LP.

MIROSLAV VITOUS - *INFINITE SEARCH*
Joe Henderson (sax), Herbie Hancock (electric piano), John McLaughlin (guitar), Miroslav
Vitous (bass), Jack DeJohnette (drums, not -2), Joe Chambers (drums (-2)
Recorded: New York City, October 9 & 10,1969
Embryo SD524
I Will Tell Him On You (-1)/ Freedom Jazz Dance (-1)/ Infinite Search/ When Face Gets Pale/
Cerecka (-1 ,-2)/ Epilogue(-2)
unissued: London Ride
Notes: McLaughlin is not implicated in an additional track on this LP
LP also issued under the titles "MOUNTAIN IN THE CLOUDS" and "THE BASS".

MILES DAVIS - *BIG FUN*
Miles Davis (trumpet), Bennie Maupin (bass clarinet), Steve Grossman (soprano sax), Herbie
Hancock, Chick Corea (electric piano), John McLaughlin (electric guitar), Ron Carter (bass),
Harvey Brooks (electric bass), William Cobham (drums), Airto Moreira (percussion), Khalil
Balakrishna, Bihari Sharma (electric sitar, tamboura, percussion).
Recorded New York City, November 19,1969-PG 32866
Great Expectations / Mulher Laranja
Note: Great Expectations also released as excerpt on Columbia 4-45090 and 4-46074
Miles Davis (trumpet), Bennie Maupin (bass clarinet), Steve Grossman (soprano sax), Herbie
Hancock, Larry Young, Joe Zawinul (electric piano), John McLaughlin (electric guitar) Ron
Carter (bass), Harvey Brooks (electric bass),William Cobham, Jack DeJohnette (drums),
Airto Moreira (percussion), Khalil Balakrishna, Bihari Sharma (electric sitar, tamboura, per-
cussion).
Recorded New York City, November 28,1969
The Little Blue Frog (also issued as a 45rpm single Columbia 4-45090)
Miles Davis (trumpet), Steve Grossman (soprano), John McLaughlin (guitar), Dave Holland
(bass), Jack DeJohnette (drums).
New York City, March 30,1970
Go Ahead John

Note: also released as an excerpt on Columbia 4-46074
McLaughlin is not implicated on the other tracks on this 2-LP set

TONY WILLIAMS LIFETIME - *TURN IT OVER*
Larry Young (organ), John McLaughlin (electric guitar; vocals-1), Jack Bruce (bass, electric bass), Tony Williams (drums; vocals-2)
Recorded New York City, early February 1970
Polydor 24-4021
To Whom It May Concern - Them/ To Whom It May Concern- Us/ This Night This Song/ Big Nick/ Right On/ Once I Loved (-2) Nuelta Abajo/ A Famous Blues (-1 ,-2)/ Allah Be Praised

MILES DAVIS - *LIVE EVIL*
Miles Davis (trumpet), Wayne Shorter (soprano sax), Chick Corea, Joe Zawinul (piano, electric piano), John McLaughlin (guitar), Dave Holland (bass), Jack DeJohnette, William Cobham (drums), Airto Moreira (percussion), Khalil Balakrishna (sitar)
Recorded: New York City, February 8, 1970
Columbia G30954 (2LP)
Medley: Gemini/ Double Image
Miles Davis (trumpet), Steve Grossman (soprano sax), Keith Jarrett, Herbie Hancock, Chick Corea (electric piano), John McLaughlin (electric guitar), Dave Holland (bass), Jack DeJohnette (drums), Airto Moreira (percussion), Hermeto Pascoal (whistling)
Recorded New York City, June 7, 1970
Little Church
Miles Davis (trumpet), Gary Bartz (soprano sax-1 ;a~2;fi-3), Keith Jarrett (piano, electric piano), John McLaughlin (guitar), Michael Henderson (electric bass), Jack DeJohnette (drums), Airto Moreira (percussion)
Recorded: The Cellar Door, Washington, December 18, 1970
Sivad, What I Say (-1,-3), Funky Tonk (-1), Inamorata (narration by Conrad Roberts (-2)

MILES DAVIS - *DIRECTIONS*
Miles Davis (trumpet), Wayne Shorter (soprano sax), Bennie Maupin (bcl), John McLaughlin (guitar), Dave Holland (electric bass), William Cobham (drums).
Recorded New York City, February 17, 1970
Columbia KC2 36472 (2LP)
Duran
Miles Davis (trumpet), Steve Grossman (soprano), John McLaughlin (guitar), Dave Holland (electric bass), Jack DeJohnette (drums).
Recorded: New York City, February 27, 1970
Willie Nelson
Miles Davis (trumpet), Keith Jarrett (electric piano), John McLaughlin (electric guitar), Airto Moreira (percussion).
Recorded: New York City, May 21,1970
Konda
McLaughlin is not implicated on the other tracks on this 2-LP set

MILES DAVIS - *A TRIBUTE TO JACK JOHNSON*
Miles Davis (trumpet), Bennie Maupin (bcl), John McLaughlin, Sonny Sharrock(electric guitar), Dave Holland (electric bass), Jack DeJohnette(drums)
Columbia KC30455
Recorded New York City, February 18,1970
Yesternow (part 3)
Miles Davis (trumpet), Steve Grossman (soprano sax), Herbie Hancock (organ), John McLaughlin(electric guitar), Michael Henderson (electric bass), Billy Cobham(drums)
Recorded New York City, April 7,1970
Right Off (Part 1)1 Right Off (Part 3)1 Right Off (Part 4) (MD out)/ Yesternow (Part 1)
Additional: Right Off (Part 1) and Right Off (Part 2) were issued on Columbia 4-45350 as excerpts of Right Off (Part 1) and Right Off (Part 3) respectively.
Notes: On the LP the two titles 'Right off and 'Yesternow' are completed by tracks with Miles Davis playing to pre-recorded material, e.g., from the "IN A SILENT WAY" session.

MILES DAVIS - *GET UP WITH IT*
Miles Davis (trumpet), Steve Grossman (soprano), Herbie Hancock, Keith Jarrett (electric piano), John McLaughlin (electric guitar), Michael Henderson (bass), Billy Cobham (drums), Airto Moreira (percussion)
Columbia KG33236 (2LP)
Recorded: New York City, April 1970
Honky Tonk
Note: McLaughlin is not implicated in the other tracks on this 2-LP set.

JOE FARRELL - *SONG OF THE WIND*
Joe Farrell (flugelhorn, soprano, tenor sax, oboe), Chick Corea(1), John McLaughlin (guitar), Dave Holland (bass), Jack DeJohnette (drums)
Recorded: New York City, July 1 & 2,1970-CTI 5T6003
Follow Your Heart/Motion
Note: McLaughlin is not implicated in the other tracks on this LP.

LIFETIME
Larry Young (organ), John McLaughlin (electric guitar), Jack Bruce (bass, vocals), Tony Williams (drums)
Recorded: New York City, July 14,1970-Polydor 2066050 (45 rpm single)
One Word/Two Worlds

LARRY CORYELL - *SPACES*
Larry Coryell, John McLaughlin (electric guitar), Miroslav Vitous (cello, bass), Billy Cobham (drums)
Recorded: New York City, August 1970
Vanguard VSD 6558
Spaces (Infinite)/ Wrong Is Right/ Rene's Theme (LC and JM only)
Note: McLaughlin is not implicated in the other tracks on this LP.

LARRY CORYELL - *PLANET END*
Larry Coryell, John McLaughlin (electric guitar) Chick Corea (electric piano), Miroslav Vitous (bass), Billy Cobham (drums)
Recorded: New York City, August 1970 - Vanguard VSD 79367
Tyrone/ Planet End
Notes: 'Spaces' outtakes. McLaughlin is not implicated in the other tracks on this LP.

MIROSLAV VITOUS - *PURPLE*
John McLaughlin (guitar), Miroslav Vitous (bass, electric bass , electric piano), Billy Cobham (drums)
Recorded: New York City, August 25,1970
CBS-Sony SOPM 157
Water Lilies
Note: McLaughlin is not implicated in the other tracks on this LP.

WAYNE SHORTER - *MOTO GROSSO FEIO*
Wayne Shorter (soprano, tenor saxes), John McLaughlin (12-string-guitar), Dave Holland (acoustic guitar, bass), Ron Carter (bass, cello), Chick Corea (marimba, drums, percussion), Michelin Prell (drums, percussion)
Recorded: A&R Studios, New York City, August 28,1970-Blue Note BNLA 014
Moto Grosso Feio/Antiqua Nera Cruzi Iskal Montezuma
Note: McLaughlin not implicated in the other tracks on this LP.
M.Cuscuna & M. Ruppil's book 'The Blue Note Label' gives April 3,1970 as recording date.

CARLA BLEY - *ESCALATOR OVER THE HILL*
Jeanne Lee (vocals-1), Carla Bley (organ :2), John McLaughlin (electric guitar), Jack Bruce (electric bass, vocals), Paul Motian (drums)
JCOA 3LP-EOTH
Recorded: New York City, Spring 1971-
Businessmen/Rawalpindi Blues (-2)/ End of Rawalpindi (-1)/... and it's again
Note: Other musicians appear on other sections of the above titles, but were probably record-

ed on different occasions.
Jack Bruce (vocals-1), Linda Ronstadt (vocals-2), Michael Mantler (trumpet), Roswell Rudd (trombone), Jack Jeffers (baritone trombone) John Buckingham (tuba), Jimmy Lyons (alto sax), Gato Barbieri (tenor sax) Chris Woods (bar), Sharon Freeman (flugelhorn), Perry Robinson (cl-2), Carla Bley (piano; vocals-1), John McLaughlin (electric guitar), Charlie Haden (bass; vocals-2), Paul Motian (drums)
Recorded: New York City, Spring 1971-
Detective writer daughter (-1)/Why (-2)
Jack Bruce (vocals), Michael Mantler (trumpet), Dewey Redman (alto sax), Carla Bley (piano, vocals), Karl Berger (vibraphone), John McLaughlin (electric guitar), Charlie Haden (bass), Bill Morimando (cello), Paul Motian (drums)
Recorded: New York City, Spring 1971
Little Pony Soldier
Note: McLaughlin is not implicated in the other tracks on this 3-LP set.

MILES DAVIS - *ON THE CORNER*
Miles Davis (trumpet), Bennie Maupin (bcl), Dave Liebman (soprano sax), Chick Corea, Herbie Hancock, Harold Williams (piano, electric piano, synthesiser), John McLaughlin (guitar), Michael Henderson (electric bass), Jack DeJohnette (drums), Billy Hart (drums, percussion, congas), Don Alias, M'tume (congas), Colin Walcott (sitar), Badal Roy (tabla)
Columbia KC31906
Recorded: New York City, June 1,1972
On The Corner/ New York Girl/ Thinkin' One Thing And Doin' Another/ Vote For Miles
Additional: Vote For Miles (part 1) Note For Miles (Part 2) issued as 45rpm single Columbia 4-45822, excerpted from LP version
Same as above but Carlos Garnett (soprano, tenor saxes) replaces Liebman.
Recorded: New York City, June 6,1972
Black Satin/ One and One/ Helen Butte/ Mr Freedom X
Note: McLaughlin is not implicated in the other tracks on this LP

JAMES TAYLOR - ONE MAN DOG
James Taylor (acoustic guitar, vocals), Craig Doerge (piano), Daniel Kortchmar, John McLaughlin (acoustic guitar), Leland Sklar (guitarone)
Recorded: Clover Recorder, Los Angeles, Autumn 1972
Warner Bros K46185
Note: McLaughlin is not implicated in the other tracks on this LP

CARLOS SANTANA & JOHN McLAUGHLIN - *LOVE, DEVOTION, SURRENDER*
Larry Young (organ), Carlos Santana (guitar), John McLaughlin (guitar 1), Doug Rauch (bass guitar), Charles Don Alias, Jan Hammer, Billy Cobham, Michael Shrieve (drums), James 'Mingo' Lewis (percussion), Armando Peraza (congas)
Recorded: New York City, October 1972 & March 1973
Columbia KC32034
A Love Supreme/ Naima/ The Life Divine/ Let us Go Into The House of the Lord/ Meditation

SANTANA - *WELCOME*
Tom Coster (piano, organ), Richard Kermode (organ), Carlos Santana (guitar), John McLaughlin (guitar), Doug Rauch (bass guitar), Michael Shrieve (drums), Armando Peraza (congas)
Recorded: San Francisco, May 2, 1973
Columbia KC32445
Flame - Sky
Note: McLaughlin is not implicated in the other tracks on this LP

JOHN McLAUGHLIN/CARLOS SANTANA BAND - *LIVE IN CHICAGO*
Larry Young (organ), Carlos Santana, John McLaughlin (guitar), Doug Rauch (bass guitar), Billy Cobham (drums), Armando Peraza (congas)
Recorded: The Amphitheatre, Chicago, September 1, 1973
OH BOY 2-9075 (BOOTLEG)
Taurian Matador/ Let us Go Into the House of the Lord/ Meditation/ The Life Divine*/ A Love

Supreme*/Afro Blue (cover says 'Follow Your Heart')/ Flame Sky*/ Naima
Note: There are two versions of this 2-CD set. The original release (1990) is without Naima'.
Later issues (p.1991) contain this track but omit 'Taurian matador'. The artwork for both
issues is, however, exactly the same. The tracks marked with * are also available on a CD
issued by Jazz Door (JD 1250, 1994).

SRI CHINMOY - *SONGS OF THE SOUL*
Sri Chinmoy (recitation), John McLaughlin (vocals, acoustic guitar, arrangement), Carlos
Santana (vocals, acoustic guitar); others
Recorded New York City, 1975
Sri Chinmoy Lighthouse (no #) Songs Of The Soul
Note: This is a cassette with orchestral and choral pieces as well as music for solo instru-
ments to accompany Sri Chinmoy reciting his poetry. McLaughlin features on two pieces with
guitar as well (presumably) as all the choral pieces. He was also the arranger for the whole
album.

STANLEY CLARKE - *JOURNEY TO LOVE*
Chick Corea (piano), John McLaughlin (acoustic guitar), Stanley Clarke (bass)
Recorded: Electric Ladyland Studios, New York City, 1975
Nemperor NE433
Song To John (Parts 1 and 2)
Note: McLaughlin is not implicated in the other tracks on this LP.

STANLEY CLARKE - *SCHOOL DAYS*
John McLaughlin (acoustic guitar), Stanley Clarke (bass), Milton Holland (congas, triangle).
Recorded: Electric Ladyland Studios, New York City, June 1976
Nemperor NE439
Desert Song
Note: McLaughlin is not implicated in the other tracks on this LP.

STANLEY CLARKE - *LIVE 1976-1977*
John McLaughlin (acoustic guitar), Stanley Clarke (bass), Darryl Munyungo Jackson (percus-
sion).
Recorded: Electric Ladyland Studios, New York City, June 1975
Sony-Epic EK 48529
Desert Song
Note: McLaughlin is not implicated in the other tracks on this CD.

FUSE ONE
Joe Farrell (tenor sax), Jeremy Wall (synthesiser, arranger, conductor), Ronnie Foster (syn-
thesiser-1), Vic Feldman (-2), John McLaughlin (electric guitar), Stanley Clarke (bass), Leon
Chancler (drums), Paulinho Da Costa (percussion)
CTI ST9003
Recorded New York City, April 12-16 1980
Grand Prix (-1)/ To Who All Things Concern (-2)
Joe Farrell (tenor sax), Jeremy Wall (piano, synthesiser, arranger, conductor), Ronnie Foster
(synthesiser), John McLaughlin, Larry Coryell (electric guitar), Will Lee (bass), Leon Chancler
(drums), Paulinho Da Costa (percussion)
Double Steal (a)
Additional: Double steal (b) edited version of (a) issued as 45rpm single on CTI 51ST 2623
Joe Farrell (soprano), Jeremy Wall (piano, synthesiser, arranger, conductor), Ronnie Foster
(synthesiser), Vic Feldman (piano), John McLaughlin (acoustic guitar), Stanley Clarke (bass),
Leon Chancler (drums), Paulinho Da Costa (percussion)
Sunshine Lady
Joe Farrell (flugelhorn), Jeremy Wall (piano, arranger, conductor), Don Grusin (synthesiser),
John McLaughlin (acoustic guitar), Stanley Clarke (bass), Tony Williams, Michael Epstein
(drums), Paulinho Da Costa (percussion)
Friendship (a)
Additional: Friendship (b), edited version of (a) issued as a 45 rpm single on CTI 81ST 2623
Notes: McLaughlin is not implicated in the other two tracks on this LP.

PACO DE LUCIA - *LIGHT AND SHADE*
Al Di Meola, John McLaughlin, Paco de Lucia (acoustic guitar)
Recorded: Cine Salamanca, Madrid, November 26, 1980
Magnum Music MMGV 076
Morning Of The Carnival (excerpt)
Note: McLaughlin is not implicated in the other tracks on this LP

PACO DE LUCIA - *CASTRO MARIN*
Paco de Lucia, Larry Coryell (acoustic guitar), John McLaughlin (12-string guitar, guitar)
Recorded: Tokyo, December 25, 1980
Nippon-Phonogram 28PP-2
Note: McLaughlin is not implicated in other tracks on this LP. This track can be also found on the compilation CD JOHN McLAUGHLIN "COMPACT JAZZ" (Verve 516 114-2) (see below).

CHICK COREA - *MUSIC FOREVER & BEYOND*
Chick Corea (piano) John McLaughlin (acoustic guitar)
Recorded: Montreux, Switzerland, July 15,1981
GRP Records GRD-5 9819 (5CD set)
Beautiful Love
Note: McLaughlin is not implicated in other tracks on this 5-CD box set.

MILES DAVIS - *YOU'RE UNDER ARREST*
Miles Davis (trumpet; keyboards-1), Robert Irving III.(keyboards), John McLaughlin(electric guitar), Darryl Jones (bass guitar), Steve Thornton (percussion), Vince Wilburn (drums)
Recorded: Record Plant, New York City, September 22,1984-Columbia SC 40023
Ms Morrisine/ Katia Prelude (-1)/ Katia (-1)
Note: McLaughlin is not implicated in the other tracks on this LP.

BILL EVANS - *THE ALTERNATIVE MAN*
Bill Evans (tenor, soprano sax, flugelhorn, keyboards), Clifford Carter (keyboards), Mitchell Forman (piano), John McLaughlin (guitar), Mark Egan (bass guitar), Danny Gottlieb (drums), Manolo Badrena (percussion)
Recorded: New York City, January/ May 1985
Blue Note BT85111
Survival Of The Fittest/ Flight Of The Falcon
Note: McLaughlin is not implicated in the other tracks on this LP.

MILES DAVIS - *AURA*
Miles Davis (trumpet), Benny Rosenfeld, Palle Bolvig , Jens Winther, Perry Knudsen, Idrees Sulieman, Palle Mikkelborg (trumpet, flugelhorn), Vincent Nilsson, Jens Engel Ture Larsen (trombone), Ole Kurt Jensen (bass trombone), Axel Windfeld (bass trombone, tuba), Jesper Thilo, Per Carsten, Uffe Karskov, Bent Jaedig, Flemming Madsen (sax, flugelhorn) Niels Eje (oboe, engl-h), Lillian Toernqvist (harp), Thomas Clausen, Ole Koch-Hansen, Kenneth Knudsen (k), John McLaughlin, Bjarne Roupe (guitar), Bo Stief (electric bass), Niels-Henning Oersted Pedersen (bass), Lennart Gruvstedt (drums), Vince Wilburn (synthesiser, drums), Marilyn Mazur, Ethan Weisgaard (percussion), Eva Thaysen (vocals)
Recorded: Easy Sound Studio, Copenhagen, February/March 1985
CBS 463351
Intro/White/Yellow/Orange/Red/Green/Blue/Electric Red/Indigo/ Violet

RAMON PIPIN - *NOUS SOMMES TOUS FRERES*
Jean-Michel Kajdan, Herve Lavandier, Ramon Pipin (piano, synthesiser, vocals, etc.), Jean-Pierre Debarbat (sax), John McLaughlin (guitar), Steve Shehan (percussion), Clarabelle, Gabriel Feat (backing vocals)
Recorded: Studio Ramses, Paris, April 1 August 1985
Cream Records 140
Les Fadaises d'Etretat
Note: McLaughlin is not implicated in the other tracks on this LP

DEXTER GORDON - *ROUND MIDNIGHT (OST)*
Dexter Gordon (tenor sax), Herbie Hancock (piano), John McLaughlin (guitar), Pierre

Michelot (bass), Billy Higgins (drums)
Recorded: Epinay sur Seine, Paris, July 1 to 12,1985
Columbia 5C40464
Warner Bros PGV 11603 (video recording)*
Body and Soul/ Body and Soul (different take)*/ Society Red*/ Autumn In New York*/As Time Goes By*
Herbie Hancock (piano), John McLaughlin (guitar), Pierre Michelot (bass), Billy Higgins (drums)
Berangere's Nightmare/Unknown

DEXTER GORDON - *THE OTHER SIDE OF ROUND MIDNIGHT*
Dexter Gordon (tenor sax), Herbie Hancock (piano), John McLaughlin (guitar), Pierre Michelot (bass), Billy Higgins (drums)
Recorded: Epinay sur Seine, Paris, July 1 to 12,1985-Blue Note BT 85135
As Time Goes By
Notes: Same track as on the video WB PGV 11603 (cf. above).
McLaughlin is not implicated in the other tracks on this LP.

GIL EVANS - *GIL MEETS JOHN AND LEE*
Miles Evans, Shunzo Ono, Lew Soloff (trumpet), Dave Taylor, Dave Bargeron (trombone), John Clark (french horn), John Surman (bass, soprano sax), George Adams (tenor sax), Chris Hunter (alto sax, flugelhorn), Gil Evans (piano, conductor), Delmar Brown, Peter Levin (synthesiser), John McLaughlin (guitar), Joseph Payne (bass), Kenwood Dennard (drums)
Recorded: Ravenna, Italy, July 2,1986
Bootleg (no label) 4LP set
Up From The Sky/Little Wing/There Comes A Time/ Stone Free/ Goodbye Pork Pie Hat/ Bird Feathers (aka Bud and Bird) Eleven
Notes: McLaughlin is not implicated in the other 2 LP's of this 4-LP set. Also available as 2-CD set.

ZAKIR HUSSAIN - *MAKING MUSIC*
Jan Garbarek (tenor sax, soprano), Hariprasad Chaurasia (flugelhorn), John McLaughlin (acoustic guitar), Zakir Hussain (tabla, vocals, percussion)
Recorded: Rainbow Studio, Oslo, December 8-10,1986
ECM 1349
Making Music/Zakiri Water Girl/Toni/Anisia*/Sunjog/You and Me/ Sabah
Note: * did not appear on LP version

DANNY GOTTLIEB - *AQUAMARINE*
John McLaughlin (acoustic guitar) Danny Gottlieb (drums)
Recorded: Milan, Italy, 1986
Atlantic 781 806-1
Duet
Notes: McLaughlin is not implicated in the other tracks on this LP. Presumably already recorded during the sessions for *ADVENTURES IN RADIOLAND* in January/February 1986.

MILES DAVIS - *BLACK DEVIL*
Miles Davis (trumpet), Kenny Garrett (alto sax), Deron Johnson (keyboards), John McLaughlin, John Scofield (electric guitar) Darryl Jones (bass guitar), Ricky Wellman (drums)
Recorded: La Grande Halle, Paris, July 10,1991
Beech Maten BM053/2 (2CD bootleg)
Katia
Miles Davis (trumpet), Kenny Garrett (alto sax), Steve Grossman (soprano), Bill Evans (tenor sax), Deron Johnson, Chick Corea (keyboards), Joseph Foley McCreary, John McLaughlin, John Scofield (electric guitar), David Holland (bass), Darryl Jones, Richard Patterson (bass guitar), Al Foster, Ricky Wellman (drums)
Jean-Pierre
Notes: John McLaughlin is not implicated in the other tracks on this 2-CD bootleg set. 'Jean-Pierre' can be also seen in a French TV film titled *MILES DAVIS AND FRIENDS*, directed by Renaud Le Van Kim.

OTHER RECORDINGS

This section features recordings that resist easy categorisation. They include official radio recordings, as well as recordings by John McLaughlin - whether as sideman featured artist or as part of a group- which form part of a recording featuring other artists i.e. label compilations, festival recordings, jams etc. Also audio-visuals products (i.e. videos, TV programmes)

"TOP OF THE POPS - 164"
Georgie Fame (vocals, organ), Eddie Thornton (trumpet), Johnny Marshall (alto, baritone sax), Lyn Dobson (tenor sax, flugelhorn), Derek Wandsworth (trombone), John McLaughlin (guitar), Ricky Brown(bass) Jon Hiseman (drums), unknown (congas)
Recorded: BBC Radio, London; Air date: January19, 1968
BBC Transcription LP
The Ballad Of Bonnie and Clyde
Notes: This LP is shared with other artists. Both tracks also available on "TOP OF THE POPS -167"

THE GUITAR ALBUM
Compilation album featuring various artists.
Recorded in New York City, March 1971
Columbia KG31045 (2LP)
JOHN AND EVE McLAUGHLIN
John McLaughlin (acoustic guitar, vocal), Eve McLaughlin (autoharp, vocal)
Devotion
unissued: My Friend/ My Dying Soul/ God And The World

MAR Y SOL
Compilation album recorded at Mar Y Sol Festival, Vega Baja, Puerto Rico, April 3 1972 featuring various artists
Atco SD 2-705 (2LP)
MAHAVISHNU ORCHESTRA
Line-up as *The Inner Mounting Flame*
The Noonward Race

"KBFH RADIO SHOW"
Compilation radio show CD featuring various artists
Recorded Palace Theatre, Buffalo, New York, January 27 1973
KBFH KB#1
MAHAVISHNU ORCHESTRA
Line-up as *The Inner Mounting Flame* see above
Dawn

"SRI CHINMOY"
Documentary film about Sri Chinmoy
Recorded New York City, spring 1973
JOHN McLAUGHLIN AND CARLOS SANTANA
John McLaughlin, Carlos Santana (guitars), possibly others
All music composed by John McLaughlin

"BEYOND AN EMPTY DREAM"
Compilation album featuring various artists
Recorded New York City, December 1973
Charisma CAS 1101
JOHN AND EVE McLAUGHLIN
John McLaughlin (acoustic guitar 1, vocal 2), Eve McLaughlin (vocal, cello), unidentified chorus
Guru/The Name Of Truth

"ROCKAROUND THE WORLD, NO.196"
Compilation album in a series featuring various artists
Recorded; various (see under respective tracks listed above)
MILES DAVIS/ SHAKTI/ MAHAVISHNU ORCHESTRA

Miles Davis: In A Silent Way (edited)/ Spanish Key
Shakti: Lady L/ La Danse Du Bonheur
Mahavishnu Orchestra: Miles Beyond/ Celestial Terrestrial Commuters

PACO DE LUCIA/JOHN McLAUGHLIN/LARRY CORYELL - *MEETING OF THE SPIRITS*
Video recording
Recorded Royal Albert Hall, February 14, 1979
VCL Communications VHS 2770-50
Paco de Lucia, John McLaughlin, Larry Coryell (acoustic guitars)
Tres Hermanos/ Entre Dos Aguas (JM out)/ Lotus Feet (LC out)/ Morning Of The Carnival/
Meeting Of The Spirits/ Guardian Angels unissued/ Waltz For Bill Evans (PDL out)/ My
Foolish Heart/ Goodbye Pork Pie Hat/ Blues 1/ Blues 2

HAVANA JAM
Compilation album featuring various artists
Recorded Karl Marx Theatre, Havana, Cuba, March 3 1979
Columbia PC2 36053 (2LP)
THE TRIO OF DOOM
John McLaughlin (acoustic guitar), Jaco Pastorius (electric bass), Tony Williams (drums)
The Dark Prince

HAVANA JAM 2
Compilation album featuring various artists
Recorded: as above
Columbia PC2 36180
Line-up: as above
Para Orientel Continuum
unissued: Are You The One? Are You The One?

JOHN McLAUGHLIN DUO "BRATISLAVA JAZZ DAYS '85"
Recorded Bratislava, Czechoslovakia, October 25-27 (exact date unknown) 1985
Opus 9115 1810/11
John McLaughlin (acoustic guitar), Jonas Hellborg (bass guitar)
Face
Note: This 2-LP set is shared with other artists.

JOHN McLAUGHLIN AND PACO DE LUCIA
Video recording
John McLaughlin, Paco de Lucia (acoustic guitar)
Recorded Zeltmusikfestival, Freiburg, June 13,1987
No label details
Spain (excerpt)
Note: This is a documentary video about Paco de Lucia released in 1995.

JOHN McLAUGHLIN PLAYS BILL EVANS
Promotional video.
Recorded: France, September 1993 Line-up: as *Time Remembered* (see above)
We Will Meet Again
Note: This is a promotional video issued by Verve France. It shows John McLaughlin talking
about the Bill Evans record (cf. above) while 'We Will Meet Again' is played repeatedly in the
background.

CARNEGIE HALL SALUTES THE JAZZ MASTERS
Compilation album featuring various artists recorded at Carnegie Hall, New York City, April 6
1994
Verve 523150-2
Herbie Hancock (piano), John McLaughlin (acoustic guitar)

Titles by SAF Publishing Ltd

No More Mr Nice Guy: The Inside Story of The Alice Cooper Group
By Michael Bruce and Billy James (reprint due soon). The dead babies, the drinking, executions and, of course, the rock 'n' roll.

Beyond The Pale: The Story of Procol Harum UK Price £12.99 (available late 1999)
Distinctive, ground breaking and enigmatic British band from the 70s.

An American Band: A History of Grand Funk Railroad UK Price £12.99
One of the biggest grossing US rock 'n' roll acts of the 70s - selling millions of records and playing sold out arenas the world over. Hype, Politics & rock 'n' roll - unbeatable!

Wish The World Away: Mark Eitzel and American Music Club UK Price £12.99
Sean Body has written a fascinating biography of Eitzel which portrays an artist tortured by demons, yet redeemed by the aching beauty of his songs.

Ginger Geezer: Vivian Stanshall & the Bonzo Dog Band (available 2000)
Stanshall was one of pop music's true eccentrics. An account of his incredible life from playing pranks with The Who's Keith Moon to depression, alcoholism, & sad demise.

Go Ahead John!: A Critical History of John McLaughlin UK Price £12.99
One of the greatest jazz musicians of all time. Includes his work with Miles Davis, Mahavishnu Orchestra, Shakti. Full of insights into all stages of his career.

Lunar Notes: Zoot Horn Rollo's Captain Beefheart Experience UK Price £11.95
For the first time we get the insider's story of what it was like to record, play and live with an eccentric genius such as Beefheart, written by Bill Harkleroad - Zoot himself!

Meet The Residents: America's Most Eccentric Band UK Price £11.95
An outsider's view of The Residents' operations, exposing a world where nothing is as it seems. It is a fascinating tale of musical anarchy and cartoon wackiness. Reprinted to coincide with the recent world tour.

Digital Gothic: A Critical Discography of Tangerine Dream UK Price £9.95
For the very first time German electronic pioneers, Tangerine Dream mammoth output is placed within an ordered perspective.

The One and Only - Homme Fatale: Peter Perrett & The Only Ones UK Price £11.95
An extraordinary journey through crime, punishment and the decadent times of British punk band leader, Peter Perrett of The Only Ones

Plunderphonics, 'Pataphysics and Pop Mechanics The Leading Exponents of Musique Actuelle UK Price £12.95
Chris Cutler, Fred Frith, Henry Threadgill, John Oswald, John Zorn, etc.

Kraftwerk: Man, Machine and Music UK Price £11.95
The full story behind one of the most influential bands in the history of rock.

Wrong Movements: A Robert Wyatt History UK Price £14.95
A journey through Wyatt's 30 year career with Soft Machine, Matching Mole & solo artist.

Wire: Everybody Loves A History UK Price £9.95
One of British punk's most endearing and enduring bands combining Art and Attitude

Tape Delay: A Documentary of Industrial Music (out of print)
Marc Almond, Cabaret Voltaire, Nick Cave, Chris & Cosey, Coil, Foetus, Neubauten, Non, The Fall, New Order, Psychic TV, Rollins, Sonic Youth, Swans, Test Dept and many more...

Dark Entries: Bauhaus and Beyond UK Price £11.95
The gothic rise & fall of Bauhaus, Love & Rockets, Tones on Tail, Murphy, J, and Ash solo.

Titles by Firefly Publishing

Poison Heart: Surviving The Ramones UK Price £11.95
Dee Dee's crushingly honest account of life as junkie and Ramone. A great rock story!

Minstrels In The Gallery: A History Of Jethro Tull UK Price £12.99
At Last! To coincide with their 30th anniversary, a full history of one of the most popular and inventive bands of the past three decades

DANCEMUSICSEXROMANCE: Prince - The First Decade UK Price £12.99
A portrait of Prince's reign as the most exciting black performer to emerge since James Brown and Jimi Hendrix.

Soul Sacrifice: The Santana Story (due late 1999)
In-depth study of seventies Latin guitar legend

Mail Order

All Firefly, SAF and Helter Skelter titles are available by mail order from the world famous Helter Skelter bookshop. You can either phone or fax your order to Helter Skelter on the following numbers:

Telephone: +44 (0)171 836 1151 or
Fax: +44 (0)171 240 9880
Office hours: Mon-Fri 10:00am - 7:00pm, Sat: 10:00am - 6:00pm,
Sun: closed..

Postage prices per book worldwide are as follows:

UK & Channel Islands	£1.50
Europe & Eire (air)	£2.95
USA, Canada (air)	£7.50
Australasia, Far East (air)	£9.00
Overseas (surface)	£2.50

You can also write enclosing a cheque, International Money Order, or registered cash. Please include postage. DO NOT send cash. DO NOT send foreign currency, or cheques drawn on an overseas bank. Send to:

Helter Skelter Bookshop,
4 Denmark Street, London, WC2H 8LL, United Kingdom.
If you are in London come and visit us, and browse the titles in person!!

Email: helter@skelter.demon.co.uk
Website: http://www.skelter.demon.co.uk

For the latest on SAF and Firefly titles check the SAF website:
www.saf.mcmail.com